ISBN 978-0-282-86621-1
PIBN 10870354

1 MONTH OF
FREE
READING

at

www.ForgottenBooks.com

By purchasing this book you are eligible for one month membership to ForgottenBooks.com, giving you unlimited access to our entire collection of over 1,000,000 titles via our web site and mobile apps.

To claim your free month visit:
www.forgottenbooks.com/free870354

English
Français
Deutsche
Italiano
Español
Português

www.forgottenbooks.com

Mythology Photography **Fiction**
Fishing Christianity **Art** Cooking
Essays Buddhism Freemasonry
Medicine **Biology** Music **Ancient**
Egypt Evolution Carpentry Physics
Dance Geology **Mathematics** Fitness
Shakespeare **Folklore** Yoga Marketing
Confidence Immortality Biographies
Poetry **Psychology** Witchcraft
Electronics Chemistry History **Law**
Accounting **Philosophy** Anthropology
Alchemy Drama Quantum Mechanics
Atheism Sexual Health **Ancient History**
Entrepreneurship Languages Sport
Paleontology Needlework Islam
Metaphysics Investment Archaeology
Parenting Statistics Criminology
Motivational

DEATH OF REV. DR. WELLES.

[Daily Record, Sept. 25, 1902.]

With the death of Rev. Dr. Henry H. Welles, which occurred shortly after noon yesterday at Forty Fort, the Wyoming Valley loses one of its oldest residents, the community a most worthy citizen, and the Presbyterian Church one of its leading clergymen.

Rev. Dr. Welles was stricken with paralysis twelve days ago, and while he did not suffer much pain, he continued to sink gradually until the end.

Rev. Henry Hunter Welles, D. D., was the third son of Charles Fisher

REV. DR. HENRY H. WELLES.

Welles of Wyalusing, Pa., whose wife was Eleanor Jones Hollenback, daughter of Col. Matthias Hollenback, the well known pioneer merchant and Indian trader, one of the survivors of the battle of Wyoming. Through his father, who was a native of Glastonbury, Conn., Dr. Welles was descended in the seventh degree from Thomas Welles of Hartford, fourth colonial

governor of the Province of Connecticut.

Born at Wyalusing on Sept. 15, 1824, he lived the life of a farmer's son until his matriculation as sophomore at Princeton, where he was graduated in the year 1844. Subsequently he took a course of two years at the theological seminary at the same place, under the tutelage of such men as Charles Hodge and the Alexanders, Archibald and Joseph Addison; and on the 29th of August, 1850, he was licensed as a preacher by the Presbytery of Susquehanna, and began in December of the same year to supply the old church at Kingston, Pa., over which he was ordained and installed as pastor in June of the succeeding year. This, his only pastoral charge, was laid down at what he understood to be the call of duty, twenty years later, since which he has been active in the service of his Master in various local fields, wherever duty seemed to call.

In 1887 he organized a Sunday school in Forty Fort, his home, which developed into a church organization in 1895, and under his fostering care became a flourishing church, with commodious house of worship, and manse now nearing completion. This effort called forth the ceaseless devotion of his later years, and the gracious influence of his work and prayers bears fruit to-day in the lives of his neighbors.

Upon the organization of the Presbytery of Lackawanna—which at the happy reunion of the two great branches of the Presbyterian Church became the successor of the two "old school" presbyteries of Susquehanna and Luzerne, as well as of the "new school" Presbytery of Montrose—he became its first stated clerk, and during all its subsequent history has been a valuable and cherished associate of this influential division of the ecclesiastical body founded by Calvin, and illustrated in the New World by such men as Jonathan Edwards, to whose family Dr. Welles was related through his paternal great grandmother Jerusha, daughter of Samuel Edwards of Hartford. Through his paternal grandmother Prudence, daughter of Col. Elizur Talcott, he was also descended from two of the noted pioneers of Massachusetts Bay, William Pynchon and his son-in-law, Elizur Holyoke, whose interesting story is told by Dr. J. G. Holland in his book, "The Bay Path."

The honorary degree of doctor of divinity was conferred upon Mr. Welles by Lafayette College in 1894. His wife, who pre-deceased him some seven years, was Ellen Susanna, daughter of Gen. Samuel G. Ladd of Hallowell, Maine, where they were married on Oct. 12, 1849. Their three children, who all survive, are Henry H. Welles, Jr., attorney at law, of Wilkes-Barre; Theodore Ladd Welles of Niagara Falls, and Charlotte Rose Welles of Forty Fort. They leave also an adopted daughter, niece of Mrs. Welles by blood, Carrie, born Fairbanks, wife of Benjamin R. Tubbs of Kingston. Mr. Welles was a member of the Wyoming Historical and Geological Society.

The life and character of Henry Hunter Welles are well known in this community, where he has lived, loved and labored for more than half a century. Only three members of the large Presbytery of which he was so long an honored member have exceeded him in length of service, and none, it is safe to say, in faithful devotion to his life's work. Of ardent piety and unquestioning faith, it was impossible for him to swerve in the slightest degree from what he knew to be the duty line. Wholly unselfish and sincere, and living always in the way of an enlightened conscience, he illustrated through a life of seventy-eight years one of the highest types of the man, the gentleman, and the Christian.

------ ●● ------

FROM PIONEER STOCK.

[Dlaiy Record, Sept. 15, 1902.]

The death of Ira Swartwood, a descendant of people noted in the early history of Wyoming Valley, occurred on Friday at his home at Falls, Wyoming County, aged about 83 years. He was a grandson of Alexander Swartwood, who was one of the early settlers of Wyoming Valley and who at one time was a large land owner on the West Side, owning the Kingston flats and the land on which are now located the boroughs of Kingston and Edwardsville. This he sold in 1794 and, going twenty miles further up the Susquehanna, bought another large tract of land on the same side of the river, which has since been known as Swartwood Bend. This was the birthplace of Ira Swartwood, he being the eldest son of Alexander Swartwood, Jr., and Elizabeth (Sickler) Swartwood. Ira was born on Jan. 24, 1819. Mr. Swartwood

helped clear the land and it became a
rich farming country.

Deceased was married to Mary,
daughter of Horace Gray, she dying
several years ago. Six children survive,
as follows: Daniel B., at home; Delia,
wife of David Sweitzer; Almeda, wife
of Giles Sickler of Lockville; Jonathan,
Rose, wife of John Fitch, and Ira, Jr,
of Falls.

SUGARLOAF MASSACRE.

[Hazleton Sentinel, Sept. 11, 1902.].

To-day marks the one hundred and
twenty-second anniversary of the
Sugarloaf massacre, in which fourteen
brave Americans were cruelly murdered
by a band of forty British and Indians.
The Americans were returning from the
defense of Fort Rice, which had been
vigorously attacked by 300 of the enemy,
and had arrived on a clearing at the
foot of Sugarloaf Mountain, about
seven miles from Nescopeck, Luzerne
County, when they were surrounded by
the murderous band and with hatchet
and gun were hewed and shot down.
Some escaped and three were taken
prisoner. The killed were: Capt. D.
Klader, Corp. Samuel Bond and pri-
vates John Kouts, John Weaver, Balt-
zer Snyder, George P. Reinhart, Peter
Croom, George Shellhammer, Paul
Neely, Abraham Smith, Jacob Arndt,
Philip George, James McGraw and
Jacob Rowe.

Fort Rice still stands, though its history is not generally known.

FAMILY REUNION.

A reunion of the Brandon family was
held at Patterson Grove camp ground
on Thursday, October 9, 1902, which
surpassed by far anything of its kind
ever before held in that vicinity. The
gathering was composed of the children, grandchildren and great-grandchildren of William Brandon, an early
settler of Wyoming Valley and Huntington Valley. Refreshments were
served under a large tent during the
afternoon to at least 100 people, after
which brief addresses and story telling
of the early pioneers were listened to
with marked attention.

The first of the Brandons, an Irishman, to arrive here landed on our
shores during the Revolutionary
period. They settled in Connecticut,
where the subject of this sketch, William Brandon, was born shortly after
the arrival of his parents in America.

After the death of his parents William, along with others, started for the Wyoming Valley, arriving here in 1792. He remained in this valley until 1805, when he removed to Huntington Valley, where he married and settled down during his remaining years. Connected with the Brandon family is a number of the most respected families of Wilkes-Barre, Kingston, Fairmount and Huntington townships.

The children of William Brandon were thirteen in number, named as follows: Benjamin Brandon, aged 98 years, still alive and resides in Nebraska; William and James, died in Fairmount Township; Daniel, died in Chicago; Dennison, Harrison, Theresa, Silvina and Julia, died and are buried in Huntington Valley; Mrs. John Henry, died in Orangeville; Adeline and Sarah, went to Nevada years ago. They are both married and are enjoying the comforts of this life. John, the fifth son, is a resident of Wilkes-Barre. A close estimate of the grandchildren, great-grandchildren and great-great grandchildren, as given us, would be setting the number at 300. Among those assembled at the reunion on October 9, the following were noticed:

Fairmount—Mrs. William Brandon, Mr. and Mrs. George Brandon, Mr. and Mrs. J. M. Brandon, Mr. and Mrs. Mylard Brandon, Miss Evan Brandon, Mr. and Mrs. John W. Saxe, Mrs. Frank McDaniels, Miss Lulu Brandon, Mr. and Mrs. H. H. Saxe, Miss Dolly Saxe, Mr. and Mrs. John E. Smith, Mr. and Mrs. Albert Downing, Miss Vernie Saxe, Mr. and Mrs. R. G. Goss, Miss Jessie Holmes and D. C. Brandon.

Huntington Mills—Mr. and Mrs. Monroe Rood, Mrs. Lilly Roberts, H. Derr Klinetob, Mr. and Mrs. John W. Klinetob, Mrs. Harrison Brandon, Mrs. William Bisher, Nathan Klinetob, Mrs. William R. Monroe, Mr. and Mrs. Nathaniel Roberts, Miss Lenora Smith, Miss Margie Rood, Miss Leone Wilson.

Harveyville—Mr. and Mrs. James Berlew, Harry Berlew and Misses Mary, Irene and Edna Berlew.

New Columbus—Leroy Yaple.

California—Mrs. R. E. Kent.

Montana—Mrs. Robert McTaggart.

Ohio—Mr. and Mrs. Lambert Brandon.

Orange—Mr. and Mrs. Dayton Dymond and daughter.

Shickshinny—Mr. and Mrs. H. E. Campbell and Walter and Eston Campbell.

Wilkes-Barre—Mrs. Lenora Gibbons, John Brandon, Mr. and Mrs. A. W.

Baker and son, Albert, Mrs. J. B. Brittain and son, Ray Brittain.

Kingston—Mrs. Harry Covert and son.

Before bidding an affectionate farewell to each other a society was formed the object of which is to assemble annually and enjoy themselves at a reunion. The following officers were elected for the ensuing year: President, George Brandon, Fairmount; secretary, J. M. Brandon, Fairmount; assistant secretary, A. W. Baker, Waller street, Wilkes-Barre; treasurer, D. C. Brandon, Fairmount.

EPISCOPAL HISTORY.

[Daily Record, Oct. 21, 1902.]

The historical sketch read by Samuel S. Hines at St. Luke's Episcopal Church anniversary in Scranton contained much historical matter and some of it had reference to the Wilkes-Barre as well as the Scranton section. He said in part:

Lackawanna County was, up to April 17, 1878, a part of Luzerne County, and Luzerne, in 1786, after the historical and bitter controversy between Connecticut and Pennsylvania had been settled, comprised what we now know as Luzerne, Susquehanna, Wyoming, Columbia and Lycoming counties, with portions of Bradford, Sullivan and Montour.

In these early days the Protestant Episcopal Church, under the guidance of Bishop White, of revered memory, in the State of Pennsylvania, sent out her missionaries to carry the gospel of Christ and to minister to the people scattered in the primitive and wild places of settlement.

Wilkes-Barre was the important town of this section, but contained few people and was not blessed with a service of our church until 1814, when Rev. Jackson Kemper was missionary. In 1817 a church organization was formed there and a charter of incorporation obtained for St. Stephen's Protestant Episcopal Church.

A church edifice erected shortly after was consecrated by Bishop White in June, 1823.

From this time on there were occasions when the rectors of St. Stephen's carried the good news of the gospel and the inspiring services of our church to the small communities scattered through the wilderness of what is now Lackawanna County, and adjoining counties, but the record of them seems

to be absent until 1841, when we learn
of pastoral visits and services by Rev.
Mr. Claxton at various times in Slocum Hollow and Providence Township,
as well as by Bishop Alonzo Potter,
who held a first public service in what
was known as the Village Chapel in
1848.

Shortly afterward Rev. John Long, a
missionary of the Society for the Advancement of Christianity of the Protestant Episcopal Church in Pennsylvania, began his labors for our Lord
in the scattered villages and settlements in this section of Pennsylvania,
and after many changes involving dis-
comforts, which we of this day can but
faintly appreciate, located in Montrose,
Susquehanna County, as rector of the
church there, and missionary to the
little groups of people separated in the
adjoining counties. He had scarcely
become settled in his plain home when
the "good and wise bishop," as he
speaks of Bishop Potter, appointed him
to work in the unoccupied territory
between Carbondale and Wilkes-Barre,
and later, more directly in Scranton
and neighborhood. Transferring his
labors therefore to the young and
growing village of Scranton, he held
services frequently in private houses,
store rooms and halls, and a public
service in the Methodist chapel at
Providence on the evening of Aug. 5,
1851.

It may be appropriately stated here
that in that year the population in the
district now included in Scranton was
about 2,500. In the years previous the
name of our city changed with the increase of population, from Slocum Hollow, or Deep Hollow (up to 1840 with
a population of 100), to Scrantonia,
Harrison, and again Scrantonia, in
succeeding years, and finally Scranton
in 1851. Of those times, one writer remarks "the village laid no claim to
piety," and that, while Providence, or
Razorville, contained a dozen houses,
a postoffice, a grist mill, an ax factory and three doctors, two stores and
a Methodist chapel, it had no regular
minister of religion, and for a time instead of religious services on Sundays,
horse racing claimed the attention of
most of the people. Yet the influence
of the Christian teachings of former
days and all adown the years was
seen and felt in no small measure. The
Methodists, Presbyterians, Baptists,
Moravians and Roman Catholics from
the first had brought the light of the
gospel and the cross of Christ to shine
upon the waste places and in the fal-

low hearts of the people, and school
houses, barns, the shelter of trees, as
well as the personal contact, the eye
to eye approach to the people by
Christ's ambassadors, witnessed the
sowing of the good seed, to the spirit-
ual uplifting of many souls.

At the close of that first public service by Rev. Mr. Long in the Methodist chapel on Aug. 5, 1851, a meeting
of the people was held and a parish
organization formed and called St.
Luke's Church.

On Easter Day, 1852, Rev. Mr. Long
assumed charge of the parish as rector in connection with his missionary
work in Pittston, Hyde Park, Providence and Dunmore. At that period
the population of Scranton was something less than 3,000, but increasing at
the rate of 500 to 600 a year. To en-
able him to concentrate his labors
upon the work of the church in this
growing community, he decided to yield
the Pittston charge and "thus avoid, in
a measure," as he said, "that going
about which was inconvenient and a
great drawback upon the advancement
of the parish."

Largely through his efforts two lots
were obtained from the Lackawanna
Iron & Coal Co. for a church and rec-
tory on the east side of Penn avenue
between Lackawanna avenue and
Spruce street. A subscription for the
purpose had been so far successful
that ground was broken for the church
on Easter Monday, 1853, and its cornerstone laid on April 19 following. At
this ceremony there were present, besides the rector, Rev. George D. Miles
of Wilkes-Barre, Rev. G. M. Skinner
of New Milford, Rev. E. A. Mendenhall
of Salem and Rev. Mr. Hull of Elmira,
N. Y., with a goodly attendance of
citizens.

Through the efforts of Rector Long
and the kindly offices and gifts of Rev.
G. T. Bedell of Ascension Church, New
York, and the ladies of his parish and
those of St. Stephen's, Wilkes-Barre,
and from friends in Philadelphia, Baltimore and other places, added to those
of his own men and women, the work
on the new church building progressed
so steadily and favorably that a first
church service and the first session of
a Sunday school were held in the basement on the last Sunday of the following July.

The church was a frame building of
unmatched boards, with basement of
stone and brick, and of Gothic design.
It had sittings for 225 persons. Its
consecration took place on Sunday,

Nov. 13, 1853, by the Rt. Rev. Bishop Potter of Pennsylvania, assisted by Rev. George D. Miles, Rev. R. B. Duane and the rector.

Rev. Mr. Long resigned his rectorate on Sept. 29, 1858, having served the parish faithfully for six years and seven months as rector, added to the previous years as missionary.

During the months succeeding, the services of the church and the needs of the people were provided for by clergymen from Wilkes-Barre and other places. In considering the call of a successor the choice rested between Rev. Henry C. Potter, a young clergyman of Philadelphia, son of the bishop of Pennsylvania, and Rev. W. C. Robinson of Norwich, Conn., both of whom possessed qualities of heart and mind which attracted the regard of the church people, and each of whom had strong advocates among them for the rectorate. The selection settled upon Rev. Mr. Robinson, and our parish perhaps lost the record of having furnished one of the strongest and most influential bishops in the United States.

Rev. Mr. Robinson assumed the rectorate on Feb. 1, 1859, and ministered to his people as pastor until Dec. 1, 1862.

It is to the credit of the vestry that they wasted little time in calling a new rector, and on Jan. 25, 1863, Rev. A. A. Marple of Wellsboro assumed the office.

Ground was broken for the new church on July 5, 1866, on a plot of ground 178 feet in front by 160 feet in depth.

A call was extended to Rev. C. Inglis Chapin of Vergennes, Vt., and accepted by him on the 28th day of November, 1877.

A new rector entered upon his duties Oct. 1, 1879, Rev. J. Philip B. Pendleton of Washington, D. C.

Rev. Henry C. Swentzel of Honesdale accepted a call from the parish and became rector on May 25, 1885.

On Nov. 1, 1892, Rev. Rogers Israel began his service.

MANY INDIAN RELICS.

[Daily Record, Oct. 25, 1902.]

At the meeting of the Historical Society held last evening the principal feature was an exhibition of a rare collection of Indian relics and a descriptive talk on them by Christopher Wren of Plymouth. It was intensely interesting and much enjoyed by the

audience. Mr. Wren has one of the most valuable collections of this kind in this section of the State and what adds to its interest is that it is almost entirely made up of local specimens. In connection with the exhibit he spoke briefly on the stone age and the ingenuity of the Indian in implements of use to him in his daily life.

Mr. Wren exhibited two large cabinets of relics that he has gathered during the past fifteen years. Most of them he picked up in this valley, but a few of those most prized in the collection came from distant States A great number of them he picked up along the river after the flood of last March, they having been washed from their places of lodgment by the force of the water and the height it attained. Several fine specimens were gathered at the camp sites of the Indians in the valley.

Mr. Wren has given the subject considerable study and he has acquired a familiarity with the mode of life of the Indians through the medium of his relics that makes his talks on the subject highly instructive. It is his intention to present to the society the entire collection. Among the relics he exhibited were: Calumet peace pipe and the beads that go with it, tobacco pouch, individual pipe made of soapstone, an especially fine collection of spear and arrow heads that must be seen to be appreciated, knives, tomahawks, net sinkers, ceremonial stones and many others. Mr. Wren was extended a vote of thanks for his address and asked to put it in form for publication.

Charles F. Hill of Hazleton presented to the society an Indian relic that will materially add to the society's collection. It is a curiously shaped sandstone that was used by the Indians who inhabited the lower end of the county. It is in the shape of a trough and was evidently used as a receptacle for grain while it was being pounded. On one side of the stone is the following inscription: "Gravel Creek Camp, 1752." The stone was for years used as pig trough by a man named McShea.

The following were elected members of the society: Mrs. I. S. White of Rock Island, Ill., corresponding member; James P. Dickson, William S. Tompkins, Hon. Henry W. Palmer, Christopher Wren, Miss Emily Ryman, Miss Rosalys Ryman and William John Raeder, resident members; Fred Hillman and Lieut. Joseph Wright Graeme, life members.

CAME FROM AN OLD FAMILY.

[Daily Record, Oct. 21, 1902.]

The death of Mrs. Ann F. Holcomb, a member of one of the oldest families of this valley, occurred yesterday morning at 1:30 at the family home in Askam, the cause of death being heart disease. The deceased had a wide acquaintance and won the admiration of all who came in contact with her, owing to her pleasant disposition and considerate ways. She was devoted to her family and a devout member of the Methodist Church. She was born in Hamilton, Ind., in 1838, which would leave her 64 years old.

Deceased was descended from the Moister family, which was among the first settlers of Wyoming Valley. Her father was the late Rev. R. Metcalf, a prominent clergyman in his day. There remain three sons and one daughter— M. E. Holcomb of the Williams Hardware Co. of this city, L. R. and G. C. of Askam, and Mrs. George Keiser of Askam. She is also survived by two brothers—J. W. Metcalf of Forty Fort and R. R. Metcalf of Askam.

The funeral will take place to-morrow afternoon at 2 o'clock with interment in Oaklawn Cemetery. Rev. J. R. Wagner will officiate.

BURIED VALLEY OF WYOMING.

[Daily Record, Nov. 5, 1902.]

The following interesting paper accounting for the depth of the Wyoming buried valley was read before the Academy of Natural Sciences, Philadelphia, last June by Benjamin Smith Lyman:

"It has long been matter for speculation and serious practical inquiry how the ancient Susquehanna valley, buried under glacial rubbish near Wyoming and Wilkes-Barre, could be at least 110 feet deeper than the apparently lowest possible outlet of the same valley near Bloomsburg, and ninety feet deeper than the one near Sunbury, as pointed out by State Geologist Lesley in the Pennsylvania State Geological Report G 7, 1883, p. xv., and by Assistant Geologist Prof. I. C. White, at p. 26. Later, in the Summary Final Report, Vol. III., Pt. I, 1895, p. 2,019, Assistant Geologist A. D. W. Smith gives a still greater depth recently found in the buried valley, at two miles below Wilkes-Barre, namely, 220 feet below the present Bloomsburg outlet, and 200

feet below the Sunbury one. The complete understanding of the buried valley in question is of the weightiest practical importance to the operators of the Wyoming anthracite basin; for the driving of coal mines unexpectedly into the glacial rubbish full of water has repeatedly caused loss of life and property, sometimes on a large scale. The consequent consciousness of danger and uncertainty about conditions exact great caution; and, perhaps, the guarding against unknown possibilities may occasion great losses that might to some extent be avoided if only the circumstances could be better understood. Several theories have, therefore, been devised in explanation of the observed facts; but none have proved to be at all satisfactory. It has, for example, been suggested that the glacier itself, before retreating and leaving the rubbish, may have scooped out the valley to that depth. But Lesley and others have repeatedly pointed out how insignificant is and must be the erosive action of glaciers; and, furthermore, it appears highly improbable that a glacier could not only scoop out a deep valley, but carry the vast amount of eroded material over the lip of the basin. In this case, too, that lip, near Bloomsburg, is about twenty miles beyond the nearest point ever reached by the glacier. In 1883, Lesley, in the passage just cited, was momentarily persuaded that there was no escape from admitting that the result had been accomplished by "sub-glacial erosion—rivers beneath the ice sheet, charged with angular drift materials, plowing deep valley grooves in the softer coal measures." But in the Summary Final Report, Mr. Smith states that Lesley "now regards his theory of subglacial erosion as wholly inadequate." Indeed, it would be hard to conceive how subglacial rivers could have maintained an erosive current at such a depth below the outlet of the valley. Mr. Smith cites the opinion of "at least one prominent mining engineer," that the buried valley "has no connected channel, but that the deep places are formed by a series of pot holes." It is true, pot holes are a subordinate glacial feature of the buried valley, and extend below its bottom forty feet or more into the coal measures, as described by Ashburner in the State Geological Report for 1885. But it is hardly conceivable that excavations on so grand a scale, as hundreds of bore holes have shown the buried valley to be, should have been effected, like pot holes, by rapid cur-

rents of water carrying the materials comminuted by means of swiftly whirling pebbles quite beyond the limits of such enormously large hollows. The immensity of the currents required for such tremendous action is wholly inadmissable. It is hardly necessary to discuss the extravagant idea that the waters of the now buried valley escaped to the sea through some originally deep subterranean crevice or channel, now hidden farther than ever out of sight by the glacial accumulations. The idea has been resorted to merely from the absence of any other thoroughly plausible explanation, in view of the evident impossibility of hollowing out a valley and carrying off the excavated material over a distant border two hundred feet higher than the bottom. What seems, however, to be an extremely simple, natural and probable solution of the problem has hitherto been apparently altogether overlooked. The crumbling of the rock beds into folds by the contraction of the earth's crust in cooling must necessisarily have been not a mere momentary movement, but in general an extremely slow one, continuing for many ages, perhaps, to be sure, intermittently, and may probabiy still be going on, even in some very ancient basins. A comparatively trivial amount of such action in the couple of hundred thousand years since glacial times would be ample to effect the observed results. For, if the Wyoming basin had thereby been depressed by only the wholly insignificant average amount of half a foot in a thousand years, and the rock saddles, or anticlinals, near Bloomsburg and Sunbury elevated at the same rate, the whole observed result would by this time be accomplished, and the old glacial valley would be found, as it is, a couple of hundred feet lower than those lowest present outlets. A liberal allowance, too, can easily be made for the degree to which those outlets have been eroded since the glacial action, and for the fact that they are not at the very summit of the anticlinals. Yet the movement would be a trifling one. In fact, the observed phenomena appear to be simply corroborations of what might with the utmost reason have been expected to occur; and the explanation is not by any means an arbitrary supposition of regional elevation or depression, conveniently imagined in order to suit facts apparently difficult to elucidate."

MASONIC SESQUICENTENNIAL.

· [Daily Record, Nov. 5, 1902.]

In commemoration of the 150th anniversary of the initiation of the immortal George Washington into th fraternity of Free and Accepted Masons, Lodge 61, itself one of the oldest lodges in the country, held suitable commemorative exercises last evening, there being a large attendance. There was vocal music by a quartet comprising William L. Raeder, Frank Puckey, Alfred E. Burnaford and Sterling Eyer, and instrumental music by Samuel Oppenheim, Adolph Hanson, Thompson H. Rowley, Ernest M. Hungerford and Harry Ash.

WASHINGTON AS A CITIZEN.

In speaking on the above theme William L. Raeder said in part:

I appreciate with much feeling the courtesy which prompted the invitation to me to respond to the sentiment "Washington as a Citizen." It is an honor which I prize very highly, and shall always remember.

I realize my inability to paint the word picture of this sentiment in the beautiful colors and with the delicate touch it warrants. I shall therefore not attempt more than to briefly trace his career and thereafter quote a few beautifnl tributes to his character.

Mr. Raeder then briefly reviewed his life, quoted Washington as Charles Wentworth Upman, Robert Treat Paine, Timothy Dwight, Rev. William Day, George Bancroft and Thomas Jefferson wrote of him, and closed with the following tribute:

Washington, the defender of his country, the founder of liberty, the friend of man. History and tradition are explored in vain for a parallel of his character. In the annals of modern greatness he stands alone, and the noblest names of antiquity lose their luster in his presence. Born the benefactor of mankind, he united all the qualities necessary to an illustrious career. Nature made him great, he made himself virtuous. Called by his country to the defense of her liberties, he triumphantly vindicated the rights of humanity, and on the pillars of national independence laid the foundation of a great republic.

Twice invested with supreme magistracy by the unanimous voice of a free people, he surpassed in the cabinet the glories in the field, voluntarily resigned the sceptre and the sword and returned

to the shades of private life. Magnanimous in youth, glorious through life, great in death, his highest ambition the happiness of mankind, his noblest victory the conquest of himself.

Bequeathing to posterity the inheritance of his name and building his monument in the hearts of his countrymen, he lived the ornament of the eighteenth century, and died regretted by a mourning world.

WASHINGTON AS A MASON.

An address was then given by Oscar J. Harvey on "Washington as a Mason." He began by alluding to the fact that there are persons who claim that Washington was not a Free Mason. Mr. Harvey did not have to proceed very long before he had abundantly proven that these allegations were incorrect and shown that the Father of his Country was a Mason of great prominence. Mr. Harvey stated that the first denial of the fact that Washington was a Mason was made during the anti-Masonic crusade which raged in this country during the years 1826 to 1837. Even since that period, well called the dark age of Free Masonry, so rife with anti-Masonic strategems, up to the present, it has been often claimed that Washington was not a Free Mason. Quotation was made from a Boston periodical as late as May, 1885, maintaining that Washington was not a Mason.

Mr. Harvey then spoke about the national Washington Monument at Washington, with the construction of which Free Masons were more or less identified, and he related the various steps of its construction from its inception in 1833 up to the time of its completion. Congress in 1848 granted a site for the monument, which, it is said, was the very spot Washington himself had marked as early as 1795 as the place for a monument to the American Revolution. On July 4 of the same year the cornerstone was laid with Masonic ceremonies. By 1854 the structure had risen to the height of 156 feet and had cost $300.000. From all the States in the Union flowed subscriptions, and various societies contributed blocks of stone and marble. The Grand Lodge of Pennsylvania appropriated $500 and sent a block of Pennsylvania marble, which may now be seen on the inner wall of the monument. In 1852, on the day of the presidential election, contribution boxes were open at he polls throughout the country for the monument fund.

The voters of Wilkes-Barre contributed $24. It was not until 1884 that the great shaft was completed. It is the tallest structure on the globe and the most imposing simple object of great dimensions in the whole world.

Washington was made a Mason in 1752 in the lodge at Fredericksburg, Va., at which time he was 20 years old. During the Revolutionary War ten military or traveling lodges were warranted in the American army. One of these held a meeting at Wilkes-Barre in 1779, at which time Gen. John Sullivan's army was passing up the Susquehanna to chastise the savages for the destruction of Wyoming during the previous year. At one of these lodges, held at Morristown, N. J., where Washington's headquarters were then located, Washington was present and insisted in initiating to membership Lafayette, then in the twenty-third year of his age. In 1780 there was a movement on foot to nominate a grand master over all the grand lodges in the United States, and Washington was suggested for the office. The project, however, was abandoned in 1774. Washington was elected an honorary member of Alexandria Lodge in Virginia, and he served as worshipful master. After his death the name of the lodge was changed to Alexandria-Washington, which it still bears.

In 1784 Lafayette revisited this country and to Washington at Mount Vernon he presented a Masonic apron and the same was used at the dedication of the Washington Monument in 1885. It is now the property of the Grand Lodge of Pennsylvania.

About 1791 or '2 Masonic honors began to be fairly showered upon the Father of his country and it became the custom to devote the first toast at Masonic banquets to the theme "Gen. Washington." One of the most interesting incidents in Washington's Masonic life was in 1793, when, clad in Masonic insignia, he, as President of the United States and acting grand master of Masons, laid with Masonic ceremony the cornerstone of the nation's capitol at Washington.

Numerous other occurrences were related by Mr. Harvey, showing Masonic affairs in which Washington participated. When Washington died, in 1799, Napoleon Buoneparte, who was a Free Mason, ordered the minister of the interior of France to erect in the gallery of the Tuilleries in Paris the statues of the greatest men in the world's history, and Washington was included in the list.

One of the latest instances of holding Washington in Masonic veneration was in August last, in London, when the American ambassador to Great Britain unveiled a portrait of Washington in Masonic regalia.

Mr. Harvey gave an account of the funeral of Washington. On his coffin were two crossed swords and his Masonic apron. All the pall bearers were colonels in the Continental Army and were members of Alexandria Lodge. In many of the principal towns of the country memorial services were held, some of them Masonic.

In Philadelphia, as the capital of the country, more elaborate services were held than in any other city, the exercises being in pursuance of resolution of Congress. The marshal of the day was Gen. Proctor, the artillery officer who had held the traveling military lodge in Wyoming Valley twenty years earlier. Prominent in the procession was a large body of Free Masons

About the time of the death of Washington this country was believed to be on the verge of war with France. Additions were made to the regular army, and a provisional force was also raised. In January, 1799, Capt. Samuel Bowman of Wilkes-Barre was commissioned by President Adams a captain in this provisional army, and, having enlisted a company of infantry here he was ordered to march with it to New Jersey, where it was mustered into the United States service as the 3d Company of the 11th Infantry.

Capt. Bowman had been an officer in the Revolutionary army, had personally known Washington, and had sat with him in an army Masonic lodge, and with him had become one of the original members of the Society of the Cincinnati. When Lodge 61 was in Wilkes-Barre in 1794 Capt. Bowman was one of its charter members. He was master of the lodge in 1797, and secretary in 1798 and '99. Upon the occasion of the Washington funeral ceremonies at Philadelphia, Capt. Bowman marched in this procession.

Mr. Harvey's address closed as follows:

In 1799 the only newspaper published in Northeastern Pennsylvania was the Wilkes-Barre Gazette and Luzerne Advertiser, a small four page weekly, edited and published here by Josiah Wright, a member of Lodge 61. The issue of the Gazette of Tuesday, December 24, 1799, appeared with the third page printed with a heavy black border, and in the editorial column on that

page this paragraph: "Last evening,
Monday, December 23d, after our paper
went to press, we received the truly
melancholy news of the death of Lieut.
Gen. George Washington. To inform
the public of so important an event
we immediately stopped the press."

The news of this event had evidently
reached Wilkes-Barre in the weekly
mail arriving Monday evening, and
was contained in a letter from Baltimore dated December 17—which letter
is printed in the issue of the Gazette
mentioned.

At this time the small and straggling
village of Wilkes-Barre 'had not yet
been erected into a borough. The
population of Wilkes-Barre Township,
including the village, consisted of only
about 800 souls.

Lodge 61 was then in the sixth year
of its life. Its membership was, in the
circumstances, small, and its place of
meeting was at the inn of Brother
Jesse Fell, a portion of which is still
standing at the corner of Northampton
and Washington streets. Here, on the
evening of Monday, December 23, 1799,
an "adjourned meeting" of the lodge
was held, at which Brother Fell, the
W. M., "communicated to the lodge
that such information was received
that left the truth thereof beyond a
doubt, of the lamented death of our illustrious friend and brother, Gen.
George Washington." It was then resolved "that the lodge wear mourning
for three months, in memory thereof."

Four days later, Friday, December
27, being St. John the Evangelist's Day,
a quarterly communication was held at
the lodge room, ten brethren being
present. (Capt. John P. Schott, W. M.,
Eleazer Blackman, S. W.· Obadiah
Smith, J. W.; Jesse Fell, secretary;
James Campbell, treasurer; Jean Fr.
Dupuy, Tyler; Arnold Colt, S. D.; E.
Bowman, J. D.; Jonathan Hancock and
Nicholas Smith.)

The officers of the lodge were duly installed, and then the lodge "proceeded
in procession, as is usual in the Masonic
Order," to the old log court house in
the Public Square, where a eulogium
on Washington was delivered by Hon.
Rosewell Welles, a member of the Luzerne County bar. Subsequently, at an
expense of $25.33 (as is shown by the
original account of Brother Fell, in my
possession,) the members of the lodge
dined together at Brother Feli's, "In
company with a number of invited
neighbors, and spent the day in har-
mony."

Rev. Horace E. Hayden presented the lodge with a steel engraving of a rare portrait of Washington taken in Masonic regalia. Mr. Hayden stated that it was given him by his kinsman, Sidney Hayden, who had it engraved (from an original painting made in 1794) for his book, "Washington and His Masonic Compeers." Washington sat for the painting, which was made for the lodge in Alexandria, and no other engraving of it was ever made than that for Sidney Hayden. Mr. Hayden paid a glowing tribute to Washington's memory. Afterwards the worshipful master presented the engraving to the Historical Society for permanent preservation and the same was accepted by Rev. Mr. Hayden.

At the conclusion of the program there were informal remarks by some of the brethren.

John Laning exhibited two old Masonic aprons, one belonging to his great-grandfather, Matthias Hollenback, and the other to his grandfather, Dr. Charles J. Christel.

THE FRENCH REFUGEES.

[Daily Record, Nov. 15, 1902.]

At a meeting of the Historical Society held last evening Rev. David Craft, who has achieved much fame as a historian in Northeastern Pennsylvania, read another of his interesting papers on the French settlement at Asylum, the home of the unfortunate French emigrants who were driven from their beloved country during the storms of the French revolution. In his previous paper Rev. Mr. Craft confined himself to an exhaustive description of the colony of refugees, but last evening he devoted himself almost entirely to an analysis of the character of the men who were foremost in the settlement, weaving a story about them and their families that could not but appeal to the interest of his audience. Rev. Mr. Craft has delved deeply into the history of this colony of royalist exiles and considerable of the material he presents in his paper is entirely new and worthy of more than passing notice. He has spent many years in research and study and the facts he has compiled are deserving of a prominent place among the stories that have been written concerning the early development of this section of Pennsylvania.

Ex-Judge Stanley Woodward presided and there was a good attend-

ance of members and visitors. The title of Rev. Mr. Craft's paper was "A day at Wyalusing" and it was in the nature of a narrative of a visit Mr. Craft and a friend recently made to the site of the old settlement. He spent much time in describing the plot of ground, the location of the principal buildings, the cemetery and house of worship. All this was interesting, but intensely so was his treatment of the men and women who sacrificed so much to establish homes in the wilderness of Pennsylvania, where they would be safe from the fury of the storms of the social and political upheaval that threatened them in their luxurious Parisian houses. The descendants of some of these refugees are now among the most prominent families of Northeastern Pennsylvania. All of them descended from the four French colonists who refused to return to France after the disruption of the colony, the family names of these four refugees being LaPorte, Prevost, LeFevre and Homet.

Rev. Mr. Craft during the course of his paper said that it was known that a survey of the plot of ground occupied by the refugees had been made, some among the elderly people still living remembering having seen it. After a long search it was found in a drawer in the desk bought at the sale of the effects of Hon. C. L. Ward. The possession of the map made it possible to locate many of the principal buildings of the settlement and it showed that the plot embraced about 1,600 acres of land. In one corner of the map is a finely executed pen picture in which America is represented as an enthroned goddess with hands outstretched welcoming the French refugees.

Mr. Craft called attention to several errors which the map has made it possible to correct, among them being the width of the streets. The map shows that the streets were sixty-six feet in width with the exception of the principal street, which had a width of 100 feet. Parts of these streets are now used as the boundaries of the farms of the present inhabitants. The colonists maintained a ferry and a wharf for the convenience of loading and unloading the boats. Actual measurements disprove the story that a large portion of the tract was lost by being washed away by the river.

When the French people abandoned Asylum they advertised the lands for sale and the upper portion of the tract was purchased by Mr. LaPorte and the

lower by Charles Homet. These belonged to the colony, but decided to cast their lot with the new country. Extended reference was made to the heads of these two families and attention was called to their descendants.

The story of Charles Homet, the speaker said, is full of serious romance. He was born in Paris in 1769 and was attached to the royal household. Being sympathizers with the royalists they were compelled to flee from their homes. Homet fled to the Bay of Biscay, but on his arrival found that the ship on which he was to sail had left her moorings and was five miles out at sea. He plunged into the sea and swam to the ship, landing more dead than alive. Mr. Craft told of his meeting on board with his future wife, his landing at Bordentown, N. J, and his arrival at Asylum in 1794. He was put in charge of the erection of the buildings that were to constitute the new settlement.

The huge building erected for baking purposes has latterly been mistaken for the palace, which was located further down the street. It was intended to be the finest building in America, the colonists having planned it for a residence for the unfortunate Marie Antoinette. They learned her fate before its completion. Its ruins are a silent mark of the devotion of the refugees to their queen. Mr. Homet was twice married and his descendants are among the most prominent farmers and enterprising citizens of Wyalusing. By his last marriage he was the father of eight sons and one daughter. He died in 1828. The brewery built by the colonists was alluded to, the plans for its enlargement never having been carried out, owing to the abandonment of the colony. The ruins of the building indicate that it was 75 by 40 feet. The home of Francis Homet, son of Charles, is near by, as is also the little church that was built through his enterprise. The names of the streets of the settlement are not shown on the old map.

In the little cemetery there are marks of the graves of eighteen or twenty of the settlers, the white boards that marked the graves having long since disappeared. In this cemetery is the grave of Mr. Prevost, who belonged to one of the first families of France and was a member of all its prominent philanthropic and patriotic societies. Mr. Prevost was drowned while trying to ford the river when it was high. Many of his descendants are residents of the northeastern counties. The

speaker believed that some permanent mark should be placed over the burial places of these refugees. The little log chapel was an important building in the settlement. All of the colonists were Roman Catholics and in this little place of worship the sacraments were administered and the various services of the church carried out. Here also there were many christenings and some marriage ceremonies. Some of the ecclesiasts after their arrival at Asylum devoted a portion of their time to business pursuits and others entirely abandoned their ecclesiastical duties.

The head of the La Porte family, which for the past hundred years has played so conspicuous a part in the political history and business activity of Wyoming and Bradford counties, was Bartholomew La Porte, whose forefathers were leaders in the political life of France for more than two centuries. He was born in Paris in 1778. He left an only son, the late John LaPorte of Towanda. After the abandonment of the colony the elder LaPorte became the owner of about 400 acres of the tract occupied by the refugees. He died in 1836, his wife surviving him sixteen years. In 1819 he was elected county commissioner and two years later he was re-elected. His only son, John La-Porte, was in the middle of the last century one of the leading citizens of Bradford County. He was county auditor, member of the General Assembly in 1829 and 1832, during the last term speaker of the House. He also served two terms in Congress, was associate judge, surveyor general of the State and a partner in one of the largest banking houses of the county. He died in August, 1862. The LaPorte family occupied what was known at Asylum as the "Great" house for many years. It was torn down in 1846, but the site can still be recognized.

Another name prominent in the settlement was DuPont. Victor DuPont, after the breaking up of the settlement, went to Delaware to join his brother in the manufacture of gunpowder. Another family conspicuous in the settlement was Prevost. Two members of the family were in Napoleon's Russian campaign. The Prevost and DuPont families are now quite numerous in this country, the most prominent of them being the descendants of the French refugees.

The cause of the break-up of the settlement was the general amnesty decree which was adopted in 1803. This threw the doors open for the return of

the exiles and all, with few exceptions, took advantage of it, being tired of the hardships they were compelled to endure in a new country.

At the conclusion of the reading of the paper Rev. Mr. Craft was given a vote of thanks and it was decided to have the paper published in pamphlet form.

Announcement was made that at the January meeting Professor Peck of Lafayette College is to read a paper on a geological subject and that William Griffith has agreed to serve as curator of paleobotany. It was also announced that portraits of Martin Coryell and Lieut. Obadiah Gore are to be donated to the society.

REVOLUTIONARY SOLDIERS.

[Daily Record, Nov. 22, 1902.]

The event of unveiling the memorial tablets bearing the names of Revolutionary soldiers buried within the limits of Wyoming County drew a large gathering to Tunkhannock on Friday afternoon at 2:30 o'clock. As the day was pleasant, nearly every precinct in the county was represented. At the appointed hour the students of the primary and high schools marched from the school buildings by twos to the corridor of the court house, where the tablets had been placed in the walls on either side of the long hall leading to the rear of the building. A large throng awaited the arrival of the scholars and as soon as possible after their arrival the interesting program that had been arranged for the occasion was begun and carried out, as follows: Singing, "Rally, comrades," by the scholars, numbering nearly 300 trained voices; which was followed by prayer, offered by Rev. H. H. Wilbur, pastor of the M. E. Church, Tunkhannock. The presentation address was by Mrs. James Wilson Piatt of Tunkhannock Chapter, D. A. R., and was made up of well chosen words conveying the object of the presentation, which were delivered in a distinct and clear tone of voice and easy manner. The response by attorney W. Ernest Little was appreciative and instructive. The throng assembled in the court room at 3 o'clock and after order was restored all assisted in singing "Red, White and Blue." Rev. David Craft of Angelica, N. Y., the historian and orator, was introduced and held the audience well for nearly an hour and interested it beyond its anticipation. The subject was "Wyoming

County and the Revolutionary War."
His address was not only instructive
and historical, but filled with patriotism, and his delivery was clear and eloquent. The tablets are fine specimens
of workmanship, 2½ by 4 feet in size,
of pure white marble of the finest qual-
ity. The lettering, which is laid in gold
leaf, is as follows: "In memory of the
Revolutionary soldiers buried in Wyo-
ming County, by Tunkhannock Chapter,
D. A. R., November, 1902." They bear
the names of the following: William
Hooker Smith, George Reynolds, Jesse
Dickinson, Timothy Lee, Gabriel Ely,
John McMillan, Joseph Fassett, Jere-
miah Osterhout, Lemuel Vose, Job
Whitcomb, Prince Alden, James Thayre,
Josiah Rogers, Henry Love, Ebenezer
Stevens, John Whitcomb, William Jack-
son, David Loveless, David Doolittle,
Mason Fitch Aldrich, Robert Reynolds,
Ambrose Gaylord, Paul Keeler, Mark
Keeney, Israel Harding, Elisha Hard-
ing, Ebenezer Parish, Marshall Dixon,
Obadiah Taylor, Elisha Ames, John
Carney, Comfort Shaw, Isaiah Adkins,
Chandler Robinson, Samuel Hallstead
and John Seymore Jacks.

CAME FROM AN OLD FAMILY.

[Daily Record, Nov. 24, 1902.]

Mrs. Lydia Bennett Smith of Kingston,
widow of Robert N. Smith, died of general debility at her home on Plymouth
street at 7 o'clock on Sunday morning.
She was the daughter of Josiah and Sarah
Taylor Bennett and was born in Hanover Feb. 6, 1813.

The family was originally from Connecticut and was among the first settlers
of Wyoming Valley.

Mrs. Smith united with the Methodist
Church when only 12 years of age and
had always been a consistent Christian
and had endeared herself to those who
knew her best by her courage in afflic-
tion and patience in suffering.

She is survived by the following chil-
dren: Sarah, at home; J. Bennett of
Wilkes-Barre, Mrs. Perry C. Rozelle of
Mt. Zion and Samuel R., at home.

The funeral will be held on Tuesday at
2 p. m. Interment in the family plot at
Forty Fort. Services will be conducted at
the house by Rev. L. C. Murdock, assisted by Rev. F. von Krug.

Many ancestors of deceased were in the
Wyoming massacre and the history of
this valley is replete with incidents connected with the family.

MRS. JOHN CONSTINE'S DEATH.

[Daily Record, Nov. 29, 1902.]

Mrs. John Constine, one of the oldest and best known residents of this city, died suddenly last evening from apoplexy at her home, 51 Public Square. The deceased was born on Feb. 22, 1823, and had she lived until Washington's Birthday would have been 80 years of age. Her husband, who was a prominent merchant here for years, died on Feb. 10, 1882. Her son Lewis, who during life was a member of the 143d Regt., under command of the late Col. Edmund L. Dana, was killed at White Oaks Church, Va., in the year 1863. Her daughter Carrie died in 1871 and another daughter, Jennie, died in the year 1865. She is survived by five sons and two daughters—Edward, a well known merchant; Augustus, Charles, Ambrose, Samuel, Mrs. Ella, wife of attorney Joseph D. Coons, and Miss Parmelia, who resided with her mother.

The deceased was born in Pretzfeld, Bavaria, Germany, and came to this country in 1839. Her maiden name was Fannie Long and she was a sister of the late Simon Long, who died on Dec. 31 last. The only surviving member of her family is her brother, Marx Long, who is the oldest living merchant in business in this city, having passed his eighty-fifth birthday anniversary on Oct. 1 last.

The deceased had not been in the best of health for the past ten years, though she was about more or less, occasionally being confined to her bed. She and her husband first resided at what was then commonly called "Bowman's Corner," opposite Jonas Long's Sons' store. In the year 1848 they moved to 51 Public Square, where deceased resided until death.

Mrs. Constine has many relatives living in this city, New York and Philadelphia. She was the grandmother of Eugene and Bertha Constine, Mrs. Alexander Meyers of St. Louis and Miss Daisy Wasserman of this city. On Nov. 1 last she fell and broke an arm, and had been confined to her room. Yesterday she apparently felt as well as usual and the messenger of death came with scarcely any warning.

The deceased was also a sister-in-law of Rev. Henry Rubin of this city, who retired many years ago from the pulpit.

The deceased was one of the kindest of women. She had a good word for every one. It was her nature to be pleasant and cheerful. She did much

for the poor and never turned a deserving person from her door. She
cared for her family devotedly. She
was a member of B'nai B'rith Jewish
congregation.

FUNERAL OF MRS. JAMES BOYD.

[Wilkes-Barre Times.]

At 2:45 o'clock on Monday afternoon
the remains of Mrs. James Boyd, who
died at Ashley, Nov. 28, 1902, were
interred in the family plot in Hollenback Cemetery. The cortege left the
deceased's home shortly after 1 o'clock,
and included only the immediate relatives, the interment being private. For
two hours this morning, however, the
house was thrown open to the public
to take a farewell glance at the coun-
tenance of the deceased. The funeral
services at the house were in charge of
Rev. Dr. G. H. Broening, pastor of the
Ashley Presbyterian Church, and Rev.
W. J. Day of Luzerne Borough, both of
whom paid high tribute to the memory
of Mrs. Boyd. For over twenty years
Rev. Mr. Day was her pastor, and he
spoke of her noble Christian nature
and high character. The pall bearers,
representing the elders, deacons and
trustees of the Ashley Presbyterian
Church, were: Jacob Drumheller, C. D.
Geissler, Frank Gemmel, William Klap-
roth, Godfrey Smith and David R.
Hughes. On the casket was placed a
number of beautiful and appropriate
floral offerings. Relatives were present
from Mauch Chunk, Freeland and Rock-
port.

[In the death of Mrs. Boyd, Ashley
has lost one whom all admired—a
woman of noble character, a devoted
mother, who made her home a para-
dise. Few people live to enjoy sixty-
three years of married life, but Mr. and
Mrs. Boyd passed the sixty-third matri-
monial milestone before death came
and took away the wife. But this long
and upright career comes from careful
habits, a strictly religious and industrious life—a life and experience that can
well be thoroughly studied and emu-
lated by the younger generation, for,
if strictly adhered to, as in the case of
Mrs. Boyd, reward is sure to follow in
that great and mysterious beyond
where the wicked cease from troubling
and the weary find eternal rest. Mr.
and Mrs. Boyd are included among the
pioneer residents of Ashley. They
moved there when the borough was a

mere village, and have lived to see it
become a leading railroad centre, to see
its small and primitive school houses
replaced by handsome and imposing
structures; to see its old fashioned single chapel removed by the march of
time and the religiously inclined worship in four beautiful churches; they
saw the first locomotive which came to
the place, as well as the first horse car,
which plied between that town and this
city, as well as many other things
which marked the progress of the century recently closed. Surely. such lives
should be an inspiration to those entering manhood and womanhood, for they
emphasize the lesson told in that bibli-
cal passage which refers particularly to
the straight and narrow path, and the
reward which comes to those who religiously keep within its boundaries.—
Editor Times.]

GOOD WOMAN'S DEATH.

[Daily Record, Dec. 5, 1902.]

Mrs. Melinda White of Ashley died
yesterday morning at 6:30 o'clock of
pneumonia, aged 83 years, after an illness of three weeks. She was the
widow of Rev. John White, who died
in Ashley some twenty years ago. She
leaves two sons and one daughter—
druggist W. D. White and Charles B.
White, city editor of the Times, both of
Wilkes-Barre, and Mrs. Thomas C.
Williams of Ashley. She is also survived by three sisters—Mrs. Araminta
Safford of Kingston, Mrs. Elizabeth
Kidney of Wilkes-Barre and Mrs. Maria
Boyst of Port Jervis, N. Y.

Mrs. White had lived in Ashley for
over a generation, and witnessed its
growth and prosperity from the time
the stage made its daily trip through
that place until the advent of the trolley cars. Both she and her husband
were closely identified with the Methodist Church of Ashley and the present
generation does not know how much of
the present success of that denomination is owing to their untiring zeal and
faithfulness, their sacrifices and energy,
their godly lives and consecrated service.

Mrs. White was in truth a mother to
Israel, and her kindly face and lovely
character will not soon be forgotten.

She was a descendant of the old
Blackman family, the older members of
which bore a prominent part in the
Wyoming massacre. Mrs. White was of
sturdy ancestry.

DIED IN WISCONSIN.

The Janesville (Wisconsin) Weekly Gazette has the following to say about the death of Mrs. Caroline A. Downing, formerly of Wilkes-Barre:

"One of Rock County's pioneer residents crossed the borderland into the lite eternal 1902, Dec. 12, death coming to Mrs. Caroline A. Downing. The end came peacefully at the home of Mr. and Mrs. James W. Scott, with whom Mrs. Downing had made her home for the past eleven years.

"Death was the result of heart trouble and the effects of paralytic strokes, Mrs. Downing having had several shocks during the past few years. Five years ago she and her daughter, Mrs. Scott, were in a railroad accident in which Mrs. Downing's shoulder was hurt, while Mrs. Scott sustained such severe injuries to her back that she will be an invalid for life. Mrs. Downing never fully recovered from the nervous shock and for three years past she has been in very poor health. She had been confined to her bed for two weeks and was unconscious since last Thursday.

"Caroline A. Holcomb Downing was born in Wilkes-Barre, Pa., on Dec. 2, 1827, and had completed the seventy-fifth year of her life. With her husband, the late Benjamin F. Downing, and family, she came to Wisconsin in 1864, settling on a farm four miles west of this city. In 1891 she came to Janesville to make her home with her daughter, with whom she has resided ever since.

"Deceased was a devout member of the Congregational Church and was a woman of the most loyal and unselfish character. A rare devotion to her home and children, a kindly consideration for the sick and unfortunate and a readiness to serve her friends made her life beautiful and she was beloved by all who knew her.

"She was the mother of nine children, five of whom are left to mourn. They are: Mrs. John E. Graham of Canyon City, Col.; Charles B. Downing, Manitou, Oklahoma; Marvin B. Downing, Milton, Wis., and Mrs. James Bliss and Mrs. James W. Scott of this city. Nine grandchildren, two great grandchildren, one brother, Charles Holcomb of Humboldt, Kan., and one sister, Mrs. Melissa, wife of G. W. Moore of 63 Blackman street, Wilkes-Barre, Pa., also survive."

F. A. B. KOONS DEAD.

[Daily Record, Dec. 13, 1902.]

At his home at Huntington Mills, this county. yesterday morning occurred the death of F. A. B. Koons, a well known farmer and paper. manufacturer, aged nearly~72 years, after a long illness of paralysis.

Mr. Koons came from an old family. John and Anna Fellows Koons, natives of Monroe and Pike counties, were his parents and he was born in New Columbus April 7, 1831. Deceased's father was a prominent merchant and surveyor and at one time associate judge of the county. In the year 1819 he moved his family to this county, where he died Feb. 8, 1878, aged 83 years. The son graduated from the public schools and was sent to Dickinson Seminary, and when 22 years of age was engaged as a clerk with a hardware firm in Philadelphia, with which he remained two years.

Soon afterwards Mr. Koons opened a hardware store in Pittston and two years later. took a traveling tour in the West. opening a store in Harveyville after his return. He also conducted a store at Town Hill and later at Huntington Mills. In 1867 he and his two brothers built the Huntington Valley paper mills and in 1884 he purchased the share of one of his brothers and when the other died he became manager. He also owned two large farms.

Mr. Koons in 1855 married Helen R. Larned, who survives. When the Civil War broke out Mr. Koons enlisted on Nov. 8, 1861, in Co. C, 56th Regt. Pennsylvania Volunteers. He participated in the battle of Bull Run and minor engagements. He was taken prisoner and sent to Libby Prison for six weeks. For gallant service he was promoted to the rank of captain and was honorably discharged in January, 1863.

Mr. Koons was on the famous Lutz mureder jury and was the one that held the first jury on that case up so long. He was forced to give in, however, against his will on account of sickness, and because of this Lutz secured a new trial.

NEW ENGLAND SOCIETY.

[Daily Record, Dec. 20, 1902.]

As has been the custom for fifteen years the members of the New England Society of Northeastern Pennsylvania gathered around the festal board in Scranton last evening, in the Board of Trade building. There was a large attendance, some 150, and the affair

had a new feature, in that the partici-
pants instead of being seated at two or
three large tables, sat around small
tables accommodating from four to
eight persons. Consequently some very
agreeable little parties were formed.

C. H. Welles presided and the singing
of patriotic songs was led by W. J.
Torrey. Previous to the dinner, which
was served at 7 p. m., the company met
for an informal reception and to exchange the annual greetings—for the
society meets only once a year. The
speakers comprised Rev. Dr. M. W.
Stryker, president of Hamilton College,
whose topic was "The Modern Puritan;" Prof. John Tyler of Amherst College, a professor of biology, who spoke
on "The Evolution of the Pilgrim;" and
Rev. J. H. Odell, pastor of the Second
Presbyterian Church of Scranton, who
had for his theme "Old and New England."

MRS. C. I. A. CHAPMAN DEAD.

All who knew her were shocked on
Saturday on hearing news of the sudden and unexpected death of Mrs. Martha Blanchard Chapman, the estimable
wife of C. I. A. Chapman of Port
Blanchard. The deceased was almost
a daily visitor to Pittston, making the
trip on the trolley cars. About 10 a. m.
on Dec. 27, 1902, she hurried to the car
tracks, from her home on the hillside
at Port Blanchard, to go to Pittston.
The effort seemed too severe for one
of her years and she was utterly exhausted as she boarded the car. By
the time Moylan's store was reached in
Port Griffith, about one mile from her
home, it was noticed that her condition was critical and the car was halt-
ed and she was carried into the Moylan residence, but life had fled ere she
reached the house. Every effort was
made to resuscitate her but all to no
avail. Undertaker Cutler of Pittston
removed the body to the family home.

For years deceased had suffered with
heart trouble and indigestion and it is
surmised that the haste in reaching the
car aggravated the former. She was
70 years and 29 days of age, having
celebrated her 70th birth anniversary
on Nov. 29. Although advanced in
years she was ever active and few people would have correctly guessed her
age, as she was as quick and spry as
many people twenty years her junior.

She was a descendant of one of the
oldest and best known Wyoming Valley
families. Her parents, John and Sarah
Blanchard, were pioneer settlers in the

Port Blanchard neighborhood, and at one time owned a large tract of land at that place. The mother was a sister of the late George Lazarus and came from Northampton County, while the father came from New England. They were very well known in this region. Deceased spent nearly all of her life at Port Blanchard. She and her husband, C. I. A. Chapman, were married within one year of half a century ago and they have lived at Port Blanchard. Mrs. Chapman was a woman of fine characteristics and through all the years of her life her words and works had an important influence upon the community in which she lived—a good wife, a kind mother and a sincere friend. Her husband is well known throughout the upper portion of the county. He was a civil engineer, a veteran of the Civil War and a writer of wide reputation, many of his communications having from time to time appeared in the Record. On account of ill health he has lived a retired life for some years.

Deceased was a life long member of the Broad street Presbyterian Church of Pittston and was among the leading workers in all matters pertaining to the church. She was also a member of Dial Rock Chapter, Daughters of the American Revolution of West Pittston.

Besides her husband the following children survive: . Maxwell Chapman of Scranton, Blanchard Chapman of Port Blanchard, and Mrs. W. H. Dean of Wilkes-Barre, wife of Professor Dean of Hillman Academy.

SUMMER FRESHET OF 1826.

The following is clipped from the Wyoming Herald of June 30, 1826:

THE FRESHET.

The drought no longer exists—nature has assumed a different aspect. Fields of grain which a few days ago were suffering with the unusual dryness of the season, are now beaten to the earth by a long and heavy rain. The Susquehanna has for the past few days been swollen to no ordinary height. Fields of grain on its banks have been inundated with its waters, and in all probability spoiled, or very much injured. We learn there has been a great destruction of property in the neighboring townships—bridges swept away, mills and dams carried off, roads cut to pieces, etc., etc. It is to be feared that the injury done will prove extensive.

MRS. WORTHINGTON DEAD.

[Daily Record, Jan. 7, 1903.]

The Sterling (Ill.) Gazette reports the death on Dec. 27, 1902, of Mrs. Sarah Worthington, who nearly seventy years ago was a resident of Wilkes-Barre. She was nearly 96 years of age, having been born in Philadelphia in 1807. Her maiden name was McShane and she came from a cultured and refined family. She was an artist and enjoyed the pleasures of painting until past 80. She was a life long Presbyterian.

"On April 24, 1834, Sarah McShane was married to Eliphalet B. Worthington, a young editor who was publishing a paper at Wilkes-Barre, Pa. Three years later the young couple decided to move to the great West, which was attracting many. They started in early March, and a month later landed at Savanna from a Mississippi steamboat. There were no roads. Indian trails winding over the virgin prairies served to point the way, swamps and unbridged streams were frequent and the trip made in the early spring time was one of hardship for the young gentlewoman, her babe and the husband unusued to frontier hardships. They arrived safely, however, and found on the site of Sterling four log cabins. One was occupied by Mr. Worthington's brother Elijah, who had come West the year before.

"Mrs. Worthington was energetic and opened the first school in the autumn of 1838. The settlers gave her some assistance, built a building and donated her the ground on which it stood. There were ten pupils enrolled and for many years Mrs. Worthington was the village schoolmistress. The year following the opening of the school the strenuous young teacher made a further effort toward refining and elevating the community by teaching a class in the art of painting.

"In 1841 Mr. Worthington was made postmaster and continued to hold that office through three administrations. He was also deputy circuit clerk for fifteen years. In the autumn of 1871 he died.

"There were five children born to Mr. and Mrs. Worthington, who grew to maturity, but all but two of them are dead.

"She was the last survivor of five families that built their log cabins on the banks of Rock River over three score of years ago and began the strug-

gle which has borne fruit beyond their wildest dreams.

"A lady matured in a refined home in Philadelphia. She married a young editor, who with his brave bride faced the dangers of the wilderness and finally found their home here. The wolf and panther were still at home in the forests. The fear of a vengeful red man lately spoiled of his hunting grounds was not unfounded. The prairies were trackless wastes of swamp and waving grass, the woods were thickets of untouched growths of tree and brable. The trail of the red man was the only path, and the only sounds were those of nature's voices."

Previous to her marriage, as the Record learns from S. H. Lynch, Miss McShane kept a select school in Wilkes-Barre, about 1830.

Her uncle, Francis McShane, in 1811 started a cut nail factory on Franklin street, above Market. It was quite a success and reduced the price of wrought nails, then in use. He married Miss Fanny Bulkeley, who after his death become the wife of Henry F. Lamb.

Elijah Worthington published the Anti-Masonic Advocate here about 1830-32, but sold to Eliphalet and emigrated to Illinois, where Eliphalet followed him with his young wife.

The Worthington family lived at Harvey's Lake, Joseph H. being their father. Mrs. Worthington's mother was a sister to Edward Lynch, a former cashier of the Wyoming Bank. Her youngest sister, Mary McShane Lawrence, is the only survivor of the family and lives at Jersey City, N. J.

SELIGMAN BURGUNDER DEAD.

[Daily Record, Jan. 12, 1903.]

Seligman Burgunder, one of the oldest and best known citizens of this city, who retired from business pursuits about eleven years ago, died at his home, 441 South River street, late yesterday afternoon of heart trouble, complicated with stomach ailment, from which he had been suffering for some months past. He was 79 years of age and up to the time he was taken ill he enjoyed fairly good health.

.The deceased was a brother of B. Burgunder, who resides on Northampton street, and an uncle of Herman Burgunder, doing business on South Main street.

The deceased was united in marriage on Sept. 15, 1852, to Miss Regina Long, a sister of the late Jonas Long and the late Isaac Long. She is now in her 77th year and on Oct. 14, 1902, they celebrated their fiftieth wedding anniversary. The marriage ceremony was performed by Rabbi Strasser, the first rabbi of the synagog on South Washington street.

Mr. Burgunder at that time was one of the town's progressive young business men, having arrived here in the autumn of 1851 from Wurzburg, Bavaria, Germany, where he was born in 1824. He associated himself in the butchering business with his brother, Bernard Burgunder, but shortly afterward withdrew from the firm and after a brief residence in Baltimore and Cumberland, Md., he returned to this city to engage in the meat business on his own account, and by hard and diligent work he was remarkably successful in this undertaking. It was a great undertaking in those days for any merchant to launch a business here, for Wilkes-Barre then was only a small village. The first cargo of anthracite coal had yet to pass beyond the mountains of Luzerne County, and what is now our busy Public Square was then hardly more than the common meeting place for plain country folk, who came to Wilkes-Barre with the products of their farm to exchange for the merchants' wares. Old Ship Zion, a public market, a Strong house and an unpretentious house occupied various sites on the present court house plot. Mr. Burgunder's place of business was then on the site now occupied by the Laning building, and here for twenty-five years he carried on the meat business with great success, numbering among his patronage the best families of the town.

About eleven years ago he retired from active business pursuits, having acquired during his long and honorable career enough of this world's goods to assure himself and family a comfortable existence for the remainder of their lives.

Aside from his wife, who survives him, are three children: Mrs. Samuel Pragheimer, residing now at Mount Sterling, Kentucky, where her husband is engaged in business; Miss Carrie Burgunder and Abraham L. Burgunder, residing in Wilkes-Barre. There are two granddaughters, Misses Maud and Mabel Pragheimer.

HISTORICAL SOCIETY MEETING.

[Daily Record, Jan. 17, 1903.]

There was a large attendance last evening at the meeting of the Historical Society, before which Dr. Frederick B. Peck, professor of geology at Lafayette College, delivered a learned illustrated discourse on the "Atlantosaur and Tritanotherium beds of Wyoming." Though the lecture was in great part scientific, the speaker with the assistance of a large number of steropticon views made it sufficiently plain to be interesting and instructive to the layman. Most of the lecture was devoted to the results of several weeks' dinosaur hunting and to a description of the frightful looking monsters of this class which inhabited North America during the mesezoic age. Aside from the scientific value of the lecture it contained many interesting incidents in connection with the travels of the expedition which started out from Laramie, Wyoming, in 1899, to explore the region which furnished such a wealth of material for Professor Marsh along this same line. Pictures of the huge vertebrates, both of the carnivorous and herbiverous classes were thrown on the canvas and the audience was given an intelligent idea of the general appearance of the monsters which trod the earth at that time.

Hon. Stanley Woodward presided and in introducing the lecturer said that for reasons which would be at once manifest to the audience he would not venture to say anything on the subject of the discourse. Dr. Peck prefaced his remarks with an expression of thanks for the honor of election to honorary membership in the society, it being all the more appreciated from the fact that the membership is so small. He said that he could not boast of having had any special advantages in the study of geology in the region to which he would call the attention of his hearers. The dinosaur beds to which he called attention lie in the Jurassic period, which geology corresponds to the mediaeval period in history.

The speaker referred to geology as the strong, lusty youth of the sciences, being less than one hundred years old.

It has radically changed the line of thought, the earth now counting its years by the scores of millions instead of by the few thousands, as in the old days. While the old geologists taught that the various formations were due to cataclysms or revolutions the modern conception of geology treats it as a succession of events. In many things, he said, the American geologists take precedence over their European brethren. Dr. Peck then went into a description of the dinosaur hunting expedition, of which he was a member, and gave an interesting recital of it and of the discoveries made concerning these strange animals. The most striking of them belong to the reptile group, which the lecturer described in detail.

They are remarkably bird-like in their formation and their remains are much more abundant in the State of Wyoming than in any other place. These animals ranged from the size of an ordinary domestic fowl or rabbit to ninety feet in length and forty tons in weight. They are so bird-like in appearance that Professor Hitchcock did not know whether or not he was dealing with birds or reptiles. The finest discoveries of the carnivorous dinosaur remains were made in the Come bluffs. The largest of the herbivorous variety which ever trod the earth was about ninety feet long, twenty-five feet in height and forty to fifty tons in weight. They rarely used their front feet and have, therefore, often been taken for bipeds. The last dinosaur slide shown by Dr. Peck represented the last of the race. It did not live during the Jurassic period but at the close of the cretaceous age.

The dinosaur expedition was sent out by the Union Pacific R. R. It started out from Laramie, Wyoming, and consisted of eighty-five individuals, representing thirty-five institutions.

The only business before the meeting was to elect the following members:

Resident—Frederic E. Zerbey, J. C. Powell and Miss Martha A. Maffet.

Corresponding—Stewart Culin, curator of archeology of the University of Pennsylvania; Charles Johnson, curator of Wagner Free Institute, Philadelphia.

Honorary—Dr. Frederick B. Peck, professor of geology of Lafayette College.

WILKES-BARRE IN 1830.

Rev. Dr. Baab of California, a resident of Wyoming Valley seventy-four years ago, writes as follows in the Herald and Presbyter concerning Wilkes-Barre:

There was a public square in the centre of Wilkes-Barre, and on it were four buildings—the Court House, the Hall of Records, the Meeting House and the Academy. But the Meeting House was not a free place of worship. It was occupied by the Presbyterians, whose pastor was Rev. Nicholas Murray, afterwards known as "Kerwin" from his letters to Archbishop Hughes. The pulpit in this church was ten feet or more above the floor, and reached by a winding stairway. It was box-like, and we could see only the head and arms of the preacher. Above it was a sounding board. The pews were high-backed, so that in looking over the congregation one could see only their heads. Every pew had a door, and there were locks on some of the doors, so that only the owner and his family could get in. There were a few pews back near the door for strangers or for residents who were not pew-holders; but most of these classes sat in the galleries. There were no ushers to seat people, and no such hospitality as we find in the most of our Protestant churches to-day. We sat during the singing, which was led by a precentor, and stood up during the prayer. The collections were not taken on plates as now, but in little bags, each fastened to the end of a long rod, so that the deacons could reach to the remotest person in the long pews. Everybody was expected to go to church at least once on the Sabbath, and families, as the bell tolled, marched in in solemn procession, and all sat together in the family pew.

The Sunday school hour was devoted especially to hearing the scholars recite portions of Scripture which they had memorized during the week. For every ten verses memorized the scholar received a blue ticket. When he had ten blue tickets he was entitled to red one, and when he had ten red ones he received a copy of the New Testament.

Though the academy on the public square belonged to the city it was not a free school. The trustees elected the teacher and fixed the rate of tuition; but the salary depended upon what the teacher could collect. He sent out bills once in three months. The boys and girls were together in all the classes. Special attention was given to Latin. We were put into the Latin grammar as soon as we could read, and I was translating the Historia Sacra before I was 9 years old. For any slight offense we were feruled on the right hand so severely that it was sore and painful for many hours. The boys and girls of to-day would rebel against such treatment. We had only Saturday afternoons as a half-holiday. Saturday morning was devoted to the writing and reading of compositions, and Wednesday afternoon to declamations.

Maj. Wandell of Mehoopany died at his home in that place on Sunday evening, Jan. 25, as the result of a fall from a hay stack on Jan. 17. The deceased was a son of John G. and Vina Mowrey Wandell, who came to Mehoopany from Albany, N. Y., in 1806, and settled on the place owned by the deceased and where he was born in 1816 and where he has continuously resided. He was one of seventeen children of whom only one survives, Johnston H. Wandell of Mehoopany.

In 1835 while working on the West Branch he was hurt, resulting in the loss of his left leg below the knee. He was a hard working and industrious man and was well known. He is survived by his wife, who was Mary Barnhart, and four children: Schuyler and Derrick of Mehoopany, Mrs. Vina Allen and Mrs. Rose Myers of Jenningsville. The funeral was held at the Baptist Church in Mehoopany on Tuesday, Jan. 27, and was conducted by Rev. T. E. Phillips, with interment in Vaughn Cemetery.

ANCESTORS IN MASSACRE.

The Wyalusing correspondent sends the following:

Andrew Jackson Elliott, a prominent farmer, died at his home at Merryall, three miles out of town, on Sunday morning, his death resulting from a paralytic stroke received several weeks ago. Mr. Elliott, whose age was 74, is survived by his companion and nine adult children, one daughter, Miss Arminda, being a missionary in the Canton field, China, working under the foreign board of the Presbyterian Church. The funeral will be held at the homestead on Wednesday at 2 p. m., Rev. M. L. Cook conducting the services.

The Elliotts are pioneers here, having come from the Wyoming Valley shortly after the massacre, in which they took a prominent part, displaying great courage in defense of the fort. Joseph, a grandfather of the subject of this notice, being one of the two who escaped the death blow of cruel Queen Esther at Bloody Rock. Joseph having been captured by the savages, by superhuman strength wrested himself from the grasp of the fiendish horde, plunged into the Susquehanna, across which he swam to the opposite shore, though severely wounded while in the stream.

MASSACRE ANCESTRY.

[Daily Record, Feb. 19, 1903.]

The Wyalusing correspondent of the Record sends the following:

Capt. John G. Brown of Sugar Run, near here, died on Monday afternoon. after a long illness, aged 71 years. The captain's ancestors participated in the Wyoming battle at the time of the massacre, those of them surviving the conflict settling in these parts at an early day.

In 1862 Mr. Brown was acting deputy sheriff of this county, but at the call of President Lincoln for 300,000 men that summer he at once entered the army, becoming captain of Co. I, 141st Regt., Pa. Vols. His command was early assigned to the Army of the Potomac, in which it served till the close of the war, there being in the service hardly a regiment that suffered a decimation equal to that of the 141st. At Gettysburg the captain was shot through his neck, the minnie ball making a dangerous wound that nearly cost the brave officer his life, the effects of the shot causing serious suffering many years later.

Returning from the army, Capt. Brown engaged in farming. a pursuit he followed the rest of his life. He was temperate, industrious and exceedingly unassuming, it being a rare thing for him to mention his experiences in army life. He received a small pension, but not at all commensurate with his rank or disability. He was twice married, his first wife, a daughter of the late John Morrow, dying in early life. He was a Mason, a lifelong Republican and an adherent of the Presbyterian faith. His farm was well tilled and his home, which commanded a fine view of the river valley, offered a liberal hospitality to all who came under its inviting roof, Mrs. Brown being a delightful entertainer.

The deceased is survived by his companion and six children, three sons and three daughters, all nearly grown up.

RHOADS FAMILY REUNION.

The annual reunion of the Rhoads family took place yesterday at the Rhoads Hotel at Harvey's Lake and among those present were: Eugene Rhoads and wife of Shenandoah. Byron Rhoads cf Pittsburg, George R. Rhoads of Providence, R. I.; James Rhoads, son William and daughter Kathlyn of Allentown and Mr. and Mrs. Mace of Brooklyn, N. Y.

A New Year dinner was served at 2 o'clock and luncheon at 9 o'clock in the evening. The entire family was present with the exception of Aaron Rhoads and wife of Providence, R. I., who for the first time in the history of the reunions could not be present.

There were also twenty guests aside from the family. After dinner the party went on the lake, each with a pair of skates, and enjoyed skating on the ice until sundown. The affair was one of the most pleasant reunions the family has ever held.

SOME GENEALOGY.

Harry and John Hines, accompanied by their father, ex-Senator W. H. Hines, returned from Ithaca, N. Y., where they were the guests of their grandfather, J. R. Wortman, one of the oldest and best known citizens of that city. During Senator Hines's stay there he spent most of his time looking up the history of the family. The great-great-grandfather of Senator Hines's two sons was Abram Wortman. He was married to Polly Gordon, who was connected with the Gordons of the Wyoming Valley. At the time of the Wyoming massacre the Gordons were settled at Kingston, coming from Monmouth, N. J. At the time of the massacre Abram Wortman was in the Revolutionary War and his wife, Polly Gordon Wortman, lived in Kingston, with her five children. After the massacre she took the children and walked over the mountain towards Stoddartsville, and thus made her way back to New Jersey with some difficulty, having lost one of the children in the forest for some time. Senator Hines's wife was Ida Wortman, whose ancestors had taken up a lot of land where Kingston Borough is now located, but left after the massacre and never returned to this valley. The relationship of the boys goes back into the late L. D. Shoemaker and the late E. C. Wadhams families through the Starr family, which originally came from England with the Plymouth colony, the latter family now being scattered far and wide. Many of the descendants are prominent in New York City.

Harry Hines is now 17 years of age and is a student at Hillman Academy and John, who is known at home and by all his comrades as "Jack," is 10 years of age, attending the Sisters' school.

HISTORICAL SOCIETY.

[Daily Record, Feb. 12, 1903.]

A dreary rain was falling but it did not prevent the Historical Society holding its yearly meeting last evening, the occasion being the forty-fifth anniversary of the founding of the organization. President Stanley Woodward was in the chair. Rev. Dr. Jones offered prayer. Sidney R. Miner read the minutes.

The following officers were elected for the ensuing year:

President—Hon. Stanley Woodward.

Vice Presidents—Rev. Henry L. Jones, S. T. D.; Hon. J. Ridgway Wright, Col. G. Murray Reynolds, Rev. Francis B. Hodge, D. D.

Corresponding Secretary and Librarian—Rev. Horace Edwin Hayden.

Recording Secretary—Sidney R. Miner.

Treasurer—F. C. Johnson.

Trustees—Hon. Charles A. Miner, S. L. Brown, Edward Welles, Richard Sharpe, Andrew F. Derr.

Meteorologist—Rev. F. B. Hodge, D. D.

Curators—

Archeology, J. Ridgway Wright.
Numismatics, Rev. H. E. Hayden.
Geology, William R. Ricketts.
Paleobotany, William Griffith.
Paleozoology, Joshua L. Welter.

E. F. Payne was elected to membership.

Daniel Edwards Newell (the young son of T. L. Newell) was elected to life membership.

Rev. Mr. Hayden exhibited a gavel made by S. Y. Kittle of wood brought from the South Sea Islands, the gavel having been used by W. D. White in laying the cornerstone of the new Federal building. It was a gift to the society.

A paper by A. F. Berlin of Allentown was read by Christopher Wren, describing an Indian spear, which was shown. It is of jasper and was found in Wyoming Valley, near the monument. It is about six inches long and undoubtedly was chipped out from material obtained at a jasper quarry in Lehigh County, ten miles from Allentown. Mr. Wren described a visit to the jasper quarries of Lehigh County. He also exhibited specimens of jasper

fragments showing the evolution of the spear head—the raw material in all stages of being chipped up into finished implements. These were found by Mr. Wren in Wyoming Valley, as were various discoidal stones used as hammers for chipping the flint.

TREASURER'S REPORT.

The report of the treasurer, Dr. F. C. Johnson, showed the general accounts as follows:

Receipts.

Balance, Feb. 11, 1902	$ 451.49
Interest on bonds	1,000.50
Transfer from savings account	2,011.85
Dues of members	810.00
G. B. & F. Hillman bond	200.00
From county commissioners	200.00
	$4,673.84

Expenditures.

Salaries, etc.	$1,192.74
Wright fund, interest	50.00
Reynolds fund, interest	50.00
Ingham fund, interest	26.50
Lacoe fund	100.00
Furniture and frames	50.59
Collector of dues	19.00
Postage and incidentals	140.02
Publications and printing	310.00
Books	140.00
Address and stereopticon	35.00
Webster Coal Co. bond and int.	1,017.78
Westmoreland Club bonds	200.00
Plymouth Bridge Co. bond and int.	1,042.37
Balance	299.84
	$4,673.84

Savings Account.

The treasurer reported that there had been paid into the savings account, $300 for the Zebulon Butler fund and $1,400 from the following life members at $100 each:

F. M. Kirby, Miss Edith Reynolds, Wm. T. Payne, Mrs. A. F. Derr, Miss A. B. Phelps, Miss Rosa Troxell, Maj. E. A. Hancock, Mrs. Mae Turner Conyngham, Thomas Graeme, Dr. L. H. Taylor, Mrs. W. P. Ryman, H. H. Ashley, J. E. Patterson, T. L. Newell.

Of this, $1,644 has been applied to the purchase of bonds. Balance in savings account, $101.

Investments.

Water Co. bonds ....$ 7,000
Plymouth Bridge Co. bonds 6,000
Miner-Hillard Milling Co.............. 1,500
Sheldon Axle Co........................ 1,000
People's Telephone 1,000
Webster Coal Co....................... 3,000
United Gas & Electric 1,000
Westmoreland Club 300

$20,800

All at 5 per cent. except Westmoreland Club bonds, which were received as life membership fees.

REPORT OF CORRESPONDING SECRETARY.

Rev. Horace E. Hayden submitted his report as corresponding secretary. He said:

In presenting to you the annual report of this society I beg to remind you that this is the forty-fifth anniversary of the birth of the society. We are fortunate in having had for our president during the past eight years one of the four persons who, on Feb. 11, 1858, founded the society, and we trust that he will long live to honor us in that position. He himself is also to be congratulated on having held forty-five years of continuous membership in the society, an admirable example for others to emulate. Three only of his associated members of 1858 have been so long connected with the institution, Messrs. Robert Baur, John Laning and William H. Sturdevant. Twelve of our present members representing the first twelve years of our corporate existence are the four just referred to and Messrs. E. H. Chase and E. Sterling Loop of 1859, Hon. Charles A. Miner of 1864, Messrs. George R. Bedford of 1866, John W. Hollenback of 1868, and William S. McLean, George Loveland and Andrew Hunlock of 1870.

These twelve were among those members who in 1870 were invited to witness the funeral obsequies of the society, as noted in the admirable paper of Rev. Dr. Jones. The society on that occasion refused a premature burial, shook off its lethargy and took on new life. These twelve have witnessed that new life gradually developed under the zealous care of Ingham, Wright and Reynolds into one of the most useful and permanent educational factors of northeastern Pennsylvania, wide in its reputation and influence.

It is very gratifying to be able to report that the condition of the society is to-day most healthy in all its departments, limited only, as all such organizations unfortunately are, by the very small number of members who are willing or able to give it active service.

Such a society as this cannot and should not be sustained as a close corporation. It must be made useful to the public to give it stability and character. It was organized as an educator, and can succeed only as this purpose is carried out. This was more fully realized by the trustees when in 1893 they decided to open the library and museum to the public eight hours a week. This movement, which was only experimental, resulted in an increased demand for the privilege and the eight hours were extended to thirteen, and then to twenty-two, and the rooms have been opened each week day from 2 to 5 p. m. for the past two years.

The society is now, however, in a condition to meet a larger demand from the public, and at the request of the librarian the trustees have decided to open the library and museum, beginning soon after Easter, each week day from 10 a m. to 5 or 6 p. m., a period of forty-eight hours a week. This move is partly made advisable by a special public claim. The Osterhout Free Library is open to the public sixty-six hours a week. It has been the fixed purpose of these two associated libraries to avoid duplicating books. In the more than 30,000 volumes of the Free Library it is doubtful if over 500 titles are duplicated in the library of this society, which is strictly confined to American history, genealogy and geology, and has a list of nearly 20,000 books and pamphlets on these subjects. The Free Library touches on these branches of study only in a general way.

But the demand in this geological section for such literature as pertains to this department at hours when the society library is not open, has made it necessary for the free library to enlarge its geological field. This will be avoided by the extension of the hours of opening to the society library, where there are over 2,000 volumes on geology, from twenty-two to forty or forty-eight hours weekly.

The finances of the society are in such a prosperous conditon as to justify this change and to guarantee its suc-

cess. At our last annual meeting the treasurer reported our endowment fund to have reached the sum of $17,600. I have the pleasure to report to-day that we have invested in first class securities an endowment fund of $21,700. Three years ago I made an effort to increase our permanent funds by securing personal gifts to the extent of $5,000 from members interested in the work. To this end John W. Hollenback gave $1,000 conditioned on my securing the other $4,000. This condition has been fully met in the sum of $4,000 paid in and invested in five per cents. with an overplus of $700 covered by first-class securities to be paid during the present year. The $5,700 included:

Matthias Hollenback fund	$1,000
L. Denison Stearns fund	1,000
27 life membership fees	2,700
Addition to the Lacoe fund by the family	100
Dr. George Woodward for the Zebulon Butler fund	200
Additional gifts to the Butler fund..	130
Sale of publications and other books.	600
Total	$5,730

The income of the society from the invested funds will be, during the year, $1,050. That from 210 annual members will also equal that $1,050. The act of assembly authorizing the commissioners of each county to pay $200 annually to the oldest Historical Society in the county will add that amount to the income.

The necessity for the purchase of books for the library must be patent to any thoughtful person. For this purpose we have two funds only, the Harrison Wright fund and the Sheldon Reynolds fund, each $1,000, the first given for the purchase of English books of genealogy, and the second for the purchase of American vital statistics that are rare and needed for study. These two funds yield each $50 annually. The Lacoe fund of $450 and the Ingham fund of $350, the Butler fund of $350, all three of which will in a few years increase to $1,000 each, are not yet in a condition to give aid to the geological and ethnological cabinets to which they are pledged. The price of historical and geological books, which are never published in large editions, is such that $500 will rarely buy more than 100 to 150 volumes.. The publication of an annual volume of proceedings by the society, the material return the members receive for their annual dues costs the society an-

nually from $300 to $350, and while this is reduced by sale of our annual volumes the receipts from all such sales are required by the by-laws to be added to the special invested funds of the society.

"Surely such an income should suffice for this society.' Thus have several members spoken. Mr. President it is not enough. This society needs and in time will have an endowment of $50,000. For this institution is not a charity, nor is it a luxury, nor, let me emphasize, is it for the benefit of the corresponding secretary. But it is as great a necessity to the educational interests of this section of Pennsylvania as any public school or library in that section. It is the object lesson for those two great branches of learning taught in all of our schools, geology and anthropology, the science of the earth, and of those who have peopled the earth. No, Mr. President, the income of the society is not yet equal to the purpose for which you aided in founding it. It is now in a state of usefulness and prosperity that is attracting public notice. The intelligent people of this section are realizing its value and have in various ways shown a personal interest in its work. Its annual volumes have gained it a character for historical and scientific research that has called forth the commendation of our best and most distinguished societies. Northeastern Pennsylvania ought to take especial pride in its enrichment. We are working for posterity.

In the annual report for 1901 the hope was expressed that an ethnological fund of $1,000 could be secured, the interest of which could be expended in adding to our fine collection of local Indian remains a part of the many desirable specimens that are held by private persons in the Susquehanna Valley. This fund was begun on Jan. 1, 1903, by the corresponding secretary, and named as a memorial fund for that distinguished hero of Wyoming of whom Charles Miner wrote these words: "The life of Col. Zebulon Butler is the history of Wyoming." The "Zebulon Butler fund" amounts already to $350 and will be increased to $1,000 by the gifts of his descendants, remaining a continual memorial to his name. I feel personally pledged to its success, my great-grandfather having been his adjutant in the continental line.

The ethnological collection of the society is very rich in local Indian re-

mains. Our display of local Indian pottery has been pronounced one of the finest in the country. The Susquehanna section abounds with fine specimens which now and then are discovever, some to find their way into our collection, but many more to be stored away as curiosities that eventually are lost or destroyed. The various scientific societies of the United States are actively gathering up the relics of a prehistoric people, and we need a fund for the purpose of purchasing such as do not naturally drift to our society. The Griffith collection, already presented, and the Wren collection, to be placed here in the spring, will increase our number of specimens to about 14,000. The Jenkins collection and the Hollister collection have been well known for years, but while this society is the proper place for such treasures it is not certain that they will be deposited here. The Butler fund will supply an income for securing many fine individual specimens that will grace any collection. The desire to give every descendant of Col. Zebulon Butler an opportunity to add his gift to this fund has led to the discovery that there are over seventy living descendants of that distinguished continental officer.

The corresponding secretary urged the preparation of a card catalog of the library, which would cost about $700.

. Reference was made to a valuable collection of books and fossils donated by the estate of the late Col. A. H. Bowman of the United State Army. The fossils and recent shells are those secured by Maj. Bowman while dredging Charleston harbor in 1853 for the erection of Fort Sumter, of which he was the military engineer. He was also aided in his work by Dr. Charles F. Ingham With the fossil shells are several thousand fine fossil sharks' teeth. The Bowman collection now forms a part of the educational display in our geological rooms, showing the "Crust of the Earth" and arranged for the use of the schools.

We are greatly indebted to Mr. Charles W. Johnson, late curator of the Wagner Free Institute of Philadelphia and now curator of the Boston Naturia History Society, who kindly came to our city and classified and arranged the tertiary fossils without any charge for his valuable services.

In the past twelve months five meetings of the society were held. President Woodward delivered the annual

address on the "Value of coins as an historical record."

The question has been not unfrequently asked, if there is much to be done in keeping up the society. It would be a wise move if every member of the society would some time visit the rooms and ascertain where and how their annual dues are expended, for we have members who have never yet seen the inside of our building.

The corresponding secretary has received during the year 550 communications, has written 535 letters, has mailed 125 pamphlets, delivered 400 copies of Volume VII, has edited the annual volume, and done other routine work.

As librarian he reports receiving 1,143 books and 576 pamphlets; total, 1,720. Of these 188 were purchased, 220 were received by exchange, 307 by gift and 434 from the United States and Pennsylvania State governments. Of the gifts 75 are bound volumes of the Scranton Republican and of the Wilkes-Barre Leader. Hon. J. Ridgway Wright sent us 235 duplicate State documents, and Hon. G. J. Hartman 152, Hon. Charles A. Miner 29. The family of the late William P. Miner has deposited in our fire proof vault 26 bound volumes of Wilkes-Barre papers from 1797 to 1847.

The Harrison Wright and the Sheldon Reynolds Memorial Libraries have outgrown their present quarters and the cases they occupy are sorely needed for the geological cabinet. To the Wright Library has just been added a fine set of "The Gentleman's Magazine," 1731-1825, of 138 volumes, the leading magazine of history of England, and to the Reynolds Library the 35 volumes of the now rare New York Biographical and Genealogical Record.

To the Indian collection have been added by purchase and gift since the flood of a year ago, 625 specimens Among the gifts is the large sandstone mealing trough from Hunkydory Swamp. the "Gravel Creek Stone" presented by Messrs. E. L, Bullock and Charles F. Hill of Hazleton, a copper arrow head from Wisconsin by Mr. J. Bennett Smith, with other lesser but equally valuable relics. Dr. Charles W. Spayd has presented to us one of the first cases of surgical instruments ever brought to the valley. From Mrs. Charles A. Miner we have received a spinning wheel and reel once the property of Gen. W. S. Ross; and from the Davenport family of Plymouth a

wooden plough used by the family for 100 years in clearing up the land of this valley.

To our portraits we have added life-sized crayons of the late William Penn Ryman, Esq., Martin Coryell, Esq., J. Vaughan Darling, Esq., and Lieut. Obadiah Gore of the Continental Army. Lieut. Gore's portrait adds one more to the faces of the survivors of the Massacre of Wyoming, to which the only other portrait extant, that of Gen William Ross, will be soon added. Other portraits are promised.

The membership of the society now numbers: Life members 108, annual members 212, total 321.

The curator of geology and minerology desires to say that his department has added many interesting specimens, and a catalog is nearly completed.

The curator of paleozoology, or the Lacoe collection, reports an increase of 200 fossil remains to his department, some of which are from the Bowman collection. The Bowman collection, already described, while distinct from the Lacoe collection, properly belongs to the department of paleozoology and forms an important part of the exhibition case, "The Crust of the Earth," which was the work of the several curators, Ingham, Wright, Lacoe and Welter.

Mr. William Griffith of Pittston, the well known geologist, has accepted the office of curator of paleobotany, which was so many years Mr. Lacoe's special work in the society. He has lately visited Mexico and has sent to the society some valuable coal fossils from the coal mines of that republic.

The department of conchology was given up by the society several years ago, as not pertaining to the special work of our institution, and the fine collection of shells is still awaiting a purchaser. When sold the money will be added to our permanent funds.

COAL PIONEER DEAD.

The Scranton Republican has the following:

Benjamin F. Fillmore, prospector, coal operator and authority on matters pertaining to coal mining, passed away at his home in Scranton on Monday evening. The deceased was 71 years of age. Death resulted from a complication of disorders.

Mr. Fillmore was one of the earliest settlers and coal operators. He made and lost fortunes, only to spend his

last years in comfortable circumstances. His relations with the coal mining industry covered a period of over forty years, although he was not actively engaged in mining for the last decade. He discovered the coal in the Moosic Mountain range and organized the Moosic Coal Co. He also opened the West Ridge mine, afterwards controlled by the Von Storches, and at present owned by the Scranton Coal Co. His knowledge of mining made him a valuable associate in developing the industry.

He not only followed mining, but railroading. He built the extension of the Lackawanna road from Binghamton to Buffalo, a great piece of contract work. In later years he engaged in prospecting and had spent much of his time in the soft coal regions in the interest of investors. At times he was an extensive holder of real estate.

Three children survive: They are: Harry, Benjamin F., Jr., and Frank. Harry is superintendent of the Woodward colliery of the Lackawanna.

GEO. W. GUSTIN DEAD.

George Wilmot Gustin died suddenly at his home in Waymart on March 6, 1903. Deceased was born at Bethlehem on Sept. 13, 1841. When a boy he learned telegraphy at Honesdale. He was a natural artist and for many years followed the avocation at Cooperstown, Towanda and Honesdale. Paintings made by him grace the walls of many Honesdale homes. One of the largest and finest is an oil painting, "In the Hands of the Enemy," which was presented to the Honesdale G. A. R. Post by Col. Durland, and is greatly admired.

Deceased is survived by five sisters— Mrs. Thomas Nichols of Carbondale, Mrs. James B. Cooper of Shawano. Wis.; Mrs. Joseph Jones and Miss Eliza Gustin of Stockbridge, Mass.; and Mrs. Coe Durland of Honesdale. His brother, Joseph N., died in San Francisco in 1850 and another brother, Oliver D., at Honesdale in 1861. He was a great-grandson of Dr. Lemuel Gustin, one of the pioneer physicians of Wyoming Valley. His family was related by marriage to David Wilmot, the proviso's father having married for his second wife Mary Carr, an aunt of the deceased. His father, John A. Gustin, was one of the early postmasters of Honesdale.

The funeral of deceased, who united with the Episcopal Church at Wilkes-Barre when a young man, was held at Waymart, Rev. J. P. Ware officiating, and in accordance with his request his remains were interred at the old Canaan Corners Cemetery, where many of his mother's relatives rest.—Honesdale Independent.

A friend sends this tribute to the Record:

A man endowed with many of those graces and accomplishments most coveted. A soul susceptible to the last degree to every emotion which ennobles humanity and withal an artist of rarest merit—such was Gustin. How easily will Christian Charity now apply the lines of Gray—

"No farther seek his merits to disclose
Nor draw his frailties from their dread
    abode,
There they alike in trembling hope re-
    pose
The bosom of his Father and his God."
                                        C.

COLONIAL DAMES.

[Daily Record, March 10, 1903.]

The Colonial Dames held a meeting yesterday morning at the residence of Mrs. George R. Bedford, 96 West South street. A pleasing feature of the meeting was a paper on "Early Colonial Architecture," read by Mrs. Bedford. The paper was written by Miss Anna Phelps and was an interesting review of colonial buildings.

Miss Phelps in her paper reviewed the progress and style of architecture during the formative period of the country and her subject was illustrated with pictures showing the type of the buildings, the material and style of construction, and gave other interesting and historical facts connected with some of the buildings described. The subject dealt with the log houses at Plymouth, the larger and more pretentious buildings of brick and stone at Salem and Boston, the odd fashioned homes of the Dutch settlers in New York and finally the old Southern mansions of the planters in Virginia and the Carolinas.

In the early days of the New England settlement the log houses were built of heavy timbers and the apertures filled in with "daub and wattles," which was the name given to the crude form of plastering at that

time. This was found unsuited to the
severe New England climate and the
natives turned to stone and brick. Miss
Phelps finds that the houses in New
York and New England were superior
to the Southern homes until after 1800,
when the boom in cotton and tobacco
gave the planters means to build the
fine old mansions which have been so
characteristic of the South until the
Civil War. She took examples of early
Colonial architecture from each of the
thirteen colonies, and gave an interesting description of an old log house
which is still standing in Bethlehem,
Pa., and which was erected before the
Revolutionary War. It is built of logs
and recently was covered with siding.
the paper was very interesting from an
historical as well as an architectural
standpoint.

DAUGHTERS OF THE REVOLU-
TION.

[Daily Record, March 10, 1903.]

The Daughters of the American Revolution held an interesting meeting in
the Historical Society building last
evening and listened to a report of one
of their delegates to the recent national
congress of the D. A. R. held at Washington, D. C. The local society sent
two delegates. Mrs. W. H. McCartney
and Mrs. H. H. Harvey.

Mrs. Stanley Woodward, the vice
regent, presided at the meeting in the
absence of the regent, Mrs. McCartney,
who is in Virginia. Mrs. I. P. Hand
acted as secretary pro tem. in the absence of the secretary, Miss Ella Bowman, who was also out of town. There
was a good attendance of members and
Mrs. Harvey gave an interesting talk
on the proceedings of the D. A. R.
congress.

CAPT. PECKENS DEAD.

E. R. Peckens of Plymouth, brief
mention of whose death was made
Mar. 17, 1903, was born at Bridgewater,
Susquehanna County, June 16, 1831. He
was educated at Wyoming Seminary
and took the higher courses at Buck-
nell University, from which he was
graduated in the class of 1854. After
completing his education he returned
to Luzerne County and kept books for
his father at what was known as the
Black Diamond store. The breaker of
that name was the first erected in the
county and was built by the father of

deceased. After clerking for some time, he was employed in the coal department of the D., L. & W. Co. and continued with that corporation until 1861, when he enlisted as captain of Co. H, 52d Regt., Pa. Vols., under command of Col. Dodge and Lieut. Col. Hoyt, who afterwards became governor of this State. The regiment had the advance in the Peninsula campaign and was engaged in all the battles and skirmishes during the war, from Lee's Mills, April, 1862; Williamsburg, May 5; Chickahominy, May 19; reconnoissance to Seven Pines, May 24, 25 and 26; Seven Pines, May 31; Railroad and Bottoms Bridges, June 27 and 28; White Oak Swamp Bridge, June 30; Carter's Hill, July 2; Matthews Co., Nov. 22; Gioucester, Va., Dec. 14; Yorktown, Aug. 17 to Dec. 31, 1862.

Capt. Peckens resigned at Beaufort, S. C., Sept. 4, 1863, on account of ill health. Upon his return from the war he took a position in the internal revenue office at Scranton, which was then under Joseph Scranton. Here he remained three years and then opened a store in Scranton, which he conducted for a short time. He then removed to Schuylkill County, where he became superintendent of the Trembath Coal Co. He later returned to Scranton and worked for the Northern Coal Co., as clerk under Mr. Albright. There he remained until it was merged with the D. & H. Canal Co. and he was given a position as assistant superintendent, which he held until his death. He had five collieries under his constant supervision. He was married Nov. 22, 1855, and his wife and one daughter, Miss Linda, survive.

Deceased was a member of Conyngham Post, G. A. R., of this city.

JOHN B. COLLINGS DEAD.

[Daily Record, March 10 ,1903.]

The death of John Beaumont Collings, formerly a well known Wilkes-Barre resident, occurred at the Moses Taylor Hospital in Scranton yesterday morning, after failing in health for a number of years. In the course of its obituary the Scranton Times says:

Mr. Collings was one of the ablest men at the bar. Eccentric to a degree, yet he numbered among his many friends every member of the legal profession, and profound regret was felt by all when they learned of his taking off.

Mr. Collings was born in Wilkes-Barre on Dec. 17, 1846. He was a scion of one of

the most prominent and foremost families in the Wyoming Valley. Two of his grand uncles on his mother's side, Elijah and Ichabod Beaumont, were two of the few persons that escaped from England's Indian allies at the time of the Wyoming massacre.

His grandfather on his mother's side, Andrew Beaumont, was one of the able men of the country in his day and occupied a seat in Congress in Andrew Jackson's administration when the South Carolina nullification doctrine was promulgated and quelled.

One of Andrew Beaumont's sons, John C. Beaumont, after whom Mr. Collings was named, was an admiral in the United States Navy at the time of the Civil War. He was an uncle of the deceased. At the time that the Czar of Russia was the intended victim of an assassination plot in 1863 the government at Washington sent Admiral Beaumont to Moscow to convey the congratulations of this government to the czar on his escape from the assassin. Admiral Beaumont took with him his nephew, Mr. Collings, at that time 17 years of age, as his secretary.

Mr. Collings's friends have heard him relate the story many times of the manner in which they crossed the ocean and found their way to the Russian capital. They crossed the ocean in one of the little ironclad monitors, then just newly added to the navy. Mr. Collings related incidents of many narrow escapes that they had on the journey and many times thought that they would go to the bottom of the Atlantic. They succeeded in reaching Moscow, however, and Mr. Collings, with his uncle, had the pleasure of visiting the Russian court. On that occasion they visited all the principal ports of Europe and wintered in the Mediterranean.

Upon his return to this country Mr. Collings took up the study of law in the office of George R. Bedford in Wilkes-Barre. He had been previously educated in the public schools of Wilkes-Barre and in the Wyoming Seminary and Dana's Academy. He finished his course of law and was admitted to the bar of Luzerne County in the year 1870.

While he was studying law he worked as a clerk in the office of the prothonotary of Luzerne County.

Much may be said of the father of Mr. Collings. Samuel Collings was the editor of a newspaper known as the Republican Farmer, which he published in Wilkes-Barre during the forties and the early fifties. He was considered one of the able editors of the State during his time and

had a reputation as an editor that extended beyond the confines of the State.

In 1873 Mr. Collings, the deceased, was nominated by the Democrats of Luzerne County for the office of district attorney. He was defeated by a close vote. He continued prominently in his profession for some time in Wilkes-Barre and then came to Scranton. It was in the next year, 1874, that he took up the practice of his profession in Scranton. He became prominent at the start and was engaged in a number of important cases which gave him a standing at the bar.

In the year 1888 he was nominated by the Democratic party of Lackawanna County for the office of district attorney and ran against Judge Edwards for that office. The latter defeated him. He never again became a candidate for any public office, but confined himself to practice of his profession. He was associated with the late A. H. Winton in the practice of law.

During the last few years of his life he had not been engaged actively at the bar to any extent.

Mr. Collings's father once held the office of consul at Morocco and died while he was at that station. Upon the occasion of his death the Emperor of Morocco sent to the United States government an autograph letter, in which ne spoke of the worth of the consul and the manner in which he had ingratiated himself with the emperor.

————

The Scranton Truth has the following:

Mr. Collings's nearest surviving relatives are two sisters and a niece. The sisters are Mrs. Alice Winton and Mrs. Julia B. Steever, wife of Col. E. Z. Steever of the 3d United States Cavalry, now stationed in Washington on detailed duty. Mrs. G. D. Murray, wife of Dr. Murray, and daughter of Mrs. Winton, is his niece.

Col. Eugene Beaumont of Wilkes-Barre, a retired officer of the United States Army and a brother of Admiral Beaumont, is also living. He is the present head of the Beaumont family and an uncle of the deceased.

Mr. Collings was a man of courtly bearing and distinguished appearance. He was a genial companion and always had at his command a rich store of anecdotes concerning public men and events of importance in local and national affairs. Ill health prevented him from very active practice of his profession during the last two years of his life, but never broke off the friendly relations which he always had with his brother members of the bar. In politics he was an uncompromising Democrat, whom defeat could not swerve

from his party allegiance. His death is
sincerely mourned and his loss deplored
by the members of the bar.

Relatives in Wilkes-Barre are an uncle,
Col. Eugene B. Beaumont, and aunts, Mrs.
Julia C. Dougherty, Mrs. A. J. Baldwin
and Mrs. Harriet C. Davison. Mr. Col-
linger was unmarried.

MRS. GLOINGER DEAD.

[Daily Record, Aug. 5, 1903.]

The death of Mrs. Julia Beaumont
Gloninger of Lebanon, third daughter
of Hon. Andrew Beaumont, deceased,
occurred yesterday morning at 3 o'clock
at North Mountain, where she had
been spending the summer. Mrs Gloninger was the widow of Dr. Cyrus D.
Gloninger, for many years one of Lebanon's leading physicians, to whom
she was united in marriage on Dec. 23,
1851. Dr. Gloninger died on Aug. 23,
1872.

The deceased had a large acquaintance in this valley and the announcement of her passing away will be received with profound sorrow. She was
beloved by all who knew her, her heart
being ever open to the demands of
charity. Her gentle disposition, genial
humor and entertaining conversation
attracted to her both young and old,
winning for her a place in the affections
of her neighbors in Lebanon and en-
dearing her to her old Wilkes-Barre
friends.

The death of Mrs. Gloninger removes
from life's activities the last of the
daughters of Hon. Andrew Beaumont
and leaves but one survivor of the once
numerous family of Andrew and Julia
Colt Beaumont—Col. E. B. Beaumont,
U. S. Army, retired, of this city.

The following children survive: Dr.
A. B. Gloninger, a prominent physician
of Lebanon; Mrs. Mary B. Gilroy and
Mrs. Eleanor Beaumont Jordan of Oak
Lane, Philadelphia, and Cyrus Dorsey
Gloninger.

Andrew Beaumont, father of Mrs.
Gloninger, was a prominent man in
Wilkes-Barre affairs half a century
ago. He was born in 1791 at Lebanon,
Conn. Educated at the old academy
in Wilkes-Barre, he took an active part
in Luzerne county politics. His first
public office was that of revenue col-
lector and he was a little later prothonotary and clerk of the courts. At
the age of thirty he was elected to the
Legislature, served two terms and was
subsequently elected to Congress in
1834 and re-elected. He was a keen

political writer for nearly half a century. He married Julia A. Colt in 1813. He died in 1853, leaving the following children:

John Colt Beaumont, rear admiral in the U. S. Navy. Died 1882.

William Henry Beaumont, lawyer and editor, died 1874.

Eugene Beauharnais Beaumont of the U. S. Army.

Elizabeth Beaumont, married Samuel P. Collings, editor and American consul to Tangier, Africa.

CAME FROM AN OLD FAMILY.

[Daily Record, March 23, 1903.]

Yesterday morning occurred the death of Mrs. Clara C. Bulkeley in Philadelphia. Mrs. Bulkeley had been a patient sufferer for several weeks past and death was not unexpected. She possessed her faculties to the last and loving hands ministered tenderly to her wants.

Mrs. Bulkeley was born in Port Blanchard, this county, being the third child of Jeremiah Blanchard, from which family the village takes its name. Jeremiah Blanchard was the grandson of Jeremiah Blanchard, captain in command of Pittston fort on July 3, 1778. She came from old Connecticut stock. It seems that the name Jeremiah had been handed down to the eldest son of each generation.

The deceased on her mother's side was one of the grandchildren of Thomas Williams, who emigrated from Connecticut in the early history of this valley. His family played an important part in the pioneer settlement of New England and from it came the establishment of Williams College of to-day. They were the original owners of the greater part of land known as Plains.

Mrs. Bulkeley's first husband was George Hiram Stark of Plains, a lineal descendant of Gen. John Stark of Bennington fame. The issue are Mrs. John E. Sayre of this city, Misses Letitia, Harriet and Elizabeth of Philadelphia and one son, James W. of Pittston. Her second husband was the late Dr. Bulkeley of this city. No children were born to her of this marriage.

The deceased was a woman of strong friendships and generous impulses, an affectionate mother, and her home was the centre of the most earnest and heartiest affections.

MISS HANNAH P. JAMES DEAD.

[Daily Record, April 21, 1903.]

Miss Hannah P. James, librarian of Osterhout Free Library, one of the best known librarians in the United States, died yesterday morning at her home on Butler street, Dorranceton, after an illness of considerable duration, aged 67 years.

Miss James was born Sept. 5, 1835, in Plymouth, Massachusetts, of good Puritan stock, and she was a direct descendant from John Alden. She was educated in public and later in private schools and early showed a taste for good books and the best in literature. She was always of a cheerful, happy disposition and was a universal favorite from childhood up.

When the Newton, Massachusetts, library was opened Miss James entered as an assistant and became the librarian about two years later. She spent seventeen years in that library and then came to Wilkes-Barre in 1887 and opened the Osterhout Free Library, selecting the books and superintending the arrangements. The library is a monument to her labors and is known over a large part of the English-speaking world as a model library of the smaller class. Miss James directed the work systematically and the books selected show her knowledge of the needs of the public.

Miss James was a faithful worker in the Unitarian Church when at her old home, but after coming here she connected herself with and soon became a member of St. Stephen's Episcopal Church.

Miss James is survived by a sister, Mrs. Merritt of Massachusetts, and a niece.

WYOMING HISTORICAL SOCIETY.

[Daily Record, May 9, 1903.]

At a meeting of the Wyoming Historical and Geological Society last evening Dr. Frederic Corss read a brief paper on The Buried Valley of Wyoming. As the subject had been presented to the society on other occasions he did not go into details but went into some theories on the origin and formation of this geological condition, which is such a menace to anthracite mining along the Susquehanna and has on more than one occasion brought disaster, as at Nanticoke when a coal mine ran into this buried valley and death to all within was caused by the rushing quicksand. Some of the bodies covered to this day. of the victims have never been re-

The bed of this buried valley is 200

feet lower at Nanticoke than it is at Berwick, farther down the river. In the course of his remarks Dr. Corss said:

"First, if all the soil and loose material were removed from the valley it is supposed that a continuous canyon worn by the action of running water would be found from Pittston to Nanticoke, supposed to be connected by intervening but as yet unsurveyed rock cuts. Such river canyons are known in many places and are supposed to have been formed by the action of swiftly running water. Evidently an elevation of 200 feet at Berwick would have been a dam which would have prevented our canyon from being formed. It would have formed a vast pool in which sedimentation would have taken place, as did actually occur. So our buried valley remains unexplained.

"Second, that the buried valley was of pre-glacial origin is seen from the fact that it is filled with glacial drift; indeed the vast accumulation of drift which covers our bed rock must have been brought by glacial action. There is an unstratified glacial mound in Edwardsville from which I have secured some beautiful specimens of subangular striated boulders, resting on an old drift mound of pre-glacial soil, the whole higher than the flood plain upon which the village of Kingston stands."

Dr. Corss believes the Wyoming canyon was formed by natural erosion.

"The bed rock of Wyoming Valley, which of course overlies the coal, is of soft clayey structure, very susceptible to the action of water and consequently easy of erosion, while the rock under the river at Berwick is a hard Devonian formation very slightly susceptible to erosive action. Hence the canyon probably does not extend beyond the carboniferous outcrop. If it does it has not been found.

"Probably the Wyoming canyon exists above Pittston in the Lackawanna Valley, as the gorge seems to have been cut by the Lackawanna River before the Susquehanna River arrived here.

"The extensive valley between Kingston Mountain and North Mountain shows universal water action, post-glacial as the small lateral moraines are mostly washed away.

"A large body of water poured over Kingston Mountain into the valley for a period long enough to produce extensive erosion and cover Welch Hill with immense conglomerate boulders from

the conglomerate cliff above it, after which the gorges at Luzerne Borough and Pittston becoming eroded more rapidly furnished a lower outlet for the northern flood and the immense drift mounds at those places were formed.

"These mounds it should be noted lie on top of the glacial drift. The mound at Luzerne overlies the marsh, an old abandoned river bed.

"The theory has been propounded that the great northern highlands where our glacier arose, were pressed down by the weight of ice.

"If so, the surface of the carboniferous strata was no doubt somewhat elevated or pushed up at the same time. We know that the highest mountains on the earth are slowly settling. The city of Quito is now fifty feet lower than it was when this society was organized.

"These considerations seem to warrant the conclusion that the buried canyon of Wyoming was formed by slow erosion of water flowing down a continuous declivity from Forest City to Berwick and that its present low elevation was caused by a change in the shape of the earth since its formation."

Dr. Corss illustrated his remarks by reference to a model of the buried valley as made for the society some time ago by William Griffith.

At the conclusion of Dr. Corss's paper Rev. H. E. Hayden read a biographical sketch of the late Hannah P. James, prepared by a friend of the lamented librarian.

There was exhibited a woven wire vest or armor sent home by Abel Gottfried, the same having been found in the Andes in Peru. The armor has a button bearing what appears to be the word Nurnberg and a coat of arms.

There was shown a fine collection of minerals from Cornwall, England, presented by William Puckey.

S. L. Brown presided.

J. C. WILLIAMS DEAD.

[Daily Record, May 9, 1903.]

The many friends of the venerable squire John C. Williams of Plains will be grieved to learn of his death from bronchial pneumonia yesterday morning.

Mr. Williams was a son of Moses and Sara Carey Williams. He was born in old Wilkes-Barre, now Plains, May 23, 1822, and had been a lifelong resident of Plains Township.

Mr. Williams was an active worker in the Methodist Church, having united with that denomination in his nineteenth year, later being ordained as a local minister.

Mr. Williams was a prominent Republican and held many positions of honor in his native township. He was a patriotic citizen and always manifested a keen interest in local and national affairs.

Deceased was a descendent of Robert Williams, who came to this country from England is 1635 or 1637. He is survived by his wife, Mrs. Sara Clark Williams, and his only daughter, Mrs. Elizabeth Williams Chamberlain, and the following grandchildren: Harriet E., Calvin P., J. Williams, Jennie M. and Emily S. Chamberlain.

Deceased was a brother of the venerable C. M. Williams, for many years postmaster at Plainsville.

HELD A FAMILY REUNION.

The reunion of the Williams family, descendants of one of the pioneer farmers and school teachers, Jonathan Williams of Lake, now Loyalville, who went from Dallas in 1840 and who raised a large family—eight boys and three girls—took place on Thursday last. All grew to manhood and womanhood, the youngest dying at the age of 22 years. The surviving members met at the home of David M. Williams on Christmas, who with his wife and family entertained those present right royally. Those present were: Fayette Williams and wife, Lewis Williams and wife, William Williams, wife and two daughters, David M. Williams, wife, two sons and two daughters of Loyalville, C. E. Totten and husband, Jonathan Williams, wife and two daughters of Westmoor, J. E. Williams, wife and daughter, O. J. Williams, wife, son and daughter, Roger C. Williams, wife, two sons, Coray Brooks, wife, son and daughter, Frank A. Edwards, wife, two daughters, L. A. Dymond, wife, son and daughter, Peter Wintz, wife and son.

Before disbanding a permanent organization was completed: President, Myron R. Williams; vice president, Orbil Williams; secretary, Jonathan W. Williams; treasurer, L. A. Dymond; committee of arrangements, Mary Williams, Maud Williams, Carrie Williams, O. P. Williams, Lorin Williams.

DEATH OF E. TROXELL.

[Daily Record, May 13, 1903.]

Ephraim Troxell, a pioneer resident of this city and a member of an old family, died at his home, 42 South Washington street, at midnight on Monday of apoplexy, aged 80 years. The deceased had been ill since last February. He was a descendant of John Troxell, who settled in Egypt, Pa., in 1734 and who was one of the pioneer settlers of Whitehall Township. His parents were Peter and Elizabeth Mickley Troxell, and he was born in the ancestral farm house built by his grandfather, which is still standing.

Ephraim Troxell came to Wilkes-Barre in 1856, where he has since resided, and was identified with many of its enterprises and business interests. He devoted much of his time during his latter years to his milling and farming interests at Harvey's Lake and Clifton. He was interested in the Harvey's Lake Transit Co., the North Street Bridge Co. and other enterprises.

Mr. Troxell and his wife, who died in August, 1901, had been communicants at St. Stephen's Church since 1856. Two children survive, Miss C. Rosa Troxell of this city and Dr. E. R. Troxell of West Pittston.

REMINISCENCE OF JOHN STURDEVANT.

[Daily Record, May 23, 1903.]

The visit of a Wilkes-Barre lady to Carbondale last week has revived the writer's recollection of an incident in the political history of Pennsylvania in which her father was a prominent participant. His name was John Sturdevant, for many years a resident of Wyoming County. The incident referred to occurred about 1839, when Joseph Ritner was governor.

At that period the territory now included in Wyoming County was a part of Luzerne. Maj. John Sturdevant and Chester Butler were representatives in the General Assembly that year, having been elected by the Whig party. The State was largely Democratic, but owing to dissensions in that party the Whigs had elected a majority of senators and just one-half the members of the lower house. The latter body being a tie and no compromise having been effected, two separate houses were organized.

The dispute for precedence waxed hot and heavy for several days, resulting in a scrimmage which has been ever since known as the "buckshot war."

Then it was that Messrs. Sturdevant and Butler, together with a colleague named Montelius of Union County, rising above party, showed their patriotism by going over to the Democratic House and ending the controversy. Their conduct was criticised sharply by some of their party constituents, but generally they were commended for an act which undoubtedly prevented bloodshed and saved the good name of the Commonwealth.

C. E. L.

DECORATION DAY ADDRESS.

The principal event of the evening was an eloquent oration by Gustav Hahn on Memorial Day. He told of the scenes in Wilkes-Barre at the breaking out of the war and gave many facts not found in print. Mr. Hahn spoke as follows:

Thirty-eight years have elapsed since the last scenes of the civil war were enacted and the subject of our trials of our sufferings and sorrows, as well as our final triumph, has been pretty thoroughly discussed and well nigh exhausted.

It seems to me, that I am in the same predicament, as in the Sacred College of Jerusalem, called the "Sanhedrin," the young rabbis were, who whenever an ecclesiastical question came up for discussion used to be interrupted by an aged priest over whose head more than five score had passed and who invariably would say: "We have heard all of this long ago!"

But without any fear of criticism or interruption, because you would be to polite and too courteous to say, "write or print any words of disparagement, I will undertake the task."

From the very beginning of the human race, from time immemorial, men and nations, moved by feelings of gratitude and of admiration, have celebrated the memory of their great men and amongst them especially of those who, by laying down their lives, have bought and accomplished the freedom of their country.

In the narrows of Thermopylae you may see this very day the ruins of the monument, which had been erected to perpetuate the glory of three hundred Spartans, who, led by their King Leonidas, assailed the camp of the immense Persian army, that had come from over the sea to subjugate the Greek nation. All of them died as heroes with their face to the foe. Their epitaph is: "Stranger, tell the Spartans that here we rest in obedience to the laws of our country."

Upon a steep rock on one side of the Four Forest Cantons of Switzerland you see constructed of brass the figure of a lion, whose heart is pierced by a javelin. The lion is dying. The monument is placed there in honor of twelve hundred

soldiers, citizens of Switzerland, who fell fighting while they were defending the royal palace of Louis the Sixteenth, King of France. They all, facing the enemy, fell to the very last man.

But, why go so far monuments, even to Greece and Switzerland? Only a few miles from here in the field of Wyoming stands a modest monument, that contains the names of the men who, on the third day of July, 1775, sacrificed their lives for the salvation of their country. The number of the British and of their savage Indian allies out numbered the American patriots four to one and annihilated the brave and patriotic, but small army.

But wherever you go on this vast continent, you see the monuments erected to our noble and great men.

First of all you see George Washington on his spirited charger with the words: "All and everything for my country,—my country against the world!"

The statue of the hero of New Orleans, Andrew Jackson, rises before your eyes and the memorable words seem to come from his lips: "By the eternal! The Union must and shall be preserved."

Out under the foliage of the grand oaks of the park of New York is the grave and the memorial chapel of U. S. Grant, the man whose initials mean: "Unconditional surrender of the enemies of my country." But in Union Square, unadorned by a uniform and on foot, stands the high and straight form of Abraham Lincoln, the man who steered the ship of State with a steady and firm hand through the stormy and tempestuous waves of the civil war. The motto engraven upon the stone on which his noble form stands is plain and simple. The words are but few, but they denote the character of the man, as a fit representative of the American nation: "With malice to none, with charity to all!"

In the fall of the year of 1860 an election took place in which not less than four different political parties were represented.

The moderate Democracy had Stephen A. Douglass and Hersherel V. Johnson for their leaders. The Ultra Democracy was led by William C. Breckenridge, then Vice President of the United States, and Lane. The exclusively American party, Bell and Everett. The Republican party was represented by Abraham Lincoln and Hannibal Hamlin.

The latter had been elected by an overwhelming majority. But threats were made that he would not live, to be inaugurated, in the city of Washington, and really all appearances gave signs of warning and the utmost care had to be observed to get the President-elect to the city of Washington without being harmed.

On the very day of the inauguration General Winfield Scott had his artillery planted upon the roofs of the buildings of the city of Washington to protect the new administration of our government.

The strongest point of Mr. Lincoln's inaugural address is the frank and plump denial of the Secession dogma.

He said: "No! Ours is one country, made so by God and his providence. Its more perfect Union is but a step in its development, not the cause of its existence."

On the day following the inauguration Mr. Lincoln submitted to the Senate the names of the men selected for his cabinet.

This was on the fifth day of March, 1861, and Mr. Lincoln, who was a very patient man by diplomacy and by gentle means, tried to keep the Union together.

But when on the thirteenth day of April, 1861, Fort Sumter had fallen, Fort Sumter in which we here in Wilkes-Barre take a special interest, because it had been built by Doctor Ingham, a very prominent engineer and a highly esteemed citizen of Wilkes-Barre, had fallen, then there seemed to be no way to avoid a collision.

The North had rudely been awakened from its unaccountable lethargy and men of all classes assembled to prepare for the defence of the Union.

In our court house the people assembled in such masses that there was only standing room.

Mr. A. T. McClintock, the leader of the bar, presided. In came Caleb E. Wright, a cultured and accomplished gentleman, a lawyer and a preacher. He had in his hands a paper sent from the city of Charleston and he read: "The North cannot exist without us! 'Cotton is king.'"

"Cotton be damned," cried Caleb E. Wright. There were present Judge John N. Conyngham, Col. Hendrick B. Wright, Judge Henry M. Hoyt, Alexander Farnham, Judge Garrick M. Harding, W. W. Ketcham, then Senator of Pennsylvania, Charles Pike, Charles Denison, S. P. Longstreet, the Rev. Dr. Mills, Dr. Reuben Nelson of Wyoming Seminary, Rev. F. P. Hunt, Edmund L. Dana, Father Fitzsimmons, Stanley Woodward, Edward H. Chase and all the prominent merchants and business men of the city, as well as all classes of the population.

Judge Conyngham impressed upon the minds of those assembled, that their country, that the cause of liberty, was in danger, and that if the young men did not go, the old ones certainly would go. He said:

"My eldest son, dear to me as the apple of my eye, will go to-morrow with the Wyoming Dragoons."

"So will mine!" said Col. Wright.

And my son will go with the Wyoming Yeagers," said Judge Reichard.

Capt Emily said: "The Wyoming Artillerists, the oldest military company, will be ready to go in the morning."

Cant Joseph Coons said: "The Wyoming Yeagers, the second oldest company, will be there in time."

Capt. Brisbane answered for the dragoons.

In the north corner of the court room stood Capt. Bertels with his lieutenant, Patrick Lenahan. They were whispering.

Capt. Bertels said: "Will they go?" Lieut. Lenahan answered: "Every man of them!"

In the morning the Wyoming Artillerists marched up on one side of Main street, the dragoons on the other and the Wyoming Yeagers came up to Franklin street. They were met by a band of music, and when they had reached the Square, there stood Capt. Jacob Bertels and with him Lieut. Patrick Lenahan at the head of a company of one hundred bright and brave men, ready to go into fight, every one an Irishman except the captain.

We thought we were the very first to hasten to the support of the Union, but were very pleasantly surprised in finding thousands upon thousands of men who were armed and equipped and eager to join the armies of the Union.

The people were for the Union. The people of the North and even of some of the border States were loyal to the extreme. The sturdy farmer left his plough, the skilled mechanic shouldered his gun, the workingman left his shop and went into the camp, the laborer exchanged the shovel and the pickaxe for the musket, and the professional man closed his office and took his place in the ranks, and when the first proclamation of President Lincoln had been issued, more men presented themselves than were wanted or thought to be needed.

The result of the call was simply marvelous. But there were serious difficulties under which the government was laboring. The largest number of able and experienced generals, educated by the government of the United States, had left our army. Gen. Robert E. Lee, G. P. T. Beauregard, Thomas J. Jackson, afterwards called "Stonewall Jackson," John C. Breckenridge, Joseph E. Johnston, Braxton Bragg McRuder, Sidney Johnson, Simon P. Buckner, James Longstreet had left the Union Army and had entered the service of the Confederacy.

But that was not all. Our misfortunes were increased by the fact that most of our forts situated in the South or in the border States, containing an immense amount of ammunition and military stores, were by the treachery of John G. Floyd, Buchanan's Secretary of War, left in the hands of the enemy. The treasury was empty, because Godard Bailey, together with Russell Majors and Waddell, had depleted the treasury.

Most of our troops were raw, and sadly in want of military knowledge, the officers of the line mostly unskilled citizens. I recollect, that at one time when Gen. Nagle held a brigade drill, a company which had come from Pittston was sadly out of order and the general who, like Napoleon, pretended to know all the men and officers of his command and could call them by name, called out:

"Capt. Brown from White Haven! How con you, an old soldier, place your company in such a position?"

Whereupon the commander of the Pittston company advanced, saluted with his sword, then made a very profound bow and said: "General! I am not Capt. Brown from White Haven, nor am I an old soldier, I am a shoemaker from Pittston."

But one year's service made able and brave soldiers out of raw recruits.

Another cause of our misfortunes was, that Gen. Winfield Scott, a hero of many battles, had become old and infirm and unable to mount a horse or to command in person and a younger and stronger commander was needed.

The battle of Bull Run had been lost by the want of ability and of patriotism of Gen. Patterson, a man who had neither the wish, nor the courage to serve his country in the way he ought to have done.

Instead of obeying his orders to advance against Gen. Johnston to keep him from joining the Confederate forces in the battle of Bull Run, he kept at a safe distance in a location where no bullets did fly.

Yea, there was another military blunder, a thing unheard of in military history. Regiments, whose time of service was about to expire, instead of being led against the enemy were asked whether they would not stay a few days longer.

Who ever heard of such a thing before? In the whole wide world a soldier is never asked but he is commanded.

We suffered reverses, our cause seemed to be lost in the eyes of Europe and even the European states themselves did not look upon us with eyes of sympathy. The impostor, who sat upon the throne of France was willing and anxious to recognize the Southern Confederacy. England openly assisted the South in furnishing piratic vessels, crews and ammunition and necessaries of war to wipe out our commerce, to sweep our vessels from the ocean. Spain had openly recognized the Confederacy and other States, such as Russia and Italy gave us no encouragement, only Germany bought our bonds and gave us her gold for them. She had confidence in our ability and in our integrity.

In the darkest hour, when our slain covered the battlefields, when the God of battles seemed to have decided against us, when France and England had been furnishing to the South all and every kind of material used in civilized and uncivilized warfare, when the hypocritical self-imposed emperor of France had solicited Queen Victoria to join him in the recognition of the Southern Confederacy, which he did not dare to undertake to do alone and single handed, and when that grand and noble woman had given the answer: "Never and at no time will I lend my hand to the commission of this crime," when our commerce had been swept from the ocean, then like a rock in the midst of the sea our country stood the rage and

the onslaught of the hurricane. Julius Caesar said: "I and danger are two lions, but I am the older and the stronger one." And this was the case with us. After defeat, after lost battles our thinned ranks filled up by patriots rushing to the front, taking the place of those who had fallen. The American nation evinced herself possessed of an indomitable energy, yea of the fullest vigor of national manhood and of unsurpassed enthusiasm and love of their country.

The first spark of the rays of hope and of our rising sun glittered in the conquest of Vicksburg by Gen. Grant. When Mr. Lincoln had received the news of this victory and before he could communicate it to his cabinet a delegation was announced who craved admission immediately. Mr. Lincoln, who was highly pleased with the news he had received from Gen. Grant, received them. They were a delegation of prohibition men and they told the President that they knew Gen. Grant was a drinking man and that he ought to be deposed immediately. Whereupon Mr. Lincoln said: "Gentlemen, will you do me a favor."

"Certainly, Mr. President."

Then Mr. Lincoln said: "Be kind enough to ascertain what kind of liquor Gen. Grant drinks. I would like to send to my other generals of the same stuff."

The battle of Antietam, though called a drawn battle by the advocates of the lost cause, McClellan kept the field ready to renew the battle on the day following and the Confederates retreated. Then and there Jackson saved the army of Lee from annihilation, and at Fredericksburg and and at Chancellorville he was in the zenith of his glory. On May 2d, 1863, he suddenly struck the flank of the Eleventh Corps and overthrew them, but struck down by a bullet of his own men he died on the tenth day of May, 1863.

His death smote the Confederates with unspeakable anguish and filled the hearts of the Union with gratitude to the Almighty. But while Stonewall Jackson was our enemy in the field, we still must give him credit for an act of magnanimity, which was of the or one of the happiest consequences for the people of the United States.

The Union outposts and the Confederate outposts were so close together and the proximity was so great that they could easily speak together and exchange tobacco and other luxuries. On the Union side was a young man still in his teens, a sentinel. He was in a very exposed position, but he stood there firm and fearless. Stonewall Jackson saw him and admired him. When a Kentucky sharpshooter approached him and said: "General, I will fetch down this Yank." But the general said: "By no means should so brave a boy lose his life. I order you to desist." The boy's life was saved. The boy afterwards became a commissioned officer and was at the end of the war a major. He died as the President of the United States and his name was William McKinley. For

this we are indebted to the nobility of character of Stonewall Jackson.

Our success in the West gave Gen. Rosecranz a position in the hearts of a grateful country gained by his victory in the battle of Corinth.

The battle of Gettsburg brought for Gen. Meade and Gen. Hancock laurels of immortality.

The battles of the Wilderness and the strife at Petersburg, after the enormous struggle of five years, brought the war to an end, and the generosity and the magnanimity of the American people showed itself at Appamatox, when Gen. Grant refused to accept of the proffered sword of Gen. Robert E. Lee. He was the first one to present the motion to restore the Southern leader to citizenship.

The men of the North and of the South had met in deadly combat and the result was, that they regarded each other with that mutual respect and esteem which courage and gallantry inspire, and the flame of the feeling of fraternity was rekindled, when the Union men at Appomatox shared their scant rations with the starving Confederate soldiers.

The North furnished the horses to the Southern population, to resume the work of agriculture and no man, who really and honestly sought restitution to American citizenship was refused. Meanwhile Gen. Longstreet, Alexander H. Stephens and Joe Wheeler, who had returned to the Stars and Stripes, occupied honorable positions under the government of the United States. In the meetings of the Grand Army of the Republic the blue and the grey frequently mix in friendly intercourse, and the late conflict with Spain has served to more firmly unite the men of the two sections by fighting shoulder to shoulder against a foreign enemy.

And now to speak of those whom we are sorrowing for to-day. Right up here you see the picture of him after whom this post is named and the face of his brother, Charles, would be a worthy counterpart to take a place by his side. There was Joseph E. Wright, the adjutant, and afterwards captain of a company of Rush's lancers. Edmund L. Dana, the gallant colonel of the 143d; Henry M. Hoyt, colonel of the 52d, statesman, judge, general and governor, who, when at a banquet and when spoken to in a complimentary way, said: "Let all of this go! all the glory I claim is that they say about me—he was an American soldier.'"

We miss to-day the familiar face of Dr. Crawford, the surgeon of the 52. Regiment of Infantry, and Col. S. H. Sturdevant, and lastly the presence of Major Leonard, as brave a man as ever fought for his country.

But though our comrades have died, they live in the memory of a grateful nation.

This is the day set apart for them and for their memory, and I mean especially the rank and file of the American Army.

Generals and commanders have found their way into history. but also every one of the others, no matter whether his rank was high or low, whether he was a commissioned officer or whether he carried a musket, of all and every one we may say:

Though dead he liveth, he lives spoken of at the campfires of his comrades in the memory of his friends. Even the humblest soldier bears on this day upon the mount beneath which he sleeps wreath of fragrant flowers and the emblem of the American nation, the Star Spangled Banner, old glory waves over him.

This is all we can do for him, who has laid down his lifefor his country. We can celebrate him in our songs and we can hand down his name to posterity.

WYOMING REVOLUTIONARY SOLDIERS.

[Daily Record, June 16, 1903.]

The Decoration Day services conducted at Hornellsville, N. Y., May 30, 1903, were memorable in that there was unveiled a monument in memory of Revolutionary soldiers of the Canisteo Valley, many of whom had, at some time or other, lived in Wyoming Valley. The exercises were conducted by the Kanestio Valley Chapter, Daughters of the American Revolution, who unveiled, assisted by the Grand Army and others. As the list is of value to our patriotic societies, it is appended:

ABBOTT, CAPT. JAMES. "One of the patriots of 1776," from the Wyoming Valley. Buried near Arkport.

BAKER, CAPT. SAMUEL. From Connecticut. He was taken captive by the Indians and released by Burgoyne's surrender. Served in Col. Willett's Corps. Buried near Cameron.

BAKER, JEREMIAH, SR. From Connecticut and the Wyoming Valley. In Sullivan's expedition. Buried near Canisteo.

BENNETT, DAVID. Private in Van Rennsalaer's Regiment, N. Y. Line. Buried in the town of Howard.

BENNETT, SERGT. EPHRAIM SR. Sergeant, in Hawthorne's Regiment, New York Line. Buried in the town of Howard.

BENNETT, SOLOMON. In the battle of Wyoming. Private in Capt. John Franklin's company, 1780. Buried near Canisteo.

BROWN, ELISHA. Private in Wessenfels's Regiment, New York Line. Buried at Brown's Crossing.

CAREY, NATHAN. At the battle of Wyoming. Buried at Arkport.

CLOSSON, NEHEMIAH. A minute man. Private in Capt. John Wheelock's company. In the battle of Trenton. Buried at Hornellsville.

CONDERMAN, ADAM. Private in Col. Willett's Regiment, New York Line. Buried at Fremont.

CONDERMAN, LIEUT. JOHN. Entered service as private and attained the rank of lieutenant in the New York Line. Buried at Fremont.

COREY, JOSEPH. Served at the battle of Wyoming. Buried near Almond.

CROSBY, CAPT. RICHARD. Served as an officer in the Dutchess County Militia, N. Y. Line. Member of Gen. Washington's body guard. Buried at Crosbyville, now Adrian.

CROSBY, QUARTERMASTER REUBEN. Served as a private in Dubois's Regiment; as quartermaster in Field's Regiment, New York Line. Buried at Crosbyville.

DARRIN, DANIEL. A private in the Conneticut Line. Buried at Troutsburg.

DOLBY, PARDON. A private in the Conn. Line. Buried at Howard.

DOTY, LEVI. A private, minute man. N. J. Militia. Buried at Doty's Corners.

FAILING, PHILIP. Enlisted at fourteen years of age. Served under Col. Dubois and Col. Willets. Buried at Jasper.

HADLEY, JAMES. In the battle of Wyoming. Buried at Hadleyville.

HALLETT, NATHAN. Served as a private in Wessenfels's Regiment, New York Line. Buried near Canisteo.

HAMILTON, ALEXANDER. A Revolutionary pensioner. Buried in the town of Howard.

HARDING, OLIVER. Enlisted at twenty-one years of age. Served throughout the war. In the battle of Wyoming. Buried at Harding's Hill.

HILLIKER, JOHN. A Revolutionary patriot and soldier. Buried at Jasper.

HOLLIDAY, AMOS. Service began at Bunker Hill and ended at Yorktown. Buried near South Dansville.

HOLMES, SAMUEL. A private of the New York Line. Held captive by the Indians for six months, escaped

and rejoined the army. Buried at Jasper.

HURLBUT, SERGT. CHRISTO-PHER. In the battles of White Plains, Trenton, Princeton, and New Jersey campaign. Sergeant in Capt. John Franklin's Company, Pa., 1780. Buried at Arkport.

HURLBUT, NAPHTALI. Private Capt. John Franklin's company, Wyoming, Pa. Buried at Arkport.

JAMIESON, CAPT. JOHN. He equipped a company at the beginning of the war. Taken prisoner at battle of Fort Washington and confined on British prison ship. Buried near Canisteo.

KELLOGG, NATHANIEL. A Rev-olutionary soldier. Buried at Jasper.

KRUZEN, RICHARD. A soldier of the N. J. Line. Buried at Greenwood.

LACEY, ABRAHAM. A soldier of the Revolution. Buried near Burns.

LEMON, MAJ. WM. S. "He was a soldier of the Revolutionary War, where his bravery and intense devo-tion to the cause won for him the rank to which he attained, that of major." Buried near South Dans-ville.

MALLORY, NATHANIEL. An ar-dent patriot, serving throughout the Revolution and wounded in the ser-vice. Buried at Troupsburg.

MAXSON, LUKE. Served as a member of the "Home guard." West-erly R. I., during the last years of the Revolution.

MEAD, ENOS. A soldier of the Connecticut Line. Buried at Green-wood.

MORRIS, LIEUT. MASTER AN-DREW. Of the Colonial Navy. Bur-ied near Canisteo.

ORDWAY, ENOCH. Served in N. H. Line. Buried at Greenwood.

RICE, SAMUEL. Served in the Connecticut Line, enlisting at the age of fifteen. Buried at Troupsburg.

ROWLEY, JOHN. Served as a pri-vate in the Albany County Militia, N. Y. Line. Buried near Canisteo.

SIMPSON, ANDREW. A Revolu-tionary soldier. Served at Bennington when but sixteen years of age. Bur-ied at Jasper.

STEPHENS, ELIAS. In the battle of Newtown. Buried at Hornellsville.

STEPHENS, ELIJAH. Served in "The Levies," N. Y. Line. Buried near Hornellsville.

STEPHENS, LIEUT. JEDEDIAH. Served six years of the war. At Valley Forge, Germantown and Brandywine. Buried near Canisteo.

STEPHENS, JOHN. Enlisted as a boy and served in the Pennsylvania Line. Buried at Greenwood.

All these last four were from Wyoming.

STEPHENS, URIAH, JR. Served five years of the war in Pennsylvania companies. Buried near Canisteo.

STERNS, JOHN. During the War of the Revolution, while yet a boy, he drove team, carrying ordinance and commissary stores from Worcester to Boston. Buried near Canisteo.

TINSLEY, AMOS. A soldier of the Revolution. Buried at Jasper.

WILBUR, BENJAMIN. A Revolutionary soldier. Buried at Howard.

WRIGHT, JESSE. Served in the Revolution. At Lexington, White Plains and Bennington. Buried at Troupsburg.

Revolutionary soldiers who were pioneers of the Canisteo Valley, burial place unknown:

BAKER, WILLIAM. Served in the New York Line.

BENNETT, ANDREW. Private in Capt. John Franklin's company, Wyoming, Pa.

GRAY, ANDREW. Served in the Wyoming Valley, Pa.

GRIGGS, JOHN. In the battle of Bunker Hill.

JONES, ISAAC. Served in "The Levies," New York Line.

KENNEDY, HENRY. Served in the New York Line.

McHENRY, CAPT. HENRY. Served in different commands of the Pa. Line.

Addresses were made by Mrs. Benton McConnell, regent of the Kanestio Chapter, D. A. R., Mrs. Jennie Jones. a member of the chapter, Mrs. John Miller Horton, regent of the Buffalo chapter, and the tablet was unveiled by Miss Carrie Jamieson, descendant of Capt. John Jamieson, and Edward O'Connor, descendant of Lieutenant-Master Morris, both in the list above.

DEATH OF SILAS W. BENNETT.

[Daily Record, June 18, 1893.]

Silas W. Bennett, an old and esteemed resident of this city, and a member of one of the pioneer families of the valley, died at his residence, 140 South Washington street, at 7:30 yesterday morning of general debility, aged 76 years. Deceased was a former well known carpenter and builder and was engaged in the erection of many of this city's prominent buildings during the past fifty years. About ten years ago he was compelled by reason of ill health to retire from active life and had since been an invalid. He is survived by a son and daughter: M. A. Bennett and Mrs. J. Bennett Smith, both of this city; also a brother, John Taylor Bennett of South Dakota, and a sister, Mrs. Angela Ruggles of Kansas. The sister is now 95 years old and the brother 93.

Silas W. Bennett was of Revolutionary stock and was a descendant of the early pioneer families in the Wyoming Valley. He was born in Hanover township on Aug. 28, 1827. His father was Josiah Bennett and his grandfather Ishmael Bennett, who came to this valley with the Connecticut settlers before the Revolutionary War. His grandmother was Sarah Taylor, who was in the fort during the Wyoming Massacre.

Deceased was a member of the Methodist Church and was prominent in Odd Fellow circles, being a member of Wyoming Lodge. I. O. O. F. He was an exemplary citizen and active in affairs for the progress of the city.

INDIAN BURIAL URN FOUND.

The Zebulon Butler collection in the Historical Society has been enriched during the past week by the addition of a complete Indian pot, or burial urn, found some years ago under a ledge of rocks on Babb's Creek, in the southern part of Tioga County, Pa.

The urn is nine inches high and eighteen inches in circumference, well made and finely proportioned. It was purchased by the "Zebulon Butled Fund," and forms part of the Indian collection named after this pioneer hero. The collection already contains nearly 700 pieces of Indian manufacture from the Wyoming Valley, some of which are admirable specimens of their skill. This urn makes the number of complete pots in the possession of this society fifteen, forming the finest collection of Iroquois pottery in the United States.

DEATH OF FRED. MEYER.

[Daily Record, June 18, 1903.]

Frederick W. Meyer, one of Wilkes-Barre's oldest and best known residents, died yesterday morning at about 5 o'clock, after a residence in this city of over 40 years, aged 76 years. The immediate cause of death was dropsy of the heart. He had been ill for sev-

FRED MEYER.

eral months. He leaves his wife and the following children: Mrs. Jacob Schmitt, Mrs. Frank Glasser, Peter, Eugene and Frank.

Mr. Meyer was at one time on the Wilkes-Barre police force and also conducted for a time a vaudeville theatre on the old graveyard lot, North Fell street.

Some time ago the Record contained an interview with Mr. Meyer, in which he gave an interesting account of his career. These words of his are appended as his obituary:

"I have had what may possibly be thought an interesting career, which includes ups and downs. First let me say that I don't think I have an enemy in the world. I was born at Ansbach, Middlefrancken, Bavaria. My father was Peter Herman Meyer and my mother's maiden name was Doretta von

Schlumbach, a sister of the father of
Col. Alexander Schlumbach, formerly
of this valley. My father, who died in
1856, was for years a forester in the
employ of the Bavarian government,
and at the time of his death was head
forester, having been appointed by
King Ludwig, at Augsburg, although
he had served in this capacity at Ansbach.

"In my early days I attended school
at Ansbach and also Augsburg. I was
counted a splendid scholar and being
advanced I was favored with the appointment as a cadet for the Third
Bavarian Infantry, and at the age of
17 was accepted as a regular soldier,
being allowed to enter the regular service at my own request. I served the
full term of three years, and then
withdrew, my father having died in
the meantime. About the time I left
the service Louis Milhauser, a friend
of the family, decided to emigrate to
America and he brought me along with
him. We arrived in New York, having sailed from Hamburg in June. 1858.
Louis Milhauser came direct to Honesdale from New York and I accompanied him. Mr. Milhauser started a general store, while I secured employment
in the tannery, and he is still living
and conducting the same business in
Honesdale.

"While in Honesdale I became acquainted with Miss Margaret McCasey,
a sister of Capt. McCasey, who was an
officer in the Civil War, and we were
married. Early in 1859 I determined
to remove to Wilkes-Barre, and after
commencing housekeeping on South
street I was fortunate in securing employment with Baer & Stegmaier at
the old brewery, which stood near the
wire bridge at South and Canal streets.
After a few months I was hired by the
late Col. Hendrick B. Wright, and
while there, at his request, I was appointed a special policeman by W. W.
Loomis, who was burgess. I continued
to serve under Col. E. B. Harvey, J. B.
Stark and D. L. Patrick, who followed
Mr. Loomis. In 1866 the regular
police force was organized, consisting
of Michael A. Kearney, chief, and three
patrolmen. Peter Kintzinger, Chris
Krupp and myself. This was the old
borough. which had but only three
wards. We were paid $50 a month and
$1 for each arrest where the fine was
paid.

"I cannot tell you the exact year;
but when the prisoners were transferred from the old jail on South
Washington street to the new prison

on Water street I was induced by County Commissioner Frank Louder to resign from the police force and take the position of watchman at the new prison. The salary was $10 a month beyond what the borough paid us. I accepted the offer and helped transfer the prisoners to their new quarters. I soon regretted the change. It was terribly lonesome up there, as, you know, I had been used to lively times in those days about town. So, after nine months of it I resigned, although warden Robert May offered to pay me extra out of his own pocket if I would remain.

"I then had a property and was induced to buy one of the lots sold by the city on the site of the abandoned cemetery. There's where I made a mistake. I bought one and erected a building on Fell street, starting a saloon, and afterwards erected Meyer's Opera House. The venture was a failure, as the hard times came on and I could not weather the storm; this resulted in my losing what I had saved— and more, too. As quick as I was forced out of the business John Mahoney, who was then in council, secured my reappointment to the police force under B. F. Myers, who was chief. I served for many years, or until I was disqualified for service by rheumatism. Since then I have been unable to do anything.

"My wife is still alive and still enjoys fairly good health. Eleven children were born to us. You remember Fred, the son who served several years as a policeman. A good son, too. We lost him and some others. That is about all I can tell you concerning my life, which has been sometimes a pleasant and other times a rough voyage."

Frederick W. Meyer has helped many a man when in needy circumstances. has always endeavored to perform his duty and aimed to be a good citizen.

H. C. GATES DEAD.

[Daily Record, June 23, 1903.]

H. Carlisle Gates, one of Wilkes-Barre's well known residents, father of city clerk Fred H. Gates died on Monday morning at his home, 216 Hanover street, aged 76 years and 8 months. He was identified with the early iron industry in this valley and was connected with concerns that have branched out to be great plants.

Mr. Gates was born in Kingston in 1826 in a house which is still standing.

Deceased was a son of Nathaniel Gates, who married Ruth Richards, whose father, David Richards, came on horseback from Connecticut a few days before the beginning of the last century, along about 1794.

H. Carlisle Gates learned his trade as a molder in the old foundry of Laning & Marshall when 18 years old, and being ambitious, at an early age he established a foundry business of his own, purchasing the old stone foundry of Joseph Van Leer on Hanover and Race streets, which prospered under his management and which he conducted for many years, giving employment to a number of men. Some years ago he sold his interest in the foundry to the Vulcan Iron Works and retired from business. He had two brothers and a sister, John, Courtland N. and Mrs. John Horton, all of whom are now dead.

The deceased is survived by three daughters and a son: Mrs. J. M. Norris, Mrs. Philip Staufer, Miss Mary C. Gates and Fred H. Gates.

The funeral was held on Wednesday morning from the residence at 10 o'clock and was private. Interment was in Forty Fort Cemetery.

Mr. Gates was a highly esteemed man and he had many interesting stories to tell of the early days in this vicinity. He saw Wilkes-Barre and its suburbs grow up from small communities and was identified with many of the progressive movements of his time.

SHORTEST WILL.

The will of the late John Brown of Ashley, noted in the papers, is not the shortest on record, that of Sarah K. Miner of Wilkes-Barre being still briefer. Her will was probated with Register S. L. French Aug. 19, 1874, and is as follows:

"Emily R. Miner is my heir.

"Sarah K. Miner."

The will was written on one sheet of note paper with a lead pencil, and on the envelope enclosing the will were the words: "Read this when I am dead."

Miss Sarah Miner was a sister of the late William P. Miner, founder of the Record. She was blind and was of great assistance to her father, Charles Miner, in his preparation of the History of Wyoming. She accompanied her father in all his visits to the old settlers, searching for information, and her keen memory was of great value to her father when he came to write up his notes at the end of the day.

The will is perhaps the shortest on record—in fact it could hardly be shorter, containing only three words exclusive of the names.

THE FRENCH AT ASYLUM.
[Daily Record, June 20, 1903.]

The romance of the settlement on the upper Susquehanna by refugees who had fled from France during the French Revolution has been told by various writers, but by none so fully as in a recent volume of 150 pages by Mrs. Louise Welles Murray, corresponding secretary of the Tioga Point Historical Society. The most elaborate chronicler previous was Rev. David Craft. and Mrs. Murray has quoted largely from him. The book is entitled "The Story of Some French Refugees and Their Asylum, 1793-1800," and is dedicated to the memory of Elizabeth Laporte, the author's mother, who is a descendant of Bartholomew Laporte, one of the founders of Asylum. Mrs. Elizabeth Laporte married Charles F. Welles, brother of J. W. Hollenback and Edward Welles of Wilkes-Barre. The author of the volume is the wife of Millard P. Murray (brother of Charles F. Murray of Wilkes-Barre) and she is a sister of Mrs. A. H. McClintock of this city.

As the author says, the history of the colony and the brave Frenchmen connected with it is as pure a bit of romance as the imagination could desire. The settlement of Asylum was the direct outcome of the French Revolution of 1789 and later. The kingdom of Louis XVI was overthrown by a popular uprising and as a result of the reign of terror the nobility began to leave France in ever increasing numbers. Those who made their escape were fortunate, as two or three years later a wholesale slaughter of the nobility began. As the revolution progressed and power passed from one party to another, the bands of fugitives grew larger and a movement set in, with the young republic of the United States as the objective point. The United States was still hardly more than a wilderness, yet she was already enjoying that liberty for which France was so vainly striving.

Soon after their arrival in this country they purchased a large tract of land on the upper Susquehanna, in the State of Pennsylvania. In this effort at settlement they were largely aided by Robert Morris, the financier of the American Revolution. The pioneers of

the party struck across the country from Philadelphia to Northumberland, and then made their way up the Susquehanna to Wilkes-Barre. This was in 1793. Here they made the acquaintance of Matthias Hollenback, proprietor of several trading posts along the upper Susquehanna, to whom they delivered a letter from Robert Morris, who not only vouched for their integrity, but who guaranteed any draft they might make.

Leaving Wilkes-Barre, the explorers continued up the river to a point in what is now Bradford County (then Luzerne), near Towanda. There the French found a desirable tract of 2,400 acres occupied by Connecticut settlers. As the territory was also claimed by Pennsylvania it was necessary for the agents of the French to buy title from both Pennsylvania and Connecticut. It appears that even after paying for the land twice the French company was at a cost of only 15 cents an acre. The conveyances from Pennsylvania and Connecticut were executed in 1794.

The name of Asylum, or, as the French wrote it, "Azilum," was given to the plot. The original map is in possession of the Bradford County Historical Society. Here was laid out a town covering 300 acres. In the centre was a market square containing two acres. In addition to the 2,400 acres at Asylum the French bought 100,000 acres of wild land on the Loyal Sock Creek, which was divided among the town purchasers. Subscribers who cleared this wild land were paid $9 per acre out of the common funds. The fine character of the roads which were built attracted much attention, as did the landscape gardening of the French.

An Asylum company was organized in 1794. It had great expectations, but was impractical and a failure. The capital stock was to consist of 1,000,000 acres in 5,000 shares of 200 acres each, but a lack of money nipped the enterprise in the bud. Building was a most difficult business, as all the lumber and other supplies had to be pushed up the river from Wilkes-Barre in flatboats, four or five days being required for an ordinary trip. Early in the life of the colony financial troubles began and the French were not able to meet their obligations. Winter came on before any houses were completed. Under these circumstances it was fortunate that many of the intending settlers had not yet arrived. The French were glad to use the log huts of their Yankee neighbors. It was a long and dreary winter

and at times the question of a food supply was very pressing. In the spring the tide of emigration again set in. What a dreary prospect was opening up before these exiled aristocrats on arriving at such a primitive settlement in the heart of a lonely wilderness! Accustomed to the luxuries of Parisian life or the tropical luxuries of the West Indies, fancy the change to rude log houses in a gloomy forest, and Wilkes-Barre (which was the only source of supply) seventy-five miles away.

But here, at least, they were safe from Robespierre and the guillotine. The thirty dwelling houses were not palatial. Indeed, they were built of logs. The Yankee settlers, who were poor in the extreme, thought these log cabins were palaces, since they had chimneys, staircases, window glass, shutters, and even porches and summer houses. Quaint little shops rose around the square, and a small chapel, and even a theatre. The houses had floors and, as a rule, were papered. Some of them had furniture brought from France, jealously hoarded even until to-day by descendants.

And the exiles were ever looking forward to the coming of their queen—she, too, a royal fugitive. It had been hoped that the king, too, would find refuge there, but even while the Susquehanna fugitives were building a retreat for Louis XVI and his queen, Marie Antoinette, both had fallen victims to the headsman's ax in bloody Paris.

The nearest grist mill was at Wilkes-Barre, as was the nearest postoffice. The settlers built for themselves a horse power mill and a ferry and a wharf, and established a weekly express to Philadelphia by a messenger traveling on horseback. This express service was maintained for several years. Though the French settlers were disappointed in not being able to give shelter to Louis XVI and the queen, yet they did entertain some distinguished visitors. Talleyrand was there in 1795, as was Louis Phillippe, afterward King of France, accompanied by his two brothers, who had been visiting Niagara Falls.

It could hardly have been expected that these people, accustomed to the luxury of the life of the nobility in France, should readily adapt themselves to this strange new life in the wilderness. They were entirely unfitted for subduing a forest. Their hours were spent in feasting and in hunting

and dancing and in picnics. Their Yankee neighbors were thoroughly disgusted with this gay life, which, they saw, must be a precursor of ultimate failure. They breakfasted late, dined at 4 o'clock, drank wine or brandy with their dinner and kept late hours. The colony dragged out a forlorn existence for about ten years. We find that one of the settlers, John Brevost, was advertising in the Wilkes-Barre Gazette in 1801 that he was about to open at Asylum a school for teaching the French language. The price of tuition and boarding all children between the ages of 10 and 16 years was set down as sixty bushels of wheat per year, to be delivered at Newtown, Tioga, Asylum or Wilkes-Barre, one-half every six months.

When the revolution was over and Napoleon invited the exiles back to France they were very glad to go. When the postman brought the news of Napoleon's magnanimity the people shouted until they were hoarse and hugged each other in true French fashion. Days were spent in feasting and rejoicing, and the majority prepared to return as fast as they could secure the means. The settlers sold most of their lands to certain of their own number who had determined to make America their permanent home. The abandoned houses gradually went to decay and in a few years hardly a trace of them remained. To-day not a trace remains except in the old French road, a few country roads where streets were laid out, and the names of Laporte and Homet, families who still have many influential representatives in Northeastern Pennsylvania.

Probably no unsettled country ever saw in its midst a colony representative of so much brilliancy and suffering as this, with its nobles, court gentlemen, soldiers, clergy, together with many a lesser light who had suffered in the crash. Here Royalists, Constitutionalists, Republicans, aristocrats and plebeians found a common bond in the scars which adversity had left upon them. For there were few among them who had not lost friends or property. Their hearts were ever in France, and their ears strained for every scrap of precious news. And when opportunity came they were ready once more to share the fortunes of their beloved country,—to work, fight or die for her.

This volume is more than a narrative —it presents biographies and genealogies of the leading refugees, portraits,

maps, autographs, reprints of documents and much other valuable material concerning an historical event of which most people know very little.

JOSIAH J. McDERMOTT DEAD.

Josiah J. McDermott of 81 North Fell street, one of the bravest soldiers of the Civil War, who saw much of the hardest kind of service, died June 20, 1903, at the age of 74 years, after a long and tedious illness. For about twenty-five years he was employed as night watchman at the Dickson Works. Prior to that he was watchman for seven years at the Laning & Price plant.

JOSIAH McDERMOTT.

About a year ago Mr. McDermott was forced to give up work owing to rheumatism and stomach trouble. His wife survives him, also two sons and a daughter —Edward S. of Wilkes-Barre, Louis, a soldier in the Philippines, and Mrs. Benjamin Bush of Ashley.

Mr. McDermott came of a family of soldiers, many of his relatives having seen service. He was born in Bath. Northampton County, in 1828, and came to this city at the age of 5 years. Wilkes-Barre was then a small village. He served

with distinction in the war with Mexico
and later enlisted in the United States
Infantry in 1855 under Capt. Frank Bowman and went to Oregon. Until a year
before the Civil War broke out he was a
member of the infantry, and after being
honorably discharged he sought private
life as a carpenter, that being his trade.
When the Civil War began he enlisted in
the Wyoming Artillerists under Capt.
Emly. He served three months and then
received his discharge and enlisted in the
23d Pennsylvania Volunteers, which was
composed of fifteen companies. They had
been in service only a short time when
five companies of the regiment were
transferred to the 6st Pennsylvania. In
this regiment he served during the remainder of the war.

Mr. McDermott's Civil War record is
filled with deeds of courage. A number
of time he was in the thick of battle and
was hit by bullets. He suffered also considerably from exposure and ailments induced by it clung to him through life.
During one of the battles he was shot in
the arm and it was badly crippled.

Mr. McDermott's ancestors were also
of military inclinations. Both his great-
grandfathers served in the Revolutionary
War. His great-grandfathers' brothers
were also soldiers and they served in
many battles.

Deceased's father, William McDermott,
died at the age of 97 years and 2 months.
His grandmother lived to be 101 years of
age; his sister, Mrs. Mary A. Parker of
Brooklyn, N. Y., is now 78 years of age;
a brother, William of Baltimore, is 71
years of age. Two of his aunts died at
the ages of 60 and 72 years respectively,
an uncle at the age of 90 years, and he
has an aunt living who is 87 years old.

Mr. McDermott was an unassuming,
courteous man and his friends admired
him for having the qualities of true manhood.

STROH REUNION.

[Daily Record, June 23, 1903.]

The fourth annual reunion of the
Stroh family was held on Friday, June
19, at Rand Park, Falls, Wyoming
County. The members of the family
assembled in the Lehigh Valley station
at Wilkes-Barre and boarded the extra
car which was attached to the 9 a. m.
train. At Pittston another large delegation of the family boarded the train.
Carriages were waiting at the Falls
depot to convey the elder members of
the family to the park. The weather
was fine, except a short shower in the

afternoon. Owing to the recent rains the Falls were looking their best. The heavy pines and cedars added much to the beauty of the grove and their fragrance was a delight to all while enjoying their dinner.

Those present were: George H. Stroh, Mrs. Sarah Stroh and daughters Minnie and Bessie Stroh, Centremoreland.

Mrs. Martha Stroh, Miss Catherine Stroh, W. J. Stroh, William Stroh and Robert Stroh, Charles Bryant, Mrs. Charles Bryant, Miss Edith Bryant and Richard Bryant, H. N. Pettebone, Mrs. H. N. Pettebone, Mrs. Bonham, Miss Martha Bonham, Misses Grace and Lizzie Bonham, Master Harry Bonham, Miss Augusta Bonham and Miss Marian Kridler Bonham, Mrs. Fred Stock, Lewis Coombs, Mrs. Lewis Coombs and children, Gertie, Bertie and Willard Coombs, Mrs. W. T. Pettebone, John B. S. Keeler, Mrs. John B. S. Keeler and children, Edith, John, Fred, William and Robert Keeler, Mrs. Stephen Stroh and daughters Maud and Ruth Stroh, Mrs. Charles Learn, Mrs. Sheldon Evans, Dr. Mathers, Mrs. Mathers and Howard Mathers, Mrs. Herman Fishkorn and Mrs. Jacob Stock, Forty Fort.

Dr. A. F. Lampman, Mrs. A. F. Lampman, Dr. William Petty, Mrs. William Petty, Miss Anna Petty, Master Byron Petty, Miss Elizabeth Petty, Miss Sarah Dennis, Mrs. Leona Richards, Mrs. Wilson Callendar and Miss Lena Callendar, Wilkes-Barre.

Miss Mary Petty, Berwick.

Mrs. Mary Oplinger, Miss Sarah J. Oplinger, Miss Mary E. Oplinger, Prof. J. W. Oliver and Master Charles R. Collins, Nanticoke.

Miss Mary J. Mathers, Luzerne Borough.

J. C. Jackson, Mrs. J. C. Jackson, Frank Jackson, Harvey's Lake.

Dr. Byron H. Jackson, Mrs. Byron H. Jackson and Byron Hubbard Jackson, Jr., Mayfield, Lackawanna County.

Miss Maud Bryant, Vienna, Fairfax County, Va.

Miss Mollie Barber, Phillipsburg, N. J.

Frank Stroh, Mrs. Frank Stroh, South Eaton.

Milton W. Petty, Mrs. Milton W. Petty and children, Misses Mildred N. and Sibyl R. Petty and George E. Petty; B. F. Reed, Mrs. B. F. Reed, Miss Marjorie Reed, Nicholas Reed, Willis Reed, Mrs. Willis Reed, Miss Mildred Reed, William Klipple, Mrs. William Klipple, Walter Klipple, Miss

Sarah Klipple, Miss Mary Klipple, N.
G. Reed, Mrs. N. G. Reed, Milwaukee,
Lackawanna County.

Norman Wagner, Mrs. Norman Wagner, Harry Wagner, Miss Helen Wagner, Sayre, Bradford County.

Miss Anna Wagner, Miss Myrtle
Wagner, Pittston.

Miss Anna Watts, Wilkes-Barre.

Mrs. William Shelly and Master Robert Shelly and Master Robert Shelly,
Carverton.

Simon Decker, Mrs. Simon Decker,
Miss Norma Decker, Rev. Mr. Wrigley,
Mrs. Wrigley, Capt. Turner, Miss Turner, Ralph Vanolinda, Mrs. Martha
Swartwood, Mrs. Victor Shelly, Roland
and William Shelly, Falls.

An important event of the day was
the business meeting, which consisted
of reading of reports. In the absence
of the secretary and treasurer, Miss
Mary Bell Jackson, who has entered
the Brooklyn Hospital, Brooklyn, N. Y.,
to study to be a nurse, the reports were
read by the president, Prof. Joseph W.
Oliver, followed by roll call, which was
responded to by 114 people, the largest
number which has ever attended a reunion of the family. Then came election of officers, which resulted as follows: President, Prof. Joseph W. Oliver,
Nanticoke; vice president, Dr. William
Petty, Wilkes-Barre; secretary, Miss
Catherine Stroh, Forty Fort; treasurer,
Miss Edith Bryant, Forty Fort; historian, Miss Mary E. Oplinger, Nanticoke. All voted to hold the next reunion on Saturday, June 18, 1904, at
the home of Mr. and Mrs. John B. S.
Keeler, Wyoming avenue, Forty Fort.

The historian then read some of the
family history and an interesting letter containing the history of the part
of the Stroh family in Mauch Chunk.
The most striking facts of the history
were as follows:

Many of the family have died at or
near 70 years of age. This verifies
God's word as taught in Psalms 90:10:
"The days of our years are three
score years and ten."

There have been no removals from
the family by death or entrances into
it by birth or marriage during the past
year.

The given names have been the same
for many generations, namely, David,
Henry, Benjamin, William, Peter, John,
Amos and George.

The great desire for education, patriotism and religion which existed in
our ancestors has increased in the present generation and is manifested by
the large number of university, col-

lege, seminary, normal, hospital and high school graduates in the family. The war records show that it has given many of its sons for the cause of freedom, and the two great religious denominations, Methodist and Presbyterian, have enrolled nearly every member of the family.

Recitations were given by Miss Norma Decker, Miss Millie Petty, Miss Helen Wagner, Miss Mildred Reed and Master Charles Collins; music, "Under the Southern skies," Miss Maud Stroh, Miss Augusta Bonham, Mrs. Fishkorn; patriotic song, Capt. Turner, who is noted for singing himself and friends out of Libby prison.

MISS MARTHA BENNETT DEAD.

The announcement on June 27, 1903, of the death at Birmingham, Mich., of Miss Martha Bennet of this city caused deep and sincere regret among the friends who heard it. Miss Bennet over a year ago was stricken with paralysis at her home on South River street and was confined to the house for about half a year. While she was improving she was seized with another slight attack, but also recovered from that so that she was able to go out doors. Several months ago she went to Michigan and the change seemed to do her good. The news of her death, therefore, was a big and sorrowful surprise to those who thought she was getting along nicely. She intended spending the summer on the farm of an uncle with her cousins, the Misses Sly.

Miss Bennet was born in Wilkes-Barre June 24, 1865, and she was a daughter of Charles and Sarah (Sly) Bennet, both deceased. Her father was a prominent laywer of the Luzerne County bar and was actively engaged in the coal industry when it was being opened up in this valley. He enlisted capital from the larger cities in the mining enterprises and was instrumental in securing the right of way for the railroads that sought entrance into the valley. Mr. Bennet took advantage of his knowledge of mining operations and accumulated considerable property. His wife was a native of Michigan.

Miss Bennet was prominently connected with a number of the local benevolent institutions and the extent of her charitable work can scarcely be realized. She was instrumental in starting the Young Women's Christian Association and her tireless work and financial assistance are largely responsible for the maintenance of that excellent institution. She was also instrumental in founding the Branch Y. W. C. A. on the Heights and it was named for her. These assosiations in her death lose the best kind of a friend. Miss Bennet was also actively engaged in church work and only recently she paid off a mortgage of $2,000 on Bennet Presbyterian Church at Luzerne Borough. The Edwardsville Y. W. C. A., the kindergarten for children of foreign parents at Luzerne Borough, the United Charities and other institutions have been greatly assisted by her.

It is to women such as she that the community owes a debt of deep gratitude. Their wealth does greater good than to gratify their own pleasure. She was honored while living and her many friends delighted to spend an hour or two in her company at her hospitable and cheerful home. In her death her name will live in the hearts of those who knew her, for she has done something that will evermore cause her memory to be cherished. She lived for others as well as for herself.

Deceased is survived by one sister, Miss Sarah Bennet of this city, by an uncle, George Sly of Birmingham, Mich., and by the following cousins: Misses Martha, Addie, Emma and Lottie Sly of Birmingham.

To her beneficence to a large degree is the Young Women's Christian Association indebted, and the main branch of this institution was known and is called the "Martha Bennet branch." The Borough of "Bennet," across the river, was called after and in honor of this young woman and it was her joy to largely support, for a time at least, the church in that now thriving borough. She was a generous contributor to the United Charities, to the First Presbyterian Church of this city, ot which she was a devoted member, and to its various subordinate organizations.

The number of young women who were the recipients of her bounty was legion and in Miss Bennet the poor of this city found a deserving friend.

IDE REUNION.

[Daily Record, June 30, 1903.]

At a reunion of the Ide family held at Fernbrook Park, near Dallas, on Wednesday the following interesting historical sketch was read:

Nicholas Ide of England, the last old countryman of the American family of Ides, died early in the seventeenth century, leaving a widow and one son. Nicholas, born in 1620. The widowed mother afterward married Thomas Bliss of Bellston, near Oakhampton, Devonshire, England. The latter belonged to a family of substantial farmers and land owners of Bellston, who because of their Puritan views and opposition to the court and clergy suffered persecution under the government of Charles I.

The family finally decided to sacrifice the comforts of their English home for the trials and hardships of a new country, that they might be free to worship God in their own way. Accordingly, in 1636, Thomas Bliss, with his wife, formerly Mrs. Ide, the lad Nicholas and three or four other children, came to America and joined the former's uncle at Braintree, near Boston.

In 1637 the family went to Hartford, Conn., it being the year after pastor Thomas Hooker, with his people and their flocks, had gone through the wilderness to Hartford and formed the settlement there. They remained there about three years, and then moved back to Weymouth, also near Boston. Religious dissensions arising in the congregation, including Thomas Bliss and his family, they left the place and settled at Rehobeth. Young Nicholas lived in Rehobeth the remainder of his life.

His name first appears in the Rehobeth record as drawing land, April 9, 1645. He afterward participated in subsequent divisions and transfers of land in Rehobeth and Attleborrow, which lies immediately north of Rehobeth. He was admitted as a freeman in 1648. In 1652 he was fined £25 by the general court of the colony of New Plymouth for selling a gun to an Indian. He pleaded inability to pay and in 1657 the court ordered that on payment of the "sum of £5 in good wampum" the balance of the fine should be remitted. He was "surveyor of the highwales" from 1662 to 1674. He is the only Ide that appears on the list of freemen of New Plymouth in 1658 and 1670. He was one of the original settlers and

one of the first land owners there, and owner of considerable land. Was active in the early settlement. Was one of a committee to settle disputes with King Philip, the Indian chief.

In the records the name is variously spelled Hide. Hyde, in the earlier, and Ide. Iyde, Iyd, Jyde.

He married a daughter by a former marriage of his stepfather, Thomas Bliss, and to them were born, all in Rehobeth, the following children:

Nathaniel, born Nov. 11, 1647.

Mary, born Dec. 10, 1849; married Samuel Fuller.

John, born 1652; served in King Philip's war, being in the "Narragansett expedition" in 1676; died December, 1676, and was buried in Rehobeth.

Nicholas, born Nov. 16, 1654.

Martha, born October, 1656; married Samuel Fuller, 1681; died August, 1700.

Elizabeth, born April 6. 1658.

Timothy, born October, 1660.

Dorothy, born May 14, 1662.

Patience, born May 25, 1664; married Samuel Carpenter, 1683, at Rehobeth.

Experience, born October, 1665.

Mary, wife of Nicholas, died or was buried Nov. 3, 1676. Nicholas died Oct. 18, 1690. Both buried at Rehobeth.

Nehemiah Ide was a descendant of Nicholas Ide of Rehobeth, Mass., from which place his people emigrated to Stockbridge, Mass., where Nehemiah was born, Nov. 24, 1746. During the Revolutionary War he enlisted as a private in Capt. Thomas Williams's company of "minute men," Col. John Paterson's regiment, which marched, April 22, 1775, from Stockbridge and West Stockbridge to Cambridge in response to the alarm of April 19, 1775. Served thirteen days, then reenlisted May 5 under the same officers and served three months and four days. Mustered out Aug. 1 and returned home in October. He obtained in payment an order for a bounty coat or its equivalent in money, dated Fort No. 3, Charleston, Oct. 27, 1775. Had a continuous service around Boston of nearly four months, and including the battle of Bunker Hill. Also sergeant in Capt. David Pixley's (Stockbridge, company, Capt. John Brown's regiment, engaged June 30, 1777, service to July 26, 1777, twenty-seven days.

During the war, an officer being wounded, his comrades set him up by the side of a tree. They saw that his wounds were fatal and asked him if he had any message to send home to his family. He requested that Nehe-

miah Ide, who was a friend of his, should marry Mary Bennett, his intended wife.

Mary Bennett was a daughter of Sarah Corkin. After the war they became acquainted and were married, as the dying officer requested. To them were born, in Stockbridge, Mass., the following children, eight in number: Sarah, born March 10, 1780, died Feb. 23, 1783, aged 3 years; Elijah, born Oct. 21, 1781; Silas, born Oct. 7, 1783, died March 1, 1800; Nathaniel, born Jan. 2, 1786; William, born May 19, 1788; John, born June 14, 1790; Nehemiah, born March 7, 1793; Oliver, born March 2, 1798.

In 1800 he, with Amos Brown and David Churchwell, bought, Sept. 16, of Lemuel Walker of Hanover, Luzerne County, 160 acres of land situated in Bedford Township, now Lehman, for which they paid, half in cash, $187, being a trifle less than $1.17 per acre, and received a deed which was recorded the next day, Sept. 17, and witnessed by Alfred Ruggles and Annis Walker. Ide and Brown, accompanied by the former's eldest son, Elijah, remained the balance of the summer and erected a log cabin near the present home of Luther and Crawford Ide, and returned to Stockbridge.

The following spring Nehemiah Ide brought his family to the new home, making the journey with oxen, having in the meantime buried a son, Silas, at Stockbridge. With his six sons, now entering manhood, they soon subdued the forests and made for themselves fine farms and comfortable homes. He was a deacon in the Baptist Church at Kingston and attended the services at that place, making the trip, a distance of nine miles, on horseback.

He died Feb. 8, 1823, and his remains lie in the cemetery at Idetown, near his home. His wife, Mary Bennett, died Nov. 16, 1851, being nearly 96 years old.

Our ancestors left us a better inheritance than wealth, that of a strong Christian character that dared to sacrifice home and comfort to their conviction of duty and brave the terrors and hardships of life in a wilderness inhabited only by savages that they might be free to worship God in the way that seemed to them right. They had the strength to be true to their convictions of right at whatever cost.

But it is well for us to remember that we cannot receive the reward for their virtues. We are neither better

nor worse than our own character. We
need not say within ourselves "We
have Abraham to our fathers, for God
is able of these stones to raise up seed
unto Abraham."

Let us endeavor to be worthy of our
fathers and bring no dishonor to the
fair name they have left us.

WYOMING COMMEMORATIVE AS-SOCIATION.

One of the finest days that could be
imagined favored the Wyoming Commemorative Association in its exercises at the foot of the monument July
3, 1903. The day was a typical midsum-
mer one, and it was delightfully tem-
pered with cooling zephyrs. The platform was decorated with flags and
roses. Barrels with cold spring water
were provided, the seating was ample
and the canvas canopy was so spread
as to afford ample shade. The attendance was larger than usual. Alexander's band of men interspersed the program with stirring selections and the
address—well, it was pronounced one
of the finest ever heard on a similar
occasion. Dr. Griffis has a charming
delivery and nobody had any difficulty
in hearing him. His analysis of the
importance which Sullivan's expedition played in the Revolution was fine
and he demonstrated that it ranked
second only to Saratoga and Yorktown.
This feature of the subject was so
graphically portrayed that all present
got an entirely new conception of Sullivan's expedition.

After a band selection, Rev. George
E. Guild, D. D., of Scranton being ab-
sent, the invocation was pronounced by
Rev. Horace E. Hayden.

In making his annual address as
president Benjamin Dorrance delivered
some stirring patriotic utterances. He
welcomed all present in the name of
the Wyoming Commemorative Association and expressed appreciation of the
beautiful weather vouchsafed. He denied that this is a mutual admiration
society, denied that there is any intention to celebrate, but said that rather
is the idea to mourn—to commemorate
the brave lives and the heroic deaths
of the fathers—of them who fought and
died that we might have liberty to
honor an event which had so much to
do with winning our independence. We
want the fathers and mothers to im-
press on the children of this country
that there are other things more important than money-making or self-
aggrandizement, or self-advancement.

We are Americans and have a duty to perform. Bring up your children in the idea that this is a country of liberty— of liberty but not of license, a liberty where one man way not strike down another who happens to stand in his way. Teach them to vote. Teach them to become American citizens in the highest sense. Teach them to learn the lesson of the flag. If you do not teach God and country there will come a reckoning, when your hearts will bleed even as the bodies of our forefathers bled on this field of Wyoming. Are you teaching them French when they can't speak English? or to dance when they don't know where Ticonderoga is, or what Brandywine means? Are you teaching them the great lesson of citizenship as exemplified in American history?

Mr. Dorrance's earnest and eloquent utterances were applauded to the echo.

The band played a bunch of national airs, the audience rising when the Star Spangled Banner was struck.

The audience rose and sang America, the band played some more and then came the addres of the day by Dr. William Elliot Griffis of Ithaca, whose theme was "History and Mythology of Sullivan's Expedition of 1779." The address will be published in full in the transactions. Following are some extracts:

DR. GRIFFIS'S ADDRESS.

The expedition of Gen. John Sullivan and his four thousand Continentals into central and western New York in 1779, which destroyed the power of the Iroquois Confederacy, though ignored or slurred over by the average historian, was one of the most important and decisive episodes in the War of the American Revolution. It was authorized by Congress, planned by Washington, and executed by Sullivan, who had some of the ablest soldiers and engineers in the Continental Army to assist him. While the loss of life was extremely small, the results, as seen in history, were astonishingly great. Beside paralyzing savagery as a united force, it stopped the flank and rear attacks on Washington's army. It opened a road into the wilderness and prepared the way, even a high way, for the civilization of the Keystone and Empire States. Its great importance and farreaching influence were recognized at the time, in the thanks of Congress, the approbation of Washington, and in the appointment of a day of thanksgiving and prayer to God.

Then, as history shows is so often the case, came the inevitable disparagement of the leader and his work, of the whole campaign and the method of conducting it. The results were belittled by closet historians. With more ignorance than knowledge, and a woeful lack of insight, the whole affair was misunderstood. This is hardly to be wondered at, considering the luxuriant growth of myth and legend, which overlaid and obscured the simple reality. Of late years critical study of contemporaneous records and matter-of-fact diaries, coupled with a painstaking survey of the ground, has given us the truth in its perspective, proportions and color. A better acquaintance with all the facts, freedom from prejudice and appreciation of the magnitude of the results, reveal the real ground of the problem as presented to Sullivan in 1779. As the greatness of the difficulties are studied and the imagination regulated by wider knowledge, all the factors considered, we do not hesitate to say that the expedition of 1779 was one of the great episodes to be reckoned in its decisive influences with Trenton and Monmouth and second only to Saratoga and Yorktown, and we place Sullivan only after Washington and Greene.

As Wyoming was by its history one of the compelling causes of this expedition and in its topography the necessary place of gathering of men and supplies, it seems appropriate on this day of celebration to take as our subject, "The history and mythology of Sullivan's expedition."

The settlement in the Valley of Wyoming, the attack by the enemy, usually called a "massacre," and the great expedition of vengeance and reprisal, which forever ruined the Long House of the Iroquois, are all links in the chain of history.

To go back to first causes, we reach the decisive year of 1609, when two men, Champlain and Hudson, representing the two contrasting and radically different types of civilization, the Germanic and the Latin, appeared in the waters of inland New York State. One incarnated New France, the other, though an Englishman, was the pioneer of New Netherland. These men, unknown to each other, were even more than forerunners of a struggle for supremacy for the possession of this continent, which was to last over a century and a half. Champlain introduced an element which divided the Indian world, and made the red man a polit-

ical factor in the contentions of Europeans. By casting in the resources of a superior civilization in an armed conflict, he arrested the long, slow course of Indian evolution and progress; for, unconsciously, he smote with paralysis Indian industry and economic systems. From the moment of the flash of his arquebus, began the degradation of the red man.

The Irquois Confederacy of Five Nations was an island in the great ocean of the Algonquin tribes that surrounded them on every side. In language, habits of life, intellectual ability and grade of civilization, the Iroquois were the superiors. Making themselves possessors of the keys of this continent, they erected that Long House, whose western door was at Niagara, its northern door at Oswego, its eastern door at Albany and its southern door at Tioga Point. With their own resources, even before the advent of the white man, they were able to dominate many tribes both far and near, and to put them under tribute. Being makers of salt, agricultural in their habits and acquirements, always rich in food supplies, and governing most of the great valleys, waterways and passes of the most valuably strategic character, they held their own grandly. Until the death-dealing bullets of Champlain's arquebusiers changed the whole current of their civilization and methods of war, they equipped themselves in bark armor and frequently fought in the open in bands and masses. That shot near Ticonderoga, on July 30. 1609, was heard throughout the Iroquois world. From that hour, these forest warriors, with one voice, swore undying hatred to the French, and at once sought out the Dutch. made the league of friendship and mutual aid, even "the covenant of Corlaer" From Fort Orange they obtained fire arms and ammunition and were soon able to dominate or terrorize a vast area of the North American Continent. Through sixteen decades or more, while the French and the British were struggling for supremacy and the Indian was a decisive political factor. the dyke reared by the Iroquois, from the Hudson to Niagara, remained unbroken by the waves of French aggression. No bribe or threat. no priest or soldier. neither prosperity nor adversity could break that dyke. The Iroquois remained loyal, first to the Dutch and then to our English fathers and their sovereign. The name of Arendt VanCurler. founder of the peace league with the

Iroquois, survives even the confederacy itself, in the names given by their descendants to-day, to their white rulers. In the United States they call the governor of New York "Corlaer," and in Canada name King Edward VII sovereign of Great Britain and Emperor of India, "Kora Kowa,,—the Great Corlaer.

Nevertheless, as Chronos devours his own offspring, so in time,—when Germanic principles triumphed over Latin and North America was to be Anglo-Saxon, after Wolfe's triumph at Quebec, the Indian ceased to be a decisive political factor. In 1776 it meant for the red man neutrality or hostility, and in either case slow destruction. For the Indian, it was a choice between two evils. The English speaking house was divided against itself.

Then both the intellect and the loyalty of the savage, who by nature is a conservative, were tried. Naturally, he took the conservative side of the argument. Perhaps he had not the mental initiative, was not intellectually able to do anything else or otherwise. At any rate, our fathers saw the impending danger. In actual forest council, the British emissaries would quote precedent, and to argument add the persuasion of more abundant whisky, arms and ammunition, kettles and beads, hatchets and mirrors, than the poorer Continentals could offer. Nevertheless our fathers in Congress employed some of the ablest men of New York, Schuyler, Herkimer and others who knew the Indians well, to win them over to friendliness or at least to remain neutral. But only the Oneidas, through Domine Kirkland, and a portion of the Mohawks were saved to the American cause. The vast majority of the Iroquois warriors sided with the King. Under such able Tories as Butler and MacDonald, and their own Brant, a chief of unusual ability, they followed the British flag to battle, not only in the open field with St. Leger, Burgoyne and others, but over the long frontier from Saratoga to Pittsburg, they lighted the torch and kept the tomahawk red. Wyoming, Cherry Valley, and the devastated hamlets in the Mohawk Valley and in central New York and Pennsylvania told the story not only of desolation and of death and the weakening of American resources and power; but from the military and strategic point of view, such active hostilities created one of the gravest of problems. Out of the heart of New York State, and navigable

almost throughout their entire length by the birch bark canoe, flowed the streams, which blending in the Delaware and Susquehanna, made easy highways to the sea. This, to the eye of Congress and Washington, meant the maintenance not only of constant rear and flank attacks upon the line of settlements and the army and the destruction of resources, so necessary in a defensive campaign, but also the formation of an enemy's granary and depot for food supplies, by which the British and their allies could be provisioned, and thus kept to the highest efficiency. The chief difficulties of the British were geography and the commissariat. Washington knew this and profited by his knowledge.

* * * *

It was absolutely necessary, then, that the Indian country should be desolated and the power of the Canadians and savages be paralyzed. No one saw the danger and the necessity more clearly than Washington. None knew better the nature of the country to be traversed and the enemy to be faced, for Washington's early training had been in the forest, and his first battles were with Indians. It was Washington who insisted that the artillery should be taken, and, despite jeers and criticism, it was taken. None knew better than he the demoralizing effects of bombs and the inability of the forest ranger, accustomed to the defense of tree trunks, to stand in force against round shot and canister. What could shatter a tree made the Indian quail.

So Congress on Feb. 27, 1779, having voted and given the order, Washington decided to detail one-third of the whole force at his command. He tendered the leadership to Gates, as courtesy bound him, who declined it. It was then at once offered by the commander in chief to one whom he trusted, and who, though not infallible in judgment or action, was swift and capable of rectifying mistakes when made—Gen. John Sullivan. Though but forty years old, he was a veteran. Interpreting aright the King's order forbidding the importation of arms into the colonies as a declaration of war, he led in December, 1774, the first American soldiers in the first hostile act against Great Britain, by capturing the fort at Piscataqua and thus obtaining the powder for Bunker Hill. After that he served at the siege of Boston, in Canada, at Trenton, Prince-

ton, Brandywine, Germantown, and at Butts's Hill, Rhode Island. as one of the most efficient and trusted of Washington's division commanders.

To form the grand army of chastisement. four brigades of infantry, one regiment of artillery, a battalion of riflemen, about 1,800 horses and a flotilla of about five hundred boats, the building of a military road from Easton to Wyoming, and the organization of a corps of three hundred pioneers, axmen, bridge builders, etc., a staff of surveyors and geographers were necessary. Besides Easton and Wyoming as bases of supplies, with a service of couriers or expresses, to keep open the line of communication. there were to be built a fort and hospital near Tioga Point. Another fort, with supplies and cattle to be sent on later. was to be erected at the foot of Seneca Lake, at the southern end of the lake country; and, perhaps, for a final dash before frost, another fortification at Honeoye would be necessary. The work to be done against the Indians was, in Washington's words, "the total destruction and devastation of their settlements." The maize land, orchards and gardens in central and western New York were to be ruined. and the forts, houses, and holy places given to the flames, so that the region would not be habitable again even by savages for possibly several years. The spirit of the Indians was to be so broken. that though they might afterward send out small raiding parties, they would no longer be able to put a large force in the field. Thus they would cease to be valuable as allies to Great Britain, or a serious element to the final solution of the problem of the Revolution.

* * * *

The punishment determined upon was severe, even to the limit of the ethics of civilization, but our fathers remembered Wyoming. It was one of the counts of the Declaration of Independence in the indictment against King George that "He (the King of Great Britain) has endeavored to bring on the inhabitants of our frontiers the merciless Indian savages. whose known rule of warfare is an undistinguished destruction of all ages, sexes and conditions."

Had this sentence been penned in 1778. after Wyoming. instead of in 1776. the indictment would have been stronger.

The Middle States, as being nearest to the ground to be invaded, were called upon to furnish the chief force. Of the four brigades, three, together with the artillery, and most of the riflemen, scouts and pioneers, were from Pennsylvania, New York and New Jersey. With these were to be joined the New Hampshire brigade, then in camp at Redding Conn., and the Sixth Massachusetts, then at Cherry Valley. The march was to be made by the right wing advancing from Schenectady, and the left wing from Pittsburg, both wings to join the main army at Tioga Point. The composition of the whole force finally gathered under Sullivan, was as follows:

The main army under Sullivan's command gathered at Easton in the spring and early summer of 1779. The Pennsylvania brigade formed the light troops under Gen. Hand—gay-hearted, impetuous and brave, the youngest of the brigadiers. Proctor's regiment of artillery (now the Second United States) with nine pieces, left the forts of the Delaware, their place being taken by Col. John Eyre and his Philadelphia batteries and men of the Pennsylvania Line. Most of the riflemen and boat men were also Pennsylvanians, though in Maj. Parr's battalion were Connecticut, Delaware, Maryland and Virginia men. The New Jerseymen had marched from Bound Brook and Elizabeth. The New Hampshiremen had crossed the Hudson from Fishkill to Newburg, and thence moved through New Jersey to Easton, some of them helping to build the military road westward from Wind Gap to Wyoming. Arriving at Wyoming they remained from the end of June until July 31st. Then supplies and stores having come up from Sunbury, the march up the Susuqehanna Valley to Tioga Point began. By Aug. 12th boats were moored and unloaded, the great camp formed and the construction of Fort Sullivan begun.

The lecturer then went into an account of the expedition, giving many interesting details, summarized as follows:

One third of the Continental army had been dispatched to devastate the fairest part of the Indian country, which object was thoroughly accomplished. Forty towns and villages, and those the most important in Iroquois land, had been laid in ashes. Two hundred thousand bushels of corn, probably the same amount of vegetables and

other food had been destroyed
and thousands of fruit trees
had been cut down. The Indian country was made virtually
uninhabitable for years. Huddled
together in reconcentration camps
near Niagara, during the unusually
severe winter of '79 and '80· the diseases
of scurvy, consumption and starvation
assisted in more than the decimation
of the savages. On the other hand,
was the exploration of one of the most
fertile and at that time best cultivated
regions along the Atlantic coast, the
opening of a path through the wilderness, the enlargement of mind and increase of knowledge gained by young
men in their impressible age, thousands of whom reentered the country
and settled as pioneers. The success
of this expedition enabled the army of
Washington to give its almost undivid-
ed attention to the front attacks of
the British army and in due time to
march to Yorktown.

* * * *

Having briefly outlined the history
of the great march which virtually destroyed the greatest Indian Confederacy on this continent, the speaker
took up what he called its parasite,
mythology. One legend is that Sullivan had lost or thrown away a certain cannon. The speaker showed
that there are no less than eleven
points along the march where this lost
piece of artillery is thought to be
buried. Great effort has been expended
in some localities to dig up the lost
gun·

There are numerous legends of the
"massacre" of Indians by Sullivan's
avengers. These growths of the imagination usually take the form of a
bayonet charge by the Continentals
and a precipitation of the redskins
over some picturesque cliff. As a matter of fact, after the battle at Newtown, near present Elmira, the majority of Sullivan's men never saw an
Indian. There were no bayonet
charges, no driving over cliffs.

More probable are the stories which
tell of relics left over from the im-
perfect destruction of Indian treasure.
which were afterwards recovered and
used by the incoming settlers.

A story long had currency that in
charging to the Battle of Newtown.
the troops rushed on shouting "remember Wyoming!" But this has little
historic support. It is not improbable.
however. that some used this battle
cry, since two companies of Wyoming

men, under John Franklin and Simon
Spalding, were in the Pennsylvania
brigade.

A legend is told of a now flourishing
poplar tree, grown from a stick thrust
into the ground by a soldier to mark
the spot which he intended on returning to settle. True to his word he
came back a decade later and located
where his poplar stick had taken root.

me of the old boats of 1779 are still
found in the rivers and at various
places are found bayonets, horse shoes
and other undoubted relics of the
march.

In conclusion the speaker said that
laying aside myth and legend the
whole route of Sullivan's march ought
to be marked with boulder or tablet.

NOTES.

Among the old settlers present was
William Dickover, who was at the
corner-stone laying 70 years ago. Another gentleman was J. M. C. Marble
of Los Angeles, Cal., who was at the
monument exercises of about 60 years
ago.

The exercises were all over by 12
o'clock and there was a general expression that they were satisfactory in
every particular.

After the exercises Mr. and Mrs.
Benjamin Dorrance entertained the
speaker and half a dozen friends at
luncheon.

The Historical Society and the several patriotic societies were duly represented in the audience.

WILKES-BARRE SEVENTY-SIX YEARS AGO.

[Daily Record, June 20, 1903.]

How the Fourth of July was celebrated in Wilkes-Barre seventy-six
years ago is thus told by the Wyoming
Herald of that date, though no information is given as to who the Wilkes-
Barre youths were who thus honored
the day:

"The following toasts were drank by
a company of young lads who met together in this town to celebrate the
Fourth of July, and who on this occasion were inspired with more patriotic
feelings than many of maturer years.
The sentiments are good and would
do honor to older and wiser heads. But
it is not so much the merit of the
toasts which induces us to publish
them as the pleasant reflection that
this meeting of youthful patriots is an
evidence that the gratitude towards

the revolutionary heroes will live in the breasts of our children when we are gathered to our fathers."

1. The Fourth of July, 1776—The day that the Americans declared themselves independent and swore in presence of their Creator that they never would return to a state of servitude.

2. The surviving heroes of the Revolution—We will cherish their memory when they shall have fallen in the last inevitable conflict.

3. The departed patriots of 1776—May the remembrance of them never fail to produce patriotic thoughts in the breast of every citizen.

4. George Washington—He who led our army from victory to victory and finally to triumph merits our everlasting veneration.

5. May happiness and prosperity attend the Western Hemisphere.

6. Success to Lafayette.

7. May America ever retain the freedom which she has gained by the valor of the heroes of the Revolution.

8. May Decatur ever be remembered as a brave man.

9. May the same be remembered of Lawrence.

10. May Washington ever be remembered as the savior of his country

11. Success to internal improvement.

12. The President of the United States.

13. If the British Lion ever presumes to set his feet on American soil, may they be hewn off with the hatchet of Liberty and the flesh picked off from his bones by the American Eagle.

The day was also celebrated by the citizen volunteers commanded by Capt. William Ross, who, after performing a number of military evolutions, dined at the house of Maj. Helme.

Seventy-six years have passed away since that youthful band of patriots so creditably celebrated the nation's birthday, and where is that band of little soldiers now? They have probably all passed over to "the other side," and there joined the great majority, including those whose memory they sought to perpetuate. O if an American citizen ever has cause to exult in the contemplation of all that is sublime in human enterprise it is in the commemoration of the deeds of those glorious patriots whose deeds these young lads were so proud to celebrate.

"Think'st thou the mountain and the storm
Their hardy sons for bondage form?

Doth our stern wintry blast instil
Submission to a despot's will?
No! we were cast in other mold
Than those by lawless power con-
    trolled."

S. H. STURDEVANT DEAD.

Samuel H. Sturdevant, one of Wilkes-
Barre s prominent merchants died at
the home of his father-in-law, Dr. J.
J. Rogers, at Huntsville on July 5,
1903, at ten minutes past 8 o'clock.
The deceased was 42 years of age and
was born at Harvey's Lake. His ailment was a complication of diseases,
from which he had been suffering for
a long time. He is survived by his
wife, Carrie Rogers, formerly of
Huntsville, and two brothers and one
sister—Miss Ellen Sturdevant of this
city, Harry of New York and Robert
of Wilkes-Barre.

Deceased was a son of the late Col.
S. H. Sturdevant, who died in Febru-
ary, 1898, and Mrs. Leah Urquhart
Sturdevant, who died in August, 1893.

In the death of Mr. Sturdevant the
city loses one of its brightest young
business men, a man known throughout the State. He was a member of
the lumber firm of S. H. Sturdevant,
doing business in this city for many
years. He came to this city with his
parents when a boy.

About a year or so ago Mr. Sturdevant went to California for a change
of climate, which, however, did him
little good. He continued in business
up to three weeks ago, when he caught
a severe cold from which he could not
rally. During his many years of business and prior to his first illness he
was always active and progressive
and took a great interest in public
affairs.

Of late he superintended the erection
of a handsome summer home at
Huntsville, which is nearly completed.
His residence in this city was at 33
Carey avenue.

Mr. Sturdevant was an ex-president
of the Ganoga Ice Co., director of the
Lake Transit Co., an ex-vice president
of the Pennsylvania Lumbermen's Association and an ardent member from
boyhood of the First M. E. Church of
this city.

MOORE REUNION.

[Daily Record, July 7, 1903.]

The Moore family held its second reunion on Saturday, June 27, at the Oneonta picnic ground at Harvey's Lake.

More than 100 relatives met and at 12 o'clock gathered around the table and enjoyed a sumptuous dinner. After dinner they boarded a steamboat and took a trip around the lake.

The meeting was then called to order and it was agreed to form a permanent organization, which was done by electing J. W. Moore of Slocum president, Lillian Moore of Wilkes-Barre secretary and Mrs. John Brodhun assistant secretary.

The next meeting will be held at the same place on the last Saturday of June, 1904.

The following were present:

Wilkes-Barre—Dr. I. H. Moore, Mr. and Mrs. W. B. Moore, Mr. and Mrs. Henry L. Moore, Mr. and Mrs. E. M. Hungerford and children Marion and Jean, Mrs. E. Enterline and son Henry, Mrs. Frank Brown, Mrs. Carle Leonard, Mr. and Mrs. John Brodhun and children Boynton, William, Flora, Nora, John, Jr., and Elizabeth, A. W. Moore, Clarence Seigle.

Ross Townishp—Mrs. Hannah Shepard, Mrs. Eliza J. Hontz, Mr. and Mrs. Giles Moore and children Cecil and Revis, Mrs. Esther Moore. Mr. and Mrs. Frank Moore and children Verge, Esther and Helen, Mr. and Mrs. Isaiah Trumbower, Mr. and Mrs. Eugene Naugle and children Viva and Niva, Mr. and Mrs. Jacob H. Moyer and son Ralph, Mr. and Mrs. Loxley Fisk and son Harry, J. N. Moore, Mr. and Mrs. Melvin Dymond and children May and Ethel.

Slocum—J. W. Moore, Ira E. Moore, Evan B. Moore, W. S. Moore, Avice Hontz.

Nescopeck—Mr. and Mrs. J. F. Birth and children May and Jennie.

Idetown—Thomas Pinder.

Bloomsburg—Mr. and Mrs. G. H. Moore and children Ila E., Bernice M., Hazel M. and Naomi C.

Dorranceton—Mr. and Mrs. John M. Harrison and children Eva and Wesley, Miss Isabella Harrison, Miss Tillie Harrison, Mrs. Samuel Harrison and daughter Mildred. Jeddie Brown.

Bowman's Creek—Mr. and Mrs. Clarence Phoenix and daughter Grace.

Tunkhannock—Mrs. Frank Major and daughter Ethel Arline.

Milwaukee, Lackawanna County—Mr. and Mrs. Frank Coon and son Samuel.

Plymouth—Mrs. Ellen Barney, Mr. and Mrs. E. Payne Dymond and children Lewis and Emily.

Forty Fort—Mrs. Tillie Moyer.

Easton—Mr. and Mrs. W. L. Mullin and son Ferris.

Pittston—Mr. and Mrs. Ray Dymond
and son Ray, Mr. and Mrs. Dana Dymond and son Elmer.

Hollow—Mr. and Mrs. Boyd Dymond
and son Clarence.

HARVEY'S HISTORY OF WILKES-BARRE.

Oscar Jewell Harvey of this city,
than whom there is no more accurate
or polished writer in Wyoming Valley,
has finished his history of Wilkes-
Barre, and it is now in press. It will
be ready for distribution to subscribers
about the first of next year.

Mr. Harvey is the author of a volume,
"A History of Lodge No. 61, F. & A.
M.," and he made out of a subject
which in most hands would be treated
as a matter of dry facts and statistics,
a most interesting series of chapters, a
volume which would as absorbingly interest one not connected with this
Masonic lodge as a member of it. Mr.
Harvey is also the author of a history
of the Harvey family and other works.

The new history of Wilkes-Barre
will have the merit of being accurate,
and this is a great consideration in a
work of this nature. Whatever Mr.
Harvey undertakes to do he does thoroughly and there never is any evidence
of superficiality in his preparations.
Where others are content with skim-
ming over facts he delves to the bottom, and in order to get at the root of
even some comparatively unimportant
event he will spend as much time in
research as many other authors would
spend in making whole chapters. It
is fortunate indeed that the writing of
the first history of Wilkes-Barre has
fallen into such hands. Combined with
thoroughness and accuracy the volume
will have the merit of being written
in pure, good English and in an entertaining style.

A prospectus regarding the work has
been issued. It is beautifully gotten
up, with two colored plates, one showing a view of Wilkes-Barre and the
Susquehanna from Ross Hill, and the
other a symbolic figure in memoriam
of Col. John Durkee—1728-1782—founder and namer of Wilkes-Barre. Other
illustrations in the prospectus are, "An
order in the handwriting of Col. Timothy Pickering," "Portion of articles
of capitulation of Fort Durkee," "Hon.
Thomas Penn," "Hon. James Hamilton," "A war party of Indians recon-
noitering," "Twelfth page of the original deed from certain Iroquois or
Six Nation chiefs to the Connecticut
Susquehanna Company," "Indians

leaving Wyoming after the battle of July 3, 1778," "Looking northwest from the site of the old Sullivan redoubt, at the rear of the German Catholic cemetery, Darling street," "Wilkes-Barre below Northampton street, as viewed from Park avenue," "A game of croquet on the river common near the Wyoming Valley Hotel in 1868."

Though called a history of Wilkes-Barre, it will really be a history of Wyoming, as up to 1800 the life of the one was inseparable from that of the other. The author promises much interesting and authentic matter—especially in the chapters relating to the Colonial and Revolutionary periods—not to be found in any previously published book dealing with the Wyoming region. The material has been derived from sources entirely unknown to earlier chroniclers, and it throws an entirely new light on many happenings in Wyoming history. All chroniclers after Miner and Chapman have been content to follow those two pioneer writers, but Mr. Harvey has struck out into new fields and has had little need to depend on any of his predecessors. It is no wonder then that drawing from new sources and from heretofore unpublished documents Mr. Harvey is able to correct many statements that, while passing current as history, have had little basis other than tradition, passed down with increasing picturesqueness from one generation to another.

Mr. Harvey has spent several years on his forthcoming volume and as all local histories are practically out of print his should be a welcome addition to hundreds of libraries, public and private.

The announcement says: "The work will contain a large amount of interesting and authentic historical matter—especially in the chapters relating to the Colonial and Revolutionary periods—not to be found in any previously published book dealing with the Wyoming region. Some of the new material forms, unquestionably, what will be looked upon as a valuable addition to the general history of this country.

"The work will comprise fifty-four chapters, containing 700 pages of text and illustrations, together with a complete index and a 'Chronological table of important occurrences.' In addition there will be over 100 pages of halftone engravings (nearly all of which will be printed from plates specially prepared for this work) on fine coated **paper.**

"The work will not be printed from stereotype plates, and only a limited edition will be issued. It will be attractively and substantially bound in maroon cloth.

"Although the expense of publication will be large, the book will be sold to subscribers at $7.50 per copy; but after all subscribers shall have been supplied the price will be advanced. An edition de luxe of 250 numbered copies printed on paper of extra quality and handsomely bound in three-quarters morocco, with gilt tops, etc., will be issued at $12.50 per copy, should a sufficient number of advance subscriptions therefor be received.

"All subscriptions should be sent to the Wyoming Historical and Geological Society, Wilkes-Barre, or to the author, Oscar J. Harvey, 36 West Union street, Wilkes-Barre, Pa."

A portion of chapter I is printed in the prospectus, and these paragraphs are taken from it:

"No attempt previous to this, so far as the writer is aware, has ever been made to write the history of Wilkes-Barre. And this fact appears most remarkable, when one realizes, in the first place, that, with the exception of Boston, New York, Philadelphia and a very few old towns of this country, there is no town in the United States whose early history is so intensely interesting and has so many strikingly dramatic events interwoven in it from its very beginning as that of this 'Diamond City' of ours; and in the second place, that there is no town in the United States—with the exception of the city of Washington—founded within the last one hundred and fifty years, that has had so many well known and eminent men identified or concerned in one way or another with its birth and early history as this same town. A cursory examination of the following pages will show the correctness of these statements to even the most careless or indifferent seeker after facts.

"In seeking out material for a work of this kind, covering a period of a century and a half, it must be obvious to the reader that the task was attended with many difficulties, the chiefest of which arose from the fact that many valuable public and private records that would not only have greatly facilitated the task, but made the results more complete and interesting, were a long time ago either lost or destroyed."

BLACKMAN REUNION.

[Daily Record, July 22, 1903.]

Some of the descendants of Elisha Blackman, one of the earliest settlers of Wyoming Valley, attended a luncheon yesterday, as the guests of Edwin H. Jones at his Glen Summit cottage. The day was a delightful one and all had a royal time. The luncheon was served at 1 p. m. and was a fine exemplification of the caterer's art. On the menu was a portrait of Elisha Blackman, son of the pioneer Elisha, himself a soldier of the Revolution and the last survivor of the Wyoming massacre. Another feature of the menu card was a historical sketch of the Blackman family by Henry Blackman Plumb.

The pioneer in America was John Blackman, born in England and came to America prior to 1640. One of his four sons, Joseph, was father of the Wyoming pioneer, Elisha Blackman.

Joseph Blackman and his wife, Elizabeth (Church), moved to Little Compton, R. I., where Elisha Blackman, one of nine children, was born Sept. 23, 1699. He married Susanna Higley, m Lebanon, Conn., to which place his father had removed in 1717, where he purchased 120 acres of land for £600. Susanna Higley was a sister of Hannah Higley, who married Capt. Joseph Trumbull, father of Jonathan Trumbull, the famous governor of Connecticut during the Revolution, the friend and adviser of Washington, and whom the latter called "Brother Jonathan." Elisha Blackman and Susanna Higley had, among other children, Elisha, born Sept. 19, 1727. He married on March 22, 1753, Lucy Polly (widow of Ebenezer Smith). They had Lucy, born Sept. 7, 1755, who married Titus Darrow; Lovina, born Sept. 7, 1757, married (in Wilkes-Barre) Darius Spafford; Elisha, born April 4, 1760, married Anna Hurlburt, Jan. 10, 1788; Ichabod, born March 24, 1762, married Elizabeth Franklin, 1786; Eleazer, born May 31, 1765, married Clarinda Hyde, 1787. From the above named descend those who are gathered at Glen Summit this 21st day of July, 1903. Elisha Blackman, who married Lucy Polly (the Widow Smith) emigrated to the Wyoming Valley in 1772. He was a lieutenant in the company commanded by Capt. William Hooker Smith of the 24th Connecticut Line stationed in the fort at Wilkes-Barre at the time of the Wyoming massacre. His son, Elisha Blackman, was in the battle of Wyoming, escaped the massacre and swam the river, fled to Wilkes-Barre, where he joined his

father, the only man left in the fort at Wilkes-Barre, the others having gone with the women and children to the mountains to show them the way towards Stroudsburg and to Connecticut. In the afternoon of the same day father and son followed. In August young Elisha returned to Wyoming with Capt. Spalding's company, and in October helped to bury the dead at Wyoming. Later he served two years with the army in Cherry Valley and on the headwarters of the Susquehanna in New York State, and in 1781 enlisted in Col. Sherman's regiment on the Hudson, being discharged in 1782. It is his picture that is presented herewith as a valiant member of the Blackman family. Eleazer Blackman, his brother, was 13 years old at the time of the invasion of the valley in 1778 by the British and Indians under John Butler, and assisted in building the fort in Wilkes-Barre by hauling the logs.

Those present: Edwin H. Jones, Malvina Jones, Amanda C. Lape, Linda D. Strome, George P. Strome, Julia Collings Dougherty, Eloise M. Dougherty, F. J. Dougher, Alice M. Dougher, Col. C. Bow Dougherty, Mrs. Anna P. Dougherty, Mr. and Mrs. Horace Horton, R. S. Westlake, Mr. and Mrs. C. B. White, Araminta Blackman Safford, George W. Blackman, Margaret E. Blackman, Edgar Zell Steever, 3d; Harriet Collings Davison, Blanche W. Emory, Elloma J. Emory, Mary A. Emory, Mary Blackman Emory, Benjamin S. Emory, Warren E. Straw, Georgia K. Straw, Charles A. Jackson, Mrs. Lillie B. Jackson, Andrew G. Raub, Mrs. Maud Baldwin Raub, Mr. and Mrs. Andrew J. Baldwin, Ira Marcy, Mr. and Mrs. H. B. Plumb, Rollin Plumb.

A permanent organization was formed by the election of George W. Blackman as president.

HON. CHARLES A. MINER DEAD.

[Daily Record, July 25, 1903.]

This morning shortly after 1 o'clock occurred the death at his home on South Franklin street of one of Luzerne county's most prominent citizens, Hon. Charles A. Miner. who came from one of Wyoming Valley's oldest and most honored families. For a couple of years Mr. Miner had been in ill health, although he was able to be about much of the time. About five weeks ago he was seized with a complication of ailments that confined

him to his home and his illness did
not yield as readily as formerly to
treatment. He gradually grew weaker
and although yesterday he was somewhat brighter than for a few days
previously, towards evening he took a
sudden turn for the worse and declined
rapidly. He was nearly 73 years of
age.

Charles Abbott Miner was a son of
Robert and Eliza (Abbott) Miner and

HON. CHARLES A. MINER.

was born in Plains Township Aug. 30,
1830. He was educated at the Wilkes-
Barre Academy and at the academy at
West Chester, Pa. Since coming of
age, and until a few years ago, when
he retired from active management,
he was engaged in the milling business on the site of the first mill built
by his maternal grandfather in 1795,
at Miner's Mills.

Mr. Miner had been prominent in
nearly all of Wilkes-Barre's industrial
enterprises. For a quarter of a century he had been a director of the
Wyoming National Bank and at his
death was its vice president. For
fifteen years he was president of the
Coalville (Ashley) street car line. He
has been president of the board of
directors of Wilkes-Barre City Hospital
almost continuously since its organiza-

tion, president of the Hillman Academy and for many years furnished the Miner prizes for the declamation contests among the pupils of that school. He was president of the Luzerne Agricultural Society, for some time was president of the State Millers' Association and an officer and stockholder in many other State and local institutions. Deceased had been a member of the Geological State Survey since 1877.

Mr. Miner represented Wilkes-Barre in the House of Representatives for three terms, from 1875 to 1880 inclusive, and in 1881 he was the Republican candidate for State Senator, but was defeated by the Democratic candidate, Hon. Eckley B. Coxe.

On Jan. 19, 1853, Mr. Miner married Eliza Ross Atherton, a daughter of Elisha and Caroline Ross (Maffet) Atherton, and to them six children were born: Col. Asher Miner, in partnership with his father in the milling business; attorney Sidney Robie Miner and Dr. Charles Howard Miner, all of whom survive; Elizabeth Miner, who died this year; Robert Miner, who died in infancy, and Ross Miner, who died in 1867. His wife also survives.

Hon. Charles A. Miner came of a family that traces its lineage back, without a break, to Henry Miner, who was knighted by King Edward III "for valorous deeds done," and who died in 1359. Descendants of this man were among the earliest comers to America, Thomas Miner settling in Connecticut in 1643. Seth Miner, a great-grandson of Thomas, born in Norwich, Conn., in 1742, was one of the earliest officers commissioned for service in the Revolutionary army. His son, Charles Miner (afterwards historian of this county), came to Wyoming Valley to look after land interests which his father, as a member of the Connecticut-Delaware Land Co., had acquired. Another son of Seth Miner, Asher Miner, came to this valley shortly afterwards and began the publication of the Luzerne County Federalist in 1801. His brother Charles was subsequently taken into partnership, and Asher went to Doylestown, Pa., where he established what is now known as the Intelligencer, and was postmaster of Doylestown for several years. Asher later went to West Chester, where he published a paper called the Village Record, which is still being published. In 1834 he returned to Wilkes-Barre, where he died in 1841. His wife was Mary, a daughter of Thomas Wright, who was born in

Ireland, and who was the founder of Miner's Mills and built the first mill there in 1795, which has been in possession of his descendants and conducted by them ever since. Of this union were born thirteen children, of whom Robert Miner, the second son, was the father of Hon. Charles A. Miner. Robert married Eliza Abbott, a daughter of Stephen Abbott, one of the early Wyoming families.

Another relative of the subject of this sketch who was prominent in this city half a century ago, was William Penn Miner, editor and farmer, who died here in 1892. William Penn Miner was a cousin of Hon. Charles A. Miner and a son of Charles Miner, editor and historian. William P. Miner and his brother, Joseph W. Miner, purchased the Wilkes-Barre Advocate (which later became the Wilkes-Barre Record) and was the editor of the paper from 1849 to 1876. William P. Miner was also prothonotary of Luzerne County from 1846 to 1849. In 1853 he started the Wilkes-Barre Record of the Times, and the Daily Record was started by him in 1873.

There were many other distinguished members of the Miner family, lawyers, journalists, authors and statesmen, who have been honorable and useful citizens in Berks, Chester, Susquehanna and Luzerne counties for over a hundred years, and the deceased, Hon. Charles A. Miner, was a worthy successor to an honored line of ancestors.

In the death of Mr. Miner Wilkes-Barre loses a citizen whom it was an honor to have in the community. He came from a family that did much for the Wyoming Valley and that was closely associated with its rise from a few straggling houses to the sisterhood of thriving communities that have made it famous. The deceased was connected with many of the local industries and in all of them his wise, conservative counsel was of great value. He grew up with many of our largest enterprises, and the mill at Miner's Mills, with which he was associated from youth, has come to be one of the largest and most prosperous in the country.

In church work Mr. Miner was also active in his time and at his death he was a warden in St. Stephen's.

As president of the board of directors of the City Hospital he was one of the stanchest supporters and warmest friends of that institution. Its interests he guarded with jealous care and

for years he was one of its most extensive contributors. Not only with money did he help largely, but every week he sent generous contributions of substantials for its support. The hospital in his death will lose a friend whose loss will be seriously felt. In line with his work for the hospital he was interested in other charities and his heart went out to the suffering and the needy. The cry of distress fell upon no unheeding ear.

He lived a good life, above the sordid and selfish interests that animate so many men of means. He followed the promptings of a heart that felt for all humanity, and in his death he leaves a memory that will always be cherished in fond remembrance.

MRS. ARABELLA LEWIS DEAD.

After an illness of only about a week's duration Mrs. Arabella D. Lewis passed away on June 20, 1903, at her home on North street. Her death was due to an injury received on Christmas Eve. She was descending a flight of stairs, when when within a step or two of the bottom she fell, sustaining a severe injury, which proved to be a fractured hip. The severe shock, together with an attack of rheumatism which complicated the case, proved too much for one of her 82 years to stand and her condition became so grave that on the tenth day she gently passed away.

In her death this community loses one of its oldiest and most highly esteemed women. Of gentle nature and unselfish disposition Mrs. Lewis was beloved by all. It may be truly said of her that she was one of the mothers in Israel. She was a life-long communicant of St. Stephen's Episcopal Church, her memory going back almost to its organization. She was a regular attendant up to the Sunday preceding Christmas. In all the relations of life, whether as wife, mother or neighbor, she was eminently faithful and her departure will be sincerely mourned by her large circle of acquaintances.

Mrs. Arabella Duncan Lewis was a daughter of George Chahoon and Mary Baker Chahoon. She was born December 9, 1820, on River street where the Wyoming Valley Hotel now stands. She was united in marriage to Josiah Lewis on September 12, 1843, by Rev. John Dorrance, D. D., pastor of the First Presbyterian Church. Her father, George Chahoon, died May 24, 1844, and her mother January 16, 1847. Her brothers and sisters died on the following dates:

Anning Owen Chahoon, February 1. 1843.

· John Chahoon, September 14, 1881.

Elizabeth Chahoon, April 14, 1861.

Ann Grant Chahoon, December 16, 1887.

Her husband, Josiah Lewis, died July 11, 1890. Children surviving Mrs. Lewis are George Chahoon Lewis and Mrs. Mary Chahoon Lewis Gross. She had resided on North street since her marriage, having commenced housekeeping in the neighboring building now occupied by Mrs. Frederick Ahlborn.

Mrs. Lewis's nephews now living are the children of her brother, John Chahoon:

George Chahoon, residing at Ausable Forks, N. Y.

Henry C. Chahoon, residing in Wilkes-Barre.

Robert I. Chahoon, Albany, N. Y.

Edward and William, Wilkes-Barre.

·Joseph Slocum Chahoon, son of her brother, Anning Owen Chahoon, died November 2, 1901.

The grandchildren are Arabella Lewis Gross, John Lewis Gross, Anna Chahoon Lewis, Ruth Hyde Lewis and Mary Squires Lewis.

———————◆———————

WILLIAMS REUNION.

The descendants of the late Jonathan Williams met at Harvey's Lake on Aug. 15 for their first reunion and had an enjoyable time. They decided to hold a reunion once a year. Those present were: Children, F. A. Williams and wife, Mrs. William Williams, D. M. Williams and wife, J. H. Totten and wife, Mrs. Edward Williams, J. W. Williams and wife: grandchildren, M. R. Williams and wife, Mrs. H. B. Williams, A. N. Williams and wife; J. E. Williams and wife, Sarah Williams, William Vaughn and wife, L. A. Dymond and wife, Roger Williams and wife, Ralph Rood and wife, Mary Williams, Loren Williams, Lillian Williams, Herbert Williams, D. W. Totten and wife, Verne Totten and wife, F. A. Edwards and wife, Nan Edwards, O. P. Williams and wife, James Williams and wife, Mrs. Stella Levan, Maud Williams, Eva Williams; great-grandchildren, Sylvia Charles, Addie and Nan Case, C. O. Brooks and wife, Bernadine Fayette, Lyman and Clara Williams, James and Myrell Jones, Bertha, Izetta, Marie and Raymond Williams, Aubrey and Donald Williams, Harold Rood, Earl and Agnes Dymond, Lavera and Alice Williams, Carmine and Mabel Edwards, Ethel and Leslie Williams, Hildreth and Esther Williams, Letha Totten; great-great-grandchildren, Madge Brooks.

OLD MUSKET FOUND.

[Daily Record, July 28, 1903.]

Relative to the finding of a musket stock bearing the date 1601, at Spring Brook, Lackawanna County, a few days ago, the Scranton Republican of yesterday says that Col. H. M. Boies of Scranton, who has a notable collection of various styled weapons of various countries and various ages, examined the old stock. He declared after a minute inspection that there is no doubt that the gun was of extremely early manufacture, but it is doubtful as to its being as old as 1601. These figures, he thinks, may be trade marks, although it is quite possible that they represent the year of its make. There is every indication, he said, that it was the property of an English soldier, and as guns were regarded as particularly valuable articles in the days which the gun appears to represent, he is inclined to the belief that it was in use by its owner at the time of its being broken.

The dents in the stock, the blood stains and break at the point where the barrel was joined, show that it was broken after a violent struggle. Apparently the soldier lost his ammunition and was forced to fight for his life, using the musket as a club. A terrific blow over the head of one assailant caused the musket to snap in twain, and, left without a weapon, he was overpowered, and as his combatants were probably Indians, his scalp was taken with a tomahawk.

So much doubt existing as to the time the weapon was used here, it is impossible to fix the time of the fight. According to Col. Boies it was probably used in the Revolutionary war, although it is possible, as has been stated, that it was in use prior to that time.

Another supposition is that the musket figured in the time of the Wyoming massacre. This was on July 3, 1778, the time of the Revolution.

MRS JOHN DOWLING DEAD.

[Daily Record, July 29, 1903.]

Mrs. John Dowling, an old resident of Wilkes-Barre and vicinity, died yesterday afternoon at 2:35 of Bright's disease at the home, 50 North Main street. Deceased had been a sufferer for the past ten years. She was about 60 years of age.

She is survived by her husband, who is employed as janitor of the Central school building, and the following chil-

dren: Mrs. C. F. Hoffman of Reynolds-
ville, Pa.; Emily A., a milliner of this
city; Fred L. of Binghamton, who is
superintendent of construction for the
Bell Telephone Co.; James F., employed
as a conductor by the Wyoming Valley
Traction Co. Two sisters of deceased
reside at Dallas, Mrs. James Garrahan
and Mrs. Edward Wagner.

Deceased was born in Plymouth.
where she resided the greater part of
her life. The family came to Wilkes-
Barre about twenty years ago. Previous to moving to 50 North Main street,
where they have lived for the past few
months, they resided at East End.

Mrs. Dowling came from one of the
oldest families in Luzerne County, belonging to colonial stock. She was a
member of the well known Pringle family. Her father was Samuel Pringle,
one of the pioneer settlers. while her
grandfather, Samuel Pringle, Sr., was
of English descent, and his wife, the
deceased's grandmother, was a Lamoreaux, of French descent. Her great-
grandmother on her mother's side was
of an historical Williams family and
she married an Ives. From this union
there were two sons, who were killed
in the Wyoming massacre, their names
being inscribed on the Wyoming Monument.

EN-ROUTE FOR MEXICO.

Among the papers of Judge Cyrus
T. Pershing, lately deceased, at his
home in Pottsville, was found a letter written to him while a student
at Jefferson College, an excerpt from
which will be of interest to Record
readers. The writer, C. C. Sheridan,
afterwards became one of the best
known physicians of western Pennsylvania and is still practicing. In re-
counting the home gossip his letter
throws a casual but most pleasant
light on some Wilkes-Barreans of
nearly 60 years ago. It will be remembered that at that time there was no
Pennsylvania Railroad. Travelers for
the west journeyed by canal up the
Juniata Valley to Hollidaysburg at the
foot of the eastern slope of the Alle-
gheny Mountains. Thence the Portage
Railroad, a system of inclined planes
and levels, similar to the gravity road
until recently operated between Carbondale and Honesdale, lifted them to
the summit and lowered them down
the western side to Johnstown on the
Conemaugh. From this point the canal
conveyed them to Pittsburg. We give
the letter exactly, not omitting the
then young physician's chill at the

name of Wyoming. The Record is under obligation to Thed Pershing, son of Judge Pershing, for the interesting document:

"Johnstown, Pa., Dec. 14, 1846.

Our town has been all excitement for a few days past in consequence of the Pa. Volunteers passing through en route for Mexico. On Friday last four companies came over and it was previously determined that the citizens should give them a supper instead of raising a purse and eating them at the rum holes. It was agreed that every citizen who was disposed to do so should say how many he could accommodate at his own table. Accordingly each citizen called out how many he would take, and before they were aware they ran short of soldiers (there being 370) before all our people were supplied. The above 370 were composed of the Pottsville company and three companies from Philadelphia, viz.: Capt. Hill's, Capt. Bennett's, and a German company, the Washington Light Infantry under Capt. Bender, a real warlike looking fellow, and he came near having a display of his military spirit under the following circumstances: The German company arrived here first. The citizens immediately marched off their respective squads to supper, and a boat was pointed out to Capt. Bender by Maj. Potts and Col. Seiper, who is commissary, in which he was told he could take his men when they returned from supper. In the meantime the cars arrived with Capt. Hill's company and their baggage was stowed in the boat which had been pointed out to Capt. Bender and a soldier left to guard it while Capt. Hill and his men were at their supper. Capt. Bender returned with his men to put them aboard, but was met at the hatch by the soldier who had been left with the baggage of Capt. Hill, who told Capt. B. that his men could not enter. Capt. B. was determined to have the boat, when the sentinel drew his bayonet and told Capt. B. he would just as soon die for his captain as his country and that he should not put his men aboard. Bender then drew a pistol to give the faithful fellow a blast when someone caught him. About this time Maj. Potts made his appearance and assured Capt. Bender that it would be all right as soon as Capt. Hill would return. Just then Hill hove in sight and the matter was adjusted by Hill shifting his baggage to another boat. What made Bender and his men the more furious was the fact that they had despised Capt. Hill's company, or at least a part of his company, as did every other company in the crowd. And for this reason: He (viz.: Hill) has some 23 men who belong

to an order in Philadelphia called the Killers, and they are nothing more nor less than a band of cut-throats and thieves. From their conduct on the other side of the mountain the companies which followed them found the doors of the citizens along the canal barred against them, to remedy which they sent a man ahead who informed the people that the Killers were coming, which so completely turned the tables that the doors were now shut against them and thrown open to the others. They are certainly a disgrace to the company, many of whom, together with most of the officers, are good men. It is to be hoped they will be turned out when they arrive at Pittsburg. So much for the first detachment.

On Saturday night about 10 o'clock the 'Wyoming (I feel my blood chilling, while I write that name) Artillerists' arrived unexpectedly. The news, however, soon spread and in a very short time they were all disposed of in squads as before, only that, in addition to a nice warm supper they were furnished with the best possible accommodations for a good night's rest. They are a noble looking company, all young men except four, and they number 123. They left their home with about 80 men, exclusive of officers; the balance they received as they came along. Amongst them is big John Martin, who clerked for the Union Line this spring. I presume you remember him, they called him the Volunteer about the warehouse. He says from the time they come within 40 miles of Santa Anna he will not shave until he strops his razor on a piece of the old chap's hide.

Your folks got a full share of the soldiers every time. Yesterday (Sunday) the three remaining companies arrived and were disposed of as before. After supper they all left. They behaved themselves like gentlmen. There was no noise or disturbance. Capt. Dana of the Wyoming Artillerists is a most amiable, but cool, determined looking man, just such a man as you could depend upon in any place—at least he looks so. But perhaps you are tired of this, etc."

THE SLAUGHTERED HARDINGS.

While employees of the Wilkes-Barre & Wyoming Valley Traction Co. were digging a hole for the erection of a pole along the sidewalk on Wyoming avenue, just outside the old Jenkins Cemetery, on Friday, they unearthed a human skull that was fairly well preserved. About ten years ago, when the traction line was established, a pole was erected a few feet away from the pole placed in position on Friday. At that time the lower bones of

a human body were found, and it is supposed that all the bones belong to the same body. Those found ten years ago were reburied just inside the cemetery fence and the skull found will be buried with them by those interested in the cemetery. It is believed that the bones are those of one of the two Harding brothers who were killed by Indians while they were at work in a field in Exeter Township shortly before the Wyoming massacre. The remains were brought to Jenkins Fort, and were buried in Jenkins Cemetery, which in olden times extended into the territory now occupied by Wyoming avenue. When the avenue was laid it out it was known that several bodies were buried in that section taken by the borough, but their exact location was not known and it was impossible to remove them within the new cemetery line.— Pittston Gazette.

WYOMING REVOLUTIONARY MILITIA.

An interesting pamphlet from the pen of Hon. Charles Tubbs of Osceola, Pa., has lately appeared, it being a reprint of a paper read by him before the Tioga Point Historical Society. The title is "The Wyoming Military Establishment, Twenty-fourth Regiment, Connecticut Militia," and it presents the history of a local regiment which played an important part in our Revolutionary history and which, until now, has not been viewed in a comprehensive light. A new feature is a list of losses sustained by Wyoming people from 1778 to 1780. Mr. Tubbs, by way of introduction, repeats briefly the contest between Pennsylvania and Connecticut over the Wyoming region, showing how the latter, inside the present limits of Pennsylvania, was an integral part of Connecticut, settled by Connecticut people, and governed by Connecticut laws. It was a Connecticut town.— Westmoreland,—attached to the Connecticut County of Litchfield, had its judge, sheriff and other officials and sent representatives to the Connecticut legislature. A bitter struggle for its possession ensued, but in the end, Pennsylvania triumphed.

Under conflicting charters from the Crown both Connecticut and Pennsylvania claimed the region. Under the Pennsylvania charter, which was the younger, came sheriffs and armed forces and drove off the Connecticut people, who claimed under a prior

charter. The disputed region was
popularly spoken of as Wyoming, but
on the Connecticut statute books it is
called Westmoreland. It embraced an
area of 5,000 square miles in present
northeastern Pennsylvania.

Having explained how the Connecticut people built up a government
within the present boundaries of
Pennsylvania, Mr. Tubbs took up the
24th Regiment of Connecticut militia,
which was organized as the Wyoming
Military establishment. By a strange
oversight this organization has received little attention from local historians.

The Wyoming people, isolated in a
wilderness infested with savages, had
from the first settlement, in 1769, de-
fended themselves with a home guard.
In 1774 the Connecticut Legislature
officially recognized the Wyoming settlements, then having a population of
about 2,000, by incorporating them into
the town of Westmoreland, a name
which may be considered as inter-
changeable with Wyoming.

The next step in the evolution of
the military establishment was in the
same year, when in town meeting assembled, the Wyoming people voted to
apply to the Connecticut Legislature
for the establishment of a regiment,
each district to have a company, ten
in all. The officers were chosen by
vote of the men of each company.
After more than a year's delay the
Connecticut Legislature established
the regiment, numbering it the 24th,
and placing it on the same basis as all
other regiments of the colony. The
colony was to pay each man 12 pence
for a day's training.

The regiment was assigned to the
sixth brigade, Connecticut State
Militia The regiment's officers were:
Zebulon Butler, colonel.
Nathan Denison, lieutenant colonel.
William Judd, major.
Col. Butler, then 44 years of age,
was a veteran of seven enlistments,
and he had served from Crown Point
to Cuba.

Lieut. Col. Denison was 10 years
younger and had seen service, though
brief, in the 3d Conn., in the French
and Indian War.

Major Judd was not a veteran.
Denison succeeded Butler as colonel
in 1777, when the latter went into the
Continental service.

Lieutenant colonels after Denison
were Lazarus Stewart and George
Dorrance.

Majors after Judd were George Dorrance and John Garret.

A complete roster of the officers, as obtained by Mr. Tubbs from the manuscript rolls, is reserved for another article in the Record.

The new regiment was organized none to soon. The Governor of Pennsylvania had made up his mind to destroy the Connecticut settlement at Wyoming, which was within the Pennsylvania County of Northumberland. Under pretence of serving sundry writs at Wyoming the sheriff of Northumberland took with him an armed force of 700 men. He called this a "posse comitatus," but it was a military expedition, commanded by one Col. William Plunket. This expedition came up the river in December, 1775, but the newly formed 24th regiment was ready for it.

Col. Butler had augmented his own regiment with the old men and boys who could be had, but his entire force was only about half that of the invader and he took position in the rocks which overlook Nanticoke, a natural defense. Col. Plunket's Pennamites made several attempts to dislodge Butler, but failed and his expedition was driven down the river in confusion. Each side lost eight or ten killed and many wounded.

Meanwhile, the outbreak of the Revolution led to a temporary lull of hostilities between Connecticut and Pennsylvania, and next year (1776) Congress ordered the raising of two companies in Westmoreland for Washington's army and each company enlisted eighty-two men. All the officers and men were taken from the ranks of the 24th militia. Twenty others enlisted under Lieut. Obadiah Gore to serve in a New York regiment, as well as ten more under Capt. Strong. Thus the 24th furnished the Continental army with 194 men in the summer of 1776.

While this depletion was going on, the town assigned to the field officers the onerous task of building forts for the large territory of 5,000 square miles.

In 1776 the Legislature enacted that the age limit should be extended so that men from 50 to 60 were no longer exempted from duty. These were formed into companies called the "alarm list," they to be attached to already existing regiments. Accordingly two companies were formed in Wyoming in 1777, Dr. William Hooker Smith being captain of one and James Bidlack, Sr., of the other. In popular

speech these supplementary companies of old men were called Reformadoes.

The year 1777 was spent by the regiment in scouting duty, as the Indians and Tories up the Susquehanna were active in distressing the patriots.

Iu 1778, owing to alarming news of a threatened invasion from the north, a third company of Continental troops was raised at Westmoreland. It was made up of men from the 24th, who thus transferred their service from the State to the United States, but it did not withdraw them from the valley. In order to increase its efficiency the regiment was drilled by two deserters from the British army, Abraham Pike and sergeant Boyd. The latter was afterwards shot as a spy by the British John Butler when he captured Wyoming.

Meanwhile, in the valley forts and blockhouses had been built, but many of the fighting men of the 24th were serving with Washington and the valley was left almost unprotected.

When the British invaded the valley Col. Denison sought to concentrate his 24th regiment, but several of the companies, so scattered were they, could not reach the valley in time. Col. Butler, of the Continental army, who was home on furlough and was pressed into command, escaped with his life, so did Col. Denison. But Col. George Dorrance was killed and so was Maj. John Garret. All the captains were killed, also three lieutenants and three ensigns. From 200 to 300 were slain on that bloody field.

"The 24th regiment was never reorganized. It was overwhelmed on the field of honor. It served three years— one for the colony, two for the State. It builded forts, it fought battles, it went down to defeat and death, amidst a wild saturnalia of blood, rapine and murder."

FITCH REUNION.

The first reunion of the Fitch family took place at Rand Park, Falls, Pa., on Thursday, Aug. 6, 1903.

Shortly after assembling threatening rain caused the managers to decide to hold the day's festivities in the auditorium and parlors of Falls Church, which was nearby. Here more than 200 of the Fitch family gathered and renewed old acquaintances, recounted reminiscences of past years, greeted relatives who had never before been seen, and offered toasts to those who were absent.

The most prominent personage present was Mrs. Mary Deubler, commonly and most affectionately known throughout the Fitch family as "Aunt Polly." Aunt Polly is an octogenarian and, being the oldest Fitch present and because of her genial and lovable character, was the centre of attraction throughout the day.

After dinner had been served to all present, all relatives repaired to the church auditorium, where an organization, with the following officers, was completed: President, Dr. A. B. Fitch, Factoryville, Pa ; first vice president, J. H. Fitch, Falls, Pa.; second vice president, G. J. Fitch, Lockville, Pa.; secretary, Albert Fitch, White's Ferry, Pa.

When this organization had been completed the president, Dr. Fitch, gave an able and interesting address on the chronology of the family.

Going back to the earliest authentic record of the Fitches in England, in 1204, where were found many who had been prominent in English history as noblemen, men of letters, jurists and officers in the English army and navy, the speaker came down to the American branch, who settled in Massachusetts and Connecticut early in the seventeen century, and lastly to the generations now living, making this portion interesting in delightful reminiscences and laughable anecdotes.

Others were then called upon, who added much to the entertainment of the gathering.

Before adjournment it was resolved by vote to hold the second annual reunion at Falls, Pa., next year, upon a date to be decided by the officers.

Following are the names of those who registered in the family register book:

Mary Deubler, Sayre; A. B. Fitch, Ada M. Fitch, Allan M. Fitch, Vivian M. Fitch, Factoryville; Cora M. Fitch, H. C. Fitch, Ernest Fitch, Avoca; Asher Fitch, White's Ferry; Floyd F. Menger, Josephine Menger, Mill City; Everett B. Campbell, Gertrude N. Campbell, Charles R. Campbell, Lindsey D. Campbell, Alexander C. Campbell, Victoria C. Campbell, Mary Frances Campbell, Theodore C. Campbell, Minooka; Mrs. A. B. Munn, Mrs. M. M. Griffin, Scranton; Mrs. Louise M. Mansfield, Lionel E. Wertman, Philadelphia; C. L. Smith, Mrs. C. L. Smith, Mrs. Lyman Swartz, Lake Winola; A. M. Dewitt, Mrs. C. M. Dewitt, Mrs. A. M. Dewitt, Bertha Dewitt, Falls; G. J. Fitch, Lockville; J. C. Menger, Mill City, Mr. and Mrs. Riley Sickler, Falls.

Rose Sickler Bloom, Frances Sickler Collamer, Wilkes-Barre; Dora Sickler Marcy, Altoona; Vera Sickler Durant, Wilkes-Barre; Victoria Sickler, Falls; Helena S. Rounds, Leroy W. Rounds, Sayre; Effie Siglin Balls, East Lemon; Eugene Rose, Ella E. Ross, Floyd Ross, Mill City: Estella E. Fitler, Sayre; Clara Keegan, Francis Keegan, Marie Keegan, Irene Keegan, Scranton.

C. S. Fitch, Alice Fitch, C. P. Fitch, F. B. Fitch, Carbondale; O. S. Fitch, Lizzie Fitch, S. Fitch, Allen Fitch, Squaretop, Albert Fitch, Sarah Fitch, Rachel Fitch, William A. Fitch, Ruth M. Fitch, Helen E. Fitch White's Ferry; Sarah Siglin Kennedy, Sayre; George Judson Fitch, Rosetta Heitsman Fitch, Ada E. Fitch Miller, Lockville.

Frank O. Fitch, Lorenzo D. Fitch, Margaret E. Fitch Swartwood, Harry W. Fitch, William Swartwood, Harriet L. Fitch Dymond, Kalista W. Fitch, Dana Dymond, Nathaniel Fitch, Pittston; J. B. Sickler, Celeolin Sickler, Perry Sickler, Emeretta Sickler, Falls; J. B. Hawker, Ella B. Hawker, Frances Verna Hawker, Vera Gertrude Hawker, Roland Hawker, Carrie Hawker, Scranton.

Lizzie Fitch, Walter Fitch, Albert Fitch, David Kresge, Lydia Kresge, Falls; Leslie Kresge, Detroit, Mich; Thomas Kresge, Joseph H. Fitch, Harold Fitch, Mrs. Chrissie Fitch, Bessie Fitch, Falls; Everett V. Fitch, Lizzie M. Fitch, Grace B. Fitch, Myrtle T. Fitch, Orlando W. Fitch, Meodnia G. Fitch, Everett V. Fitch, Scranton; S. W. Fitch, Hattie A. Fitch, Herbert Fitch (son), Helen Fitch (daughter), Sayre; Mrs. Alfred B. Fitch, Falls; Albert Clinton Fitch, Sugar City: Walter S. H. Haslam, Verna Haslam, Rose Fitch Haslam, Scranton; S. J. Fitch Menger, Esther Menger, Forster Menger, John Fitch, Rose Fitch, H. A. Odell, Mrs. H. A. Odell, Falls.

PETTEBONE FAMILY REUNION.

[Daily Record, Aug. 8, 1903.]

About ninety members of the Pettebone family, one of the oldest families in the valley, coming originally from Connecticut and settling in the Wyoming Valley about 1769, passing through the massacre times, held a family reunion at Fernbrook on Thursday. Representatives were present from Dorranceton, Forty Fort, Luzerne Borough, Kingston, Hazleton, Binghamton, N. Y., and Chinchilla, near Scranton.

After dinner a business meeting was held. George Pettebone presided. Invocation by Rev. B. P. Ripley of Forty Fort, after which secretary Jacob S. Pettebone read the record of the previous reunion and reported that two deaths and six births had occurred since the last meeting. The following officers were elected:

President, John S. Pettebone, Forty Fort.

Vice president, George Pettebone, Forty Fort.

Recording secretary, Jacob S. Pettebone, Dorranceton.

Corresponding secretary, O. B. Pettebone, Forty Fort.

Treasurer, Noah Pettebone, Dorranceton.

Entertainment committee—Mrs. John Parry, Miss Clyde Bartholomew, E. H. Pettebone, Jacob S. Pettebone.

Noah Pettebone made a few remarks and Rev. B. P. Ripley delivered an address.

The next reunion will take place Aug. 5, 1904, at the same place.

WALTER FAMILY REUNION.

[Daily Record, Aug. 25, 1903.]

The Walter family held its seventh annual reunion at Rand Park, Falls, on Thursday afternoon and it was largely attended and the program and outing greatly enjoyed. The Walter family is descended from the late Henry Walter of Newton, who came from New Jersey about seventy-five years ago. He was the father of five daughters and nine sons and his direct descendants now number over 200, the association books showing 155 registered on Thursday. The exercises at the park were opened with the singing of the hymn "Nearer, my God, to thee" and prayer by John Walter. Selar Walter then welcomed the guests in a neat speech and the following program was rendered by the younger members of the family:

Recitation, Nerva F. Walter; poem, Mrs. Melissa Davis; address, Mr. Jennings of Florida; recitation, Lena Walter; duet, Myrtle and Grace Walter; recitation, Neva F. Walter; recitation, Master John B. Raeder.

Among those who attended were: Mrs. Melissa E. Davis of Hampton, Va.; W. H. Walter and wife and daughter Neva, Benjamin Raeder and wife, Henry Raeder and wife, Robert, Elizabeth and Edith Raeder of Pittston; William W. Raeder and family of

Wilkes-Barre. E. G. Coon, wife and children of Ransom, George Coon, wife and son, George W. Raeder, wife and daughter, Rose Raeder of Milwaukie, Pa.; Mrs. John Coon of Bald Mount, H. F. and Ira Coon of Carverton, S. H. Walter, wife and children of Trucksville, B. E. Walter, J. A. Walter and family, I. D. Vosburg and wife, Arthur Walter, wife and family, Horace Rozelle and wife of Mill City; Frank Walter, wife and family, Ira Walter and family, Mrs. David Walter of Lockville; Arthur Jacoby and family, Benjamin Jacoby and family, H. Jacoby and family of Balt Mount; Mr. and Mrs. George Scott of Athens and others. The time and place for the next meeting will be decided by the officers.

RANSOM REUNION.

[Daily Record, Aug. 29, 1903.]

The members of the Ransom family held their second annual reunion at Fernbrook Park yesterday. Dinner was served at 12, and 2:30 Rev. Mr. Knipp of Plymouth delivered an address. A musical program followed. Those present were:

Mr. and Mrs. Thomas Ransom, Daisy and Gertrude Ransom, Mr. and Mrs. Harry Ransom, Ralph Ransom and daughter Mildred, Mr. and Mrs. C. C. Ransom, Flora, Mabel, Clarence and Jay Ransom, Mr. and Mrs. William Ransom and two sons, Mr. and Mrs. Joseph Ransom and son, Mr. and Mrs. G. C. Ransom, Mr. and Mrs. Frank Ransom, Mrs. Grace Ransom, Mr. and Mrs. George Ransom, Edna, Emma, Harriet, Bell and Jessie Ransom, Barton Ransom, Charles Ransom, Mr. and Mrs. Erbin Ransom, Mr. and Mrs. Corey Ransom, Mr. and Mrs. Albert Bertram, Joseph, Dora, Ralph, Boyde, Clara and Edna Bertram, Mr. and Mrs. Charles Bertram, Mr. and Mrs. Peter Bertram, Blanche and Crissie Bertram, Mr. and Mrs. Payne Major, Mr. and Mrs. Henry Harrison, Ora, Mazie and Stanley Harrison, Mr. and Mrs. Boyde Mosteller, Mabel and John Mosteller, Mr. and Mrs. David Davis and daughter Hazel, Mrs. Absolom Case, Addie, Stanley and Walter Case, Mr. and Mrs. Harry Case and children, Mrs. Garringer, Herman, Edith, Emma, Phoebe, Lina, Zelzah, Nelson, Ethel, Raymond and Henrietta, Mr. and Mrs. Charles Wilson, Mr. and Mrs. Izah Harris, Mr. and Mrs. John B. Smith, Miss Jennie Smith, Mrs. Harvey Yeager, Francis, Roscoe, Fred, Carrie and Margaret Yeager, Mrs. Andrew Levie, Mr. and Mrs. Whitney and daughter Liva, May and Florence Lamoreaux, Mrs. Maud Sutliff and daughter, Mrs. Lora Davenport and daughter, Mil-

dred and Rebecca Steevers, Miss Jennie Harter, Cora and Henry Harter, Mr. and Mrs. Fred Harloss, Robert, George, Harry and Ira Harloss, Misses Mamie, Mattie and Bertha Johnston, Alfred Johnston, Mrs. Henry Johnson and son Stanley, Mr. and Mrs. Wesley Morton, Flossie and Hazel Morton, Mr. and Mrs. Everett Besteder and daughter, Arthur Case, Mr. and Mrs. H. B. Davenport, Mrs. Record and daughter Emma, Mrs. Duncan and son, Mrs. John Record, Rev. Mr. and Mrs. Knipp and daughter, Willis Hawley, Mrs. Clarence Stevens, Miss Katherine Morgan, Mrs. John Roberts, Mrs. Kemmer, Mr. and Mrs. F. Conner, Nellie and Maud Major, Mr. and Mrs. Ransom Elston and children, Mrs. Guy Bisel, Mrs. Charles Henderson, Miss Sarah Meeker, Steven Elston, Mrs. Libbie Johnston, Mrs. Laura Price, Mrs. R. M. Johnston.

WYOMING REVOLUTIONARY MILITIA.

[Daily Record, Sept. 1, 1903.]

In his recent pamphlet on the Wyoming Military Establishment, reviewed in Record, Aug. 5, 1903, Charles Tubbs has gathered from manuscript muster rolls what we have never before had— a complete roster of the officers of the historic old 24th regiment of militia, now almost forgotten. While the local historians have made references to the companies, such references have been brief, and the 10th company, from Huntington and Salem, organized 3 years later than the others, has been entirely overlooked. Following is the roster, together with the dates of appointment:

COLONEL.

Zebulon Butler, May, 1775.
Nathan Denison, May, 1777.

LIEUTENANT COLONEL.

Nathan Denison, May, 1775.
Lazarus Stewart, May, 1777.
George Dorrance, Oct., 1777.

MAJOR.

William Judd, May, 1775.
George Dorrance, May, 1777.
John Garret, Oct., 1777.

FIRST COMPANY, WILKES-BARRE.

Captains: Stephen Fuller, Oct., 1775; John Garret, Oct., 1776; Elisha Swift, May, 1777; James Bidlack, Jr., Oct., 1777.

Lieutenants: John Garret, Oct., 1775; Asa Stevens, Oct., 1776; James Bidlack, Jr., May, 1777; Lebbeus Tubbs, Oct., 1777.

Ensigns: Christopher Avery, Oct., 1775; David Downing, Oct., 1776; Lebbeus Tubbs, May, 1777; John Comstock, Oct., 1777.

SECOND COMPANY, KINGSTON.

Captains: Nathaniel Landon, Oct., 1775; William Hooker Smith, May, 1777; Dethic Hewit, Oct., 1777; Aholiab Buck, May, 1778.

Lieutenants: George Dorrance, Oct., 1775; Flavius Waterman, May., 1777; Aholiab Buck, Oct., 1777; Elijah Shoemaker, May, 1778.

Ensigns: Asabel Buck, Oct., 1775; Dethic Hewit, Oct., 1776; Elisha Blackman, May, 1777; Asa Gore, Oct., 1777.

THIRD COMPANY, PLYMOUTH.

Captains: Samuel Ransom, Oct., 1775; Asaph Whittlesey, May, 1777.

Lieutenants: Perrin Ross, Oct., 1775; Aaron Gaylord, May, 1777.

Ensigns: Asaph Whittlesey, Oct., 1775; William White, May, 1777.

FOURTH COMPANY, PITTSTON.

Captains: Solomon Strong, Oct., 1775; Jeremiah Blanchard, May, 1777.

Lieutenants: Jonathan Parker, Oct., 1775; Timothy Keyes, May, 1777.

Ensigns: Timothy Keyes, Oct., 1775; William Shays, May, 1777; Jeremiah Bigford, May, 1778.

FIFTH COMPANY, HANOVER.

Captain: William McKarrican, Oct., 1775.

Lieutenants: Lazarus Stewart, Jr., Oct., 1775; Rosewell Franklin, May, 1777.

Ensigns: Silas Gore, Oct., 1775; Titus Hinman, May. 1777.

SIXTH COMPANY, UPPER WILKES-BARRE.

Captain: Rezin Geer, Oct., 1775.

Lieutenant: Daniel Gore, Oct., 1775.

Ensigns: Matthias Hollenback, Oct., 1775; John Hagerman, Oct., 1777.

SEVENTH COMPANY, EXETER.

Captain: Stephen Harding, Oct., 1775.

Lieutenant: Elisha Scovill, Oct., 1775.

Ensign: John Jenkins, Jr., Oct., 1775.

EIGHTH COMPANY, LACKAWAY.

Captain: Eliah Farnham, Oct., 1775. [Miner says Varnum.]

Lieutenants: John Shaw, Oct., 1775; Jonathan Haskell.

Ensign: Elijah Winters, Oct.. 1775.

NINTH COMPANY, UP RIVER.

Captains: James Secord, Oct., 1775; Robert Carr, May, 1776.

Lieutenants: John Depue (De Pui), Oct., 1775; Nathan Kingsley, May, 1776.

Ensign: Rudolph Fox, Oct.. 1775.

TENTH COMPANY, HUNTINGTON-SALEM

Captain: John Franklin, May, 1778.

Lieutenants: Frethias Wall, Oct.. 1776; Stoddart Bowen, May, 1778.

Ensigns: John Franklin, Oct., 1776; Nathaniel Goss, May, 1778,

GEORGE CATLIN.

His was the gifted eye, which grace
  still touched
As if with second nature; and his
  dreams,
His childish dreams, were lit by hues
  of heaven.
Those which wake Genius.

Eli Catlin, the grandfather of George
Catlin, was a captain in the 2d Con-
necticut Regt. of the Revolutionary
Army, then commanded by Col. Zebulon
Butler. Putnam Catlin, the father of
Geo. Catlin, was born at Litchfield,
Conn., in 1764, and entered the law
office of Uriah Tracy somewhere about
1773. In the year 1787 he removed to
Wilkes-Barre, then peopled by Connecticut settlers. It was here that he
married Polly Sutton, the mother of
Geo. Catlin, who was the mother of
fourteen children. Geo. was the fifth
one of the large family. Putnam
Catlin soon established a large practice and was considered one of the
foremost lawyers of the county. Closely identified with all the growing interests of the village and the county. His
name is frequently mentioned in matters relating to the government and
progress of the community—in fact he
was one of the leading spirits of the
then small colony of Yankees who had
emigrated from Connecticut to build
their homes in the wilds of Pennsylvania. Polly Sutton, the mother of
Geo. Catlin, was born in Exeter Township about the year 1790. Her father
was one of the brave but unfortunate
band engaged under Col. Zebulon Butler in the battle of Wyoming, July 3,
1778. She was captured by the Indians
at Forty Fort, but was subsequently
released. She and Frances Slocum,
who was abducted by the Indians,
were playmates. At an early day she
developed a fine artistic taste, which
feature was undoubtedly transmitted
to her son George. About the year
1805 Putnam Catlin removed from
Wilkes-Barre to "Hop Bottom," in the
Beech Woods, and commenced farming, leaving Geo. in Wilkes-Barre at
the home of his most intimate friend,
the late Steuben Butler, in whose
house, still standing, George painted
his first painting—an apple. Putnam
Catlin writes to his friend under date
of May 3, 1814:

"I have the pleasure of reading your
letter by the last mail in behalf of
George. The friendship you express
for him, while it evinces the goodness
of your heart, will be considered by me
as a proof of his merit while under

your immediate notice. I confess, my dear old friend, that I am at this time much perplexed in deciding how to manage the education of my children. I have already perhaps been extravagant in the indulgence of my children. Taxes are becoming enormous and war prices still continue, beside with all my pride and particularly for my children. I am obliged to consider myself as a mere farmer—a republican farmer—a beech woods farmer without a hired man in the haying season. How then am I to spare Geo. and James, too? I admit that your reasoning is just in regard to Geo., but I know not how to spare him at this time. I shall not be able to give him a public education. If he shall persist in the choice of law as a profession he will have to glean for himself. It is unpleasant to write so long faced a letter, but so good a friend ought to have good and sufficient reasons why Geo. is not more indulged at this time," etc.

In a subsequent letter dated Hop Bottom, May 15, 1814, he says:

"I pray you to admonish George frequently of the necessity of improving his time to the best advantage. I have much solicitude on his account, fearing he will not sufficiently appreciate the value of time as it flies."

Then follows a letter from George to his and his father's old friend, in which he says:

"I received yours of the 23d and acknowledge that I am under an obligation of writing a long letter for having so long neglected you. Your last letter, it seems, proceeded from that place which was once the asylum of our social enjoyments when in the long winter evenings we so happily used to talk over many important matters, and having placed our apples around the grate and seated ourselves, we enjoyed time in its pride. Such days we have seen and such I hope will soon return. Although I had despaired of the hope of residing with you this winter, I have still an anxiety and a belief that business will yet be so arranged that I shall shortly be favored with the pleasure of seeing dear old Wyoming. If not so, I must content myself in the woods," etc.

George Catlin, the son of Putnam Catlin, was born at Wilkes-Barre July 26, 1786, in the old Catlin house built by Putnam Catlin on South Main street and afterward owned and occupied by the late and venerable "Squire Dyer." Catlin was contemporary with such men as Pickering, Franklin, Gib-

son, Burnside, Dyer, Griffin and Welles, some of whom while not born in Wyoming Valley, spent their early life here and rose to eminence and distinction amidst its classic shades and its honest and primitive people. 'Tis true that the earth is the sepulchre of illustrious men. I may not in this place presume to pronounce the funeral panegyric of these extraordinary men—it has already been done by some of the master spirits of the country—by men worthy of the task, worthy as Pericles to pronounce the honor of the Athenian dead. The monuments of human greatness yield in succession to the destroying influence of time. Time knows not the weight of sleep, or weakness, and night's deep darkness has no chain to bind his rushing pinions.

George Catlin was an enthusiast in painting. He loved painting for painting's sake—it was the one object of his life. He had no time for "money making." He was like Prof. Agassiz, who when asked by one of the crowned heads of Europe to deliver a lecture before a literary society, for which he should name his own price, replied: "I have no time for money making." No. His whole soul—his every energy, was dominated by his love of his profession, his career, and his power of transferring the beautiful in nature to his canvas. Catlin and Agassiz—"par nobile fratrum"—where do you find two such men among the millions of the present day? Both have passed to "the other side" but their works do live after them. Time has not inscribed upon the sepulchre of the dead any nobler names than Catlin and Agassiz. Like sumptuous Athens and Baalbec's gilded dome, Time touched them and they perished and Genius mourns her extinguished glory. The stupendous production of art, on which Catlin inscribed his victories and which he intended as pillars of his fame, have combined and exhibited all that is sublime in artistic conception and all that is graceful in execution. Could he have attached durability to these, his triumphs would have been complete. Catlin always cherished towards the Indian the most profound and sincere friendship and it was his boast that while he had visited every tribe of Indians on the continent, he had never lost a shilling's worth of property, nor ever received a blow. He was the red man's friend and wherever he went he diffused around him gladness and joy— the eyes of the young sparkled brighter than ever at his approach—

old age, as it cast its dim glasses at
the blue vault of heaven, seemed inspired with new vigor. The flowers
looked more gay, the grass more green,
the birds sang more cheerily. He spoke
of "frontier life" as a dark and sunken
vale of wretchedness bordering the
"proud and chivalrous" pale of savage
society and said: "It is for these in-
offensive and unoffending people yet
unvisited by the vices of civilized society that I would proclaim to the
world that it is time for the honor of
our country, for the honor of every citizen of the republic and for the sake of
humanity that our government should
raise her strong arm to save the remainder of them from the pestilence
which is rapidly advancing upon them.
Many are the rudenesses and wilds in
nature's works which are destined to
fall before the deadly ax and desolat-
ing hands of civilized man. Of such
rudenesses and wilds nature has no-
where presented more beautiful and
lovely scenes than those of the vast
prairies of the West: and of man and
beast no nobler specimens than those
that inhabit them—the Indian and the
buffalo—joint and original tenants of
the soil and fugitives together from the
approach of civilized man. They have
fled to the great plains of the West and
there, under an equal doom, they have
taken up their last abode, where their
race will expire and their bones will
bleach together. My heart has sometimes almost bled with pity while
among them and witnessing their inno-
cent amusements and I have contem-
plated the inevitable bane that was
rapidly advancing upon them without
that check from the protecting arm of
government which alone can shield
them from destruction."

Mr. Catlin saw but the man. He
queried not at policies. His plea was
humanity. His creed never changed.
He thus spoke of his creed:

"I have had some unfriendly denunciation by the press and by these critics
I have been reproachfully designated as
the 'Indian-loving Catlin.' What of
this? What have I to answer? Have
I any apology to make for loving the
Indians? The Indians have always
loved me and why should I not love the
Indians?

"I love the people who have always
made me welcome to the best they had.

"I love a people who are honest without laws, who have no jails or poor-
houses.

"I love a people who keep the com-
mandments without ever having read

them or heard them preached from the pulpit.

"I love a people who never swear, who never take the name of God in vain.

"I love a people who love their neighbors as themselves.

"I love a people who worship God without a bible, for I believe that God loves them also.

"I love a people whose religion is all the same, and are free from religious animosities.

"I love a people who have never raised a hand against me, or stolen my property, when there was no law to punish them for either.

"I love a people who never have fought a battle with white men except on their own ground.

"I love and don't fear mankind where God has made and left them, for they are children.

"I love a people who live and keep what is their own without locks and keys.

"I love all people who do the best they can—and, oh! how I love a people who don't live for the love of money."

After an absence of many years from his native land Mr. Catlin returned to New York and placed his famous gallery of Indian paintings on exhibition, from where he writes to his old friend as follows:.

My Dear Ancient Comrade:

It seems strange to me after an absence of 35 years to hear the familiar sounds of names, that once were so dear to me and which amid the strange vicissitudes of my eventful life, I had almost forgotten. Your friend's conversation in his several visits to my exhibition have rekindled old associations of my boyish days and renewed the resolution which I long since made to visit the far famed and beautiful valley which gave me birth, and my present desire is to do it before long. I want to once more tread the soil of my old hunting grounds—"Bear Creek," "Ten Mile Run"—the "7-mile house"—where once in early manhood days it was my good luck to kill a panther, who measured 8 feet from tip to tip. It gives me unspeakable pleasure to learn that your health is good and that you are still in the enjoyment of life and I hope and trust that we may both be kindly spared until we can meet again in this world. The changes and the progress of your beautiful village and the melancholy exit of so many ancient friends will make me feel sad and melancholy while there, but I shall find one friend, which to me will be better than a hundred. My letter must at this time be a short one, whilst it con-

veys the assurances of a long laid up but not forgotten affection and attachment of Your old friend, Geo. Catlin.

Mr. Catlin lived to enjoy the blessings earned by a long life of energy, honor and toil—and to realize all which his fondest hopes had desired. The infirmities of life stole slowly and silently upon him, leaving still behind a cheerful and happy serenity of mind. He was a typical "gentleman of the old school"—a gentleman in instinct and culture. After having passed an almost triumphal tour of Europe—with his world-wide collection of Indian paintings and curiosities, the greatest that had ever been seen in any country. After having been the favored guest of different crowned heads of the continent he returned in triumph to his native land—in peace—in the bosom of domestic affection—in the hallowed reverence of his friends and countrymen—in the full possession of all of his faculties—he wore out the last remnant of a well spent life surrounded by an affectionate family—without a fear to darken. with scarcely a sound to disturb its close—or a cloud to shade the brightness of the slowly setting sun.

Fortunate man! Fortunate to have so lived and died. Fortunate to have gained and received the plaudits of thousands of his countrymen on both sides of the Atlantic. He had

Climbed Fame's ladder so high
That from the round at the top he
stepped to the sky.

Kronos.

CAREY FAMILY REUNION.

.[Daily Record, Sept. 3, 1903.]

Descendants of the Carey family, one of the pioneer families of the Wyoming Valley, held their annual reunion at Hanover Park yesterday and a large number were present. It is estimated that there are now a thousand descendants of the two Carey brothers, who settled in this valley among the first pioneers.

During the day an informal program was rendered. The officers of the association are as follows: President, H. D. Carey; first vice president, Bateman D. Carey; second vice president, Mrs. A. D. Smith; third vice president, W. H. Derby; secretary, Miss Estella Williamson; treasurer, Mrs. Isaac M. Jones.

The Record last year published an extended history of the family.

REGIMENTAL REUNION.

[Daily Record, Sept. 11, 1903.]

Yesterday was a great day for the surviving veterans of Capt. Rice's company of the 53d Regt., Pennsylvania Volunteers. They had with them Maj. Gen. John R. Brooke, the first colonel of the regiment. The veterans and their families, friends and neighbors, to the number of nearly a thousand, assembled in the beautiful park at Fernbrook and spent the greater part of the day in rational and wholesome enjoyment. Gen. Brooke reached the park before 10 o'clock in the morncally by his former soldiers who forty years ago fought under his command. It was an incident never to be forgotten by the veterans. He was surrounded at all times during the day by the men, who appeared to fairly worship him.

The survivors of the company (nearly all of whom live in Dallas and surrounding country) maintain an organization, and a business meeting was held in the morning. While this was in ing and was greeted most enthusiastiprogress people were constantly arriving on the trolley cars and in carriages. Scores of ladies, including the wives and daughters of the veterans, were busy during the forenoon preparing dinner, which was served in the dancing pavilion, and was free to all. Hundreds partook of the abundance of food supplied, and more than two hours elapsed before all had been served.

Shortly after 2 o'clock, the tables having been removed, the pavilion was turned into an auditorium and a meeting organized, with O. L. Roushey as chairman. Not half the people could find seats in the pavilion, and those who could not, crowded around on the outside. After singing and an invocation, the chairman introduced Col. J. D. Laciar, who delivered a brief address in which he spoke of the achievements of the Union armies as seen at the present day, and referred to the magnificent record of Gen. Brooke, both as a volunteer during the war for the preservation of the Union and subsequently as an officer in the regular army.

Admirable addresses by Judge George H. Troutman (himself a Civil War veteran), Col. C. Bow Dougherty (commander of the 9th Regt., Pennsylvania Volunteers, and in Gen. Brooke's command during the Spanish-America War), and Hon. Henry W. Palmer,

followed, interspersed with music and recitations by some young ladies of Dallas. All these addresses were enthusiastically received and were highly

GEN. BROOKE SPEAKS.

Gen. Brooke was then introduced and received an ovation. He is a calm, deliberate and exceedingly forcible speaker. His references to the experience in the field of the regiment to which most of the veterans before him were attached were touching and at times brought tears to the eyes of many in the audience, especially when alluding to the sacrifices made by the mothers, wives, daughters and sisters of the men who were fighting the battles of their country for four long, weary and anxious years.

For the Southern people he had only words of kindness. The Confederates appreciated by the audience.

were brave men and the vast majority of them believed they were right. The war with Spain cemented the Union more closely than it had been at any time since long before the Rebellion. The sons of Union soldiers and the sons of the Confederates stood side by side in the Spanish-American War. There is no sectional animosity now. We are one nation, one people, greater, more powerful, more invincible than ever before in the history of the republic. He expressed the hope that all the gallant veterans of the great war would live worthy of the matchless cause for which they were willing to make any sacrifice in the days of their young manhood. •

A storm of applause greeted the general as he closed his address, and the audience then marched past the front of the speaker's platform and warmly shook the hand of the veteran.

Among those who went to Fernbrook to meet Gen. Brooke were Col. Beaumont, Col. Ricketts and many other Civil War veterans who had met him during the Civil War.

THE SURVIVORS.

Surviving members of the regiment are as follows:

Capt. Isaac A. Howell, Wyoming.

Capt. Theodore Hatfield, Kansas.

Capt. Nathan Montany, Canton, Bradford County.

Lester Race, Lockville, Wyoming County.

Robert Hunter, Centremoreland, Wyoming County.

M. F. Newberry, Beaumont.

John Clark, Beaumont.
William Richards, Beaumont.
Norton Newberry, Beaumont.
Thomas Dymon, Dorranceton.
Frank Harding, Dushore, Sullivan County.
George W. Thompson, Luzerne Borough.
Henry Whitson, Plymouth.
Ira Lyons, Forty Fort.
Morris Hatten, Gregory.
William H. Jackson, West Pittston.
O. L. Fisher, Dallas.
Edward Pembleton. Huntsville.
Peter Kulp, Huntsville.
E. L. Hoover, Huntsville.
John Wilson, Ketcham.
Frank Westover, Plymouth.
Robert Dymon, Orange.
Capt. Walter Hopkins, San Francisco, Cal.
Perry Frantz, Dallas.
O. L. Roushey, Dallas.
William Hockenberry, 6 Lehigh street, Wilkes-Barre.
William Givens, Ashley.
Alexander Preston, Dallas.
James Tulip, Idetown.
Jabez Jackson, Laketon.
Abel Perrigo, Laketon.
James Sorber, Ruggles.
Henry Case, Ruggles.
Nelson Case, Ruggles.
Myron Strickland, Kingston.
Charles Huey, West Pittston.
Jonas Westover, Register.
Daniel McCloud, Beaumont.
John A. Folkerson, Waterton.
George Willis, Dorrance, Nebraska.
R. M. Hall, Towanda.
Edward S. Cogswell, Fairdale, Susquehanna County.
Robert Jacobs, Thompson, Susquehanna County.
Will I. Carpenter, Hartford, Susquehanna County.
Abram Hurst, West Overton, Westmoreland County.
Martin W. Anthony, Wallsville, Lackawanna County.

Charles Lathrope, Winfield, Kansas.
William Moore, Trucksville.
Benson Wardin, Plainsville, Kansas.
John Anthony, Washington, D. C.
Thomas Brown, Bloomsburg.
Ed Kirkham, Brooklyn, N. Y.
S. C. Dymon, Vassar, Michigan.

THOSE WHO DIED.

The following died during the year:
A. T. Poole, Forty Fort.
Charles Christpell, Beaumont.
Calvin Bisbing, Outlet.
Hugh Patton, Fort Shaw, Montana.

DEMOLISHING WINTER HOUSE.

[Daily Record, Sept. 22, 1903.]

I am not often overcome by "cacoethes scribendi," but at this time the fit is on.

I have this moment returned from a morning survey of my surroundings. Alas! for the heartless spirit of innovation—pardon me, I mean enterprise—the last landmark near me is going. They are tearing away the "Old Winter House," the home of that kind-hearted, venerable man so long justice in Jenkins and once my competitor for the office—Peter Winter.

I cannot give you the date of his coming to what is now the intersection of the Wilkes-Barre and Laflin roads—Inkerman village. It was probably as early as 1815, the third year of our last war with Great Britain.

At that date my stepfather, Eleazer Carey (subsequently for many years magistrate in Wilkes-Barre), was keeping the first store in Pittston and was postmaster there—his commission dating 1811.

John and Daniel Searle carried the mail in a buggy. Subsequently they were owners of the coaching line as far as "Dundaff," then looked upon as a rising young city, now utterly eclipsed by Honesdale.

It is one of the pleasing recollections of boyhood—being sent on horseback by Father Carey to procure from squire Winter a deed left in his possession and carry it to Dr. Nathaniel Giddings of Pittston. The horse was a "racker," the weather was hot and my seat was a little galling. My recollections are not overly pleasant, touching the ride, but I recollect Father Carey's directions:

"Charley, you'll pass the half-way house at John's (meaning John Carey), then Sam Saylor's store, then you'll stop at squire Winter's little black house, after that you'll get but two houses—John D. Shafer's and Ike Thompson's—and then you'll be in Pittston."

"Then you'll be in Pittston!" Yes, that was about my first entrance into Pittston, subsequently the scene of many happy days of my life.

The place from which I located "The Gravity"—the old Gravity—like its precursor at Mauch Chunk, first located by Josiah White, Erskine Hazard and Isaac A. Chapman in the year 1824. Ah! Mr. Editor, how the years rush by—do we use them aright?

Yes! they are ripping and tearing at the "Old Winter House" to-day and

soon, very soon, the worms will be ripping and tearing at us.

Let us every day try to put in one more day ripping and tearing at public and private sin.

C. I. A. C.

Port Blanchard, Sept. 19, 1903.

REUNION OF 52D REGIMENT.

[Daily Record, Sept. 25, 1903.]

The survivors of the noted 52d Regt., which includes a number of Luzerne County warriors, met in reunion at Nay Aug Park, Scranton, on Wednesday and the "boys" had a fine time. The registration list showed the following present:

Staff officers—Hugh Crawford, New York City; B. P. Walters, Factoryville; S. B. Mott, Scranton; S. T. Trace, Pittston.

Co. A—F. E. Connan, New York City; I. E. Finch, Wilkes-Barre.

Co. B—Capt. R. W. Bannatyne, Tunkhannock; D. T. Doty, Waverly, Pa.; Abraham Rinker, Wyoming; Asa H. Frear, Lake Winola; Charles Russell. Russell Hill; S. Van Sickle, Bald Mount; Thomas Griffiths, Scranton; Peter Aidred, Pittsburg.

Co. C—Utty Turner, Factoryville.

Co. D—F. E. Ransom, Chase; Joseph McCracken, Moosic.

Co. E—Joseph Harper, Scranton; A. D. Finney, Granville Centre.

Co. F—James K. Lunger, West Nanticoke; John Gurns, Moscow; Henry Harding, Tunkhannock; Andrew Singer, Clark's Green; H. N. Mott, R. B. Lindley, Factoryville; Samuel M. Sorber, Kingston.

Co. G—Henry H. King, Loyalville; W. S. Stark, Plainsville; Joseph Shimer, Wilkes-Barre; Edward Miller, Pittston, Henry Rush, Wilkes-Barre; E. E. Rozell, Brooklyn, Pa.; John Swartz, Glenwood; George Ace, Milwaukee.

Co. H—Capt. C. C. Battenberg, Archbald; Abraham Greiner, Table Rock, Neb.; W. W. Archer, Scranton; Anthony Long, Scranton; F. Pickering, Peckville; Simon Rhodes, Scranton; H. C. Miller, John Ayres, Old Forge; John Hull, Scranton, J B. Travis, Peckville; W. N. Smith, Scranton; James S. Sieger, Dunmore; Simon Ferris, Factoryville; Philitus Snedicker, Peckville; J. R. Roberts, Falls; A. G. Callum, Bald Mount.

Co. I—T. W. Hunter, Mill City; David Evans, Scranton; Patrick Hourigan, Wilkes-Barre; William D. Jones, Scranton; S. B. Williams, Wyoming; John

Smith, Scranton; John A. Schlager,
Scranton; James Jeremith, Scranton;
Edward Hall, Scranton.

Co. K—C. E. Morrison, Oneonta, N.
Y.; O. C. Sears, Peckville; Solomon
Millard, Avoca; William McClave,
Scranton; E. H. Ripple, Scranton; Pat-
rick Brown, Greeley Centre, Neb.; A.
Walker, Forest Lake; William Scott,
Binghamton, N. Y.; Edward Jones,
Carbondale; John T. Roberts, Scranton,
Andrew J. Scutt, Parsons.

Dinner was served by the Women's
Relief Corps and at 2 p. m. the business meeting was called to order by
William McClave of Scranton, president of the association. President Mc-
Clave delivered his annual address, in
the course of which he said:

"The bent forms and other indications
of declining vigor admonish us that the
time cannot be far distant when each
and all of us will have heard the final
bugle call that will summon us to be
mustered out of the activities of this
life to join the comrades who have already passed over the great divide to
join the grand army of the dead, twenty-one of whom have been mustered out
of our own association since our last
reunion, viz.: Comrades Frederick
Wagner, Scranton; John W. Taylor,
Harveyville, Pa.; Ed R. Peckens, Plymouth; William S. Hopkins, Shultzville,
Pa.; John E. Perry, Fort Pierre, S. D.;
J. W. Evans, Berwick; Daniel Warner,
Montrose; William H. Furman, Meshoppen; Thomas Crompton, Meshoppen; Benjamin Keefer, Shanksville; Edward Landis, Shanksville; Abraham
Carver, Dewey, Pa.; David Spangler,
Shanksville; Martin Lee, Carbondale;
W. S. Davis, Meshoppen; Charles Dod-
son, Jerseytown; Nathan Joslin, Water-
town; Nathaniel Green, Wilkes-Barre;
Thomas Smith, Scranton; Richard
Sheppard, Wanamie; John Poynton,
Pittston."

The report of secretary Miller showed
that there are now 482 members on the
rolls of the association. From the
treasurer came a report showing that
$128.31 was expended during the year
and that there is now $28.93 due the
treasurer.

Letters were received from the following, who were unable to attend the
reunion:

Albert Jennings, Sterling, Kan.; Rev.
E. Mangles, Ashland, Md.; Jacob Ross,
Shanksville, Pa.; S. W. Taylor, Shick-
shinny; W. D. Weber, Tremont, Neb.;
Henry M. Hoyt, Jr., Washington, D. C.;
J. P. Davis, Pittston, Ark.; J. G. Row-
land, governor of National Military

Home, Leavenworth, Kan.; W. J. Sleppy, St. Paul, Minn.; Wilson M. Bower, Lewisburg, Pa.; Joshua Fincey, Beulah, Neb.; Philip Schrock, Shanksville, Pa.; Samuel P. Cholfant, Sawtelle, Cal.; Dr. J. H. Kauffman, Minersville, Pa.; J. E. Myers, Broken Bow, Neb.; J. W. Evans, Colorado Springs, Col.; P. Rafs, Newark, N. J.

The following were elected honorary members of the association: A. McLeod Miller of Kingston, son of secretary Miller; John H. Rush of Wilkes-Barre and John A. Gilbride of Boston. All are sons of members of the regiment.

The following committees were appointed by the president:

Resolutions—S. B. Mott, Scranton; R. W. Bannatyne, Tunkhannock; Asa Frear, Lake Winola.

Auditing—Col. E. H. Ripple, Scranton; F. E. Crompton, Brooklyn, N. Y.; C. C. Battenberg, Archbald.

When the order of election of officers was reached there was a unanimous desire to have the present officers reelected, and they were again chosen. The following were elected vice presidents to fill vacancies caused by death: For Co. K, Col. E. H. Ripple; for Co. G, William Stark of Plainsville; for Co. H, Capt. C. C. Battenberg of Archbald.

The association decided to send a greeting to Col. J. C. Dodge of Dodgeville, Mass., the colonel of the 52d Regt.; a letter of sympathy to Maj. J. B. Fish of Scranton, who is ill, and a letter of condolence to Alva Dolph of Carbondale, whose son was killed on Monday.

Col. Ripple of the committee that has charge of the compiling of the history of the regiment read some highly interesting excerpts from the portions of the work which have been written. Great satisfaction was expressed over the rapidity with which the work is progressing. A vote of thanks was returned to Col. Ripple.

Short addresses were made by Mr. Gilbride of Boston, the newly elected honorary member; Capt. P. DeLacy, and Maj. O. E. Vaughn of Moscow. Capt. DeLacy invited those present to attend the reunion of his regiment, the 143d, at Carbondale on Oct. 9, and Maj. Vaughn pleaded for a county veterans' organization.

The 52d Regt. was rich in material for the ministry. The following are on its rolls: Rev. Thomas B. Janyn, Denver, Col.; Rev. Josiah Wagner, Luzerne Borough; Rev. K. Harris, Kingston; Rev. M. D. Fuller, Jermyn; Rev. Ed-

ward Manges, Oakland, Md. Rev. John Patrick of Snahomish, Wash., died on Jan. 30, 1901.

The survivors of the regiment and a number of local Grand Army men enjoyed a campfire at night. William McClave presided and the principal feature of the program was an address by Judge H. M. Edwards on the duties of good citizenship.

BRANDON REUNION.

At Patterson Grove, Luzerne County, Pa., on Sept. 10, there assembled the descendants of William Brandon and his wife, Tryphena Fuller Brandon. Despite the fact that the weather conditions were somewhat threatening, a goodly number turned out to participate in this occasion and thereby renew family affiliations. A spread for 150 persons was none too large to accommodate those who sat down to the tables. After a sumptuous repast and a general good time the meeting was called to order by J. W. Saxe and the following board of officers were elected: President, George M. Brandon; secretary, A. W. Baker; assistant secretary, Mrs. Lillian Roberts; treasurer, J. W. Saxe. This board decided upon holding the next annual meeting at Patterson Grove on the second Thursday in September, 1904; and, if stormy, then on the Saturday following. They wish to tender sincere thanks to the camp meeting association for their kind treatment while guests upon their grounds. and praise the band for the excellent music furnished. The following of kin were present:

Harveyville—W. C. Marshall and wife, George M. Brandon and wife, J. M. Brandon, wife and daughter Lulu.

Huntington Mills—Mrs. J. C. Berlew and children Marie, Edna, Harry, Arthur, Ford and Coral. Sterling Brandon and son Stanley, John W. Kleintob, wife and son Derr, Mrs. Sarah K. Wilson and daughter Leona. Mrs. Jane Monroe, J. E. Shultz, wife and son Dyson, Mrs. Mary Morroe. Mrs. Mary J. Brandon, Monroe Rood, wife and daughter Margia.

West Pittston—Mrs. Strat Brandon. daughter Elsie and son Joseph.

Milton—Dr. Harry McNeal and wife.

Shickshinny—H. E. Campbell, wife and sons Eston and Walter, Fred Baker and wife.

Rittenhouse—C. H. Marshall, wife and sons Leon and Evan, Edward Kleintob.

wife and daughter Ione, Walter Blaine, wife and sons George and Kenneth, J. W. Saxe and wife, John Smith and wife. Mrs. Maggie Boston and child Vida.

Wilkes-Barre—Mrs. Julia Baker, A. W. Baker, wife and children Lulu, Lizzie, Lenore, Florence and Albert, Jr.

Kyttle—D. C. Brandon, wife, son Herman and daughter Virgie, Harvey Wesley, wife and son Torrence, Mrs. N. G. Roberts, Mrs. T. J. Roberts, Mrs. H. R. McCern.

New Columbus—Lee Yaple, wife and son Paul.

Orange—Dayton Dymond, wife and children Oscar and Irene.

Plainsville—Mrs. C. M. Williams.

Kingston—Harry Covert, wife and sons Morris and Robert.

Berwick—D. M. Baker and sons Harry, Howard and Fred.

Orangeville—Jethro Henry and wife.

Muhlenburg—Dr. Charles A. Long, wife, daughter Freda and son Harold.

Among the visitors were noticed Mr. and Mrs. A. M. Blaine, Mrs. Bert Myers, Mrs. Henry Myers, Mrs. Garrison, Mr. and Mrs. Samuel Krickbaum, Solomon Taylor, Mrs. James Meeker, Mr. and Mrs. Chester Bisher, Mrs. Tubbs, Mrs. Robert Kyttle, Stephen Kleintob, Mr. and Mrs. Albert Downing, E. A. Fink, Dr. J. P. Hess and Mr. and Mrs. Gwinn Goss.

MRS. PRISCILLA BENNETT DEAD.

[Daily Record, Sept. 26, 1903.]

Mrs. Priscilla Lee Bennett, one of this city's most charitable and venerable women, died at Leehurst, Oliver's Mills, her summer home on the mountain, at 5:45 yesterday afternoon after a long illness of paralysis, at the ripe age of 84 years. She sank into a last peaceful sleep with the setting of the sun, after a lengthy illness which she bore with Christian fortitude. In her demise the Methodist Church has lost one of its most liberal contributors and the various charitable institutions a kindly, benevolent friend and supporter.

Wilkes-Barre loses one of the most notable women who have graced its annals, she being known the country over as one of the most liberal women in the Methodist Church. In the distribution of her wealth she has made it a habit to make her bestowments in her life time instead of providing for them in her will. Thus she has been able to enjoy the good that her money was doing.

She was born on March 14, 1819, at Hanover, Luzerne County, Pa., and was a daughter of James Stewart Lee of Hanover, who was a brother of Col. Washington Lee. She was married on Nov. 18, 1856, to Hon. Ziba Bennett of Wilkes-Barre. Though no children came to bless their union, Mrs. Bennett was yet devoted in a remarkable degree to her step-children, Mrs. Martha Bennett Phelps and George Slocum Bennett, who in turn reciprocated her maternal love

Mrs. Bennett was a member of the First Methodist Episcopal Church, Wilkes-Barre. She was identified with its Sunday school for more than forty years, and for more than thirty years was assistant superintendent, her stepson, George S. Bennett, being then and now its superintendent. So great was her interest in this work that she gave the splendid Sunday school building at a cost of $26,000, it being one of the model structures in Sunday school architecture and design.

She also gave the organ to the First M. E. Church, at a cost of $10,000; also $2,400 to build Bennett Chapel, named after her, at East End, Wilkes-Barre.

She contributed largely to the General Missionary Society of the Methodist Church, to the Women's Foreign Missionary Society and the Women's Home Missionary Society, to the church extension of the Methodist Church, to Drew Theological Seminary, besides helping numerous churches, and students preparing for the ministry and for missionary work.

Wesleyan University, Wyoming Seminary, American University at Washington, Grant University at Chattanooga, Tenn., were recipients of her bounty.

She gave largely to the local Y. M. C. A., Y. W. C. A., Home for Homeless Women, Home for Friendless Children, of which she was one of the founders, first treasurer, and for many years its president; City Hospital, Wilkes-Barre, endowing the "Washington Lee bed" at a cost of $5,000; Brooklyn Methodist Hospital; endowing the "Josephine Lee bed," Lee Library and a building at Orangeburg, S. C.; the Fennett building at Clarkson, Miss., besides many benefactions of which her family and friends know nothing.

MAJOR FAMILY REUNION.

[Daily Record, Aug. 27, 1903.]

The fourth annual reunion of the Major family took place at Fernbrook Park yesterday and was well attended. David Major of Lehman, in his eighty-fourth year, was not able to be present. He is the oldest one of the family.

The Major family, which came from England and settled in Lehman more than eighty years ago, is one of the most numerous and thrifty families of Luzerne County and has representatives in various parts of the country.

An abundance of good things burdened the tables, at least for a time.

Those present were: J. Wesley Major, C. B. Major, R. D. Major, G. B. Major, S. F. Major, Mrs. S. F. Major, Mrs R. D. Major, Mr. and Mrs. Frank Major, Mr. and Mrs. Theodore Major, Mr. and Mrs. William Major, Mrs. B. Badman and Miss Margaret Thomas Badman, Mrs. C. B. Major, Harry Major, Mrs. Major Wardell, Mr. and Mrs. Robert Milligan, Mr. and Mrs. Thomas H. Major, Mr. and Mrs. S. F. Rogers, Mrs. Rebecca Wharram Stark, Mrs. Dr. Sutliff, Mrs. C. B. Wilcox, Dr. Homer Wilcox, Mr. and Mrs. Lewis Major and three children, Mrs. Fred Major, Mrs. W. H. Freeman, Mr. and Mrs. Marshall Major and two children, Mrs. Charles Major and one child; Mrs. Frank Major, accompanied by her grandson, Jesse Major, whose father died in the Philippine war; Miss Helen Major and Dr. Deible, Mrs. Nelson Whipp, Miss Libbie Major of Keelersburg, Mrs. Gilbert Miller, Luther Major, Dr. Arthur Major, Miss Stella Major, Mrs. Fred Major, Mrs. Josephine Houghton Smith, Professor Charles Major, Miss Bessie Bishop, Austin and Theodore, sons of F. W. Major of Centremoreland; Isaac Major, Miss Lizzie Major, C. B. Wilcox, George Major and wife, Miss Martha Wilcox, Mr. and Mrs. R. B. Vaughn and daughters Helen. Florence and son Ralph, George Lazarus, Mr. and Mrs. B. C. Rice, C. D. Linskill, W. J. Honeywell, Mrs Joseph LaBarr, Mrs. Eli Parrish, Mrs. Daniel Hontz, Major Case, Mrs. Douglas Case, Levi Rice, Mrs. Asa Wardan, Miss Edith Lyon, Misses Carrie and Genevieve Schoonover.

The Ferguson family reunion occurred at Fernbrook Park on Wednesday, Aug. 26.

Upon arrival at the grounds at 7 a. m. the place had been occupied for two hours by the members of the Major family, who had taken possession of half of the pavilion and more than half the tables.

Dinner was served at 12. At 1 o'clock the tables were cleared and a business meeting was held in the park. Charles.

Perrin was elected chairman. Theron Ferguson, the retiring president, nominated S. M. Austin and he was duly elected president for the ensuing year. Charles Perrin was elected vice president; Mrs. Edward Hallock, secretary, and Mrs. Hunter, treasurer.

The receiving committee was retained; also the representatives of each tribe are to remain the same as previously. The time for the next reunion is to be the last Wednesday in August, 1904, at Fernbrook Park.

After the business meeting there was music by the orchestra. Over 200 were present, including guests. The reunion closed at 5 p. m.

Among those present were: Mrs. Wilford Osterhout of White's Ferry, John Kunkle, C. D. Kunkle, justice Newman, William Still, Calvin Perrin, Charles Perrin, Mr. and Mrs. Samuel McCarty, Major Case.

William J. Honeywell of Dallas was present at nearly 80 years of age. He assessed the property owners of Dallas when he was a young man, and now there is but one man living of those he assessed, Robert Wilson.

ROUND'S SWORD RETURNED.

[Daily Record, Oct. 2, 1902.]

The Manassas (Virginia) Journal of Aug. 7 has the following, in which mention is made of George C. Round, who was born in Kingston; where his father was a Methodist clergyman. Mr. Round was baptized in the old Forty Fort M. E. Church by Rev. Dr. George Peck:

One of the interesting incidents of the Horse Show week at Manassas was the coming of Lieut. W. Simpson Harrison of Landmark, Fanquier county, bringing a sword captured by the 17th Virginia from an officer of the 55th Pennsylvania, in the days of civil war. It seems that a few weeks ago Lieut. Harrison was in Manassas on business at the real estate office of George C. Round & Co. In swapping war stories, as veterans are wont to do, he told Lieut. Round the story of the sword and of his desire to return it to its original owner. Mr. Round, who is a native of Luzerne county, Pa., took at once a lively interest in the affair. The inscription on the scabbard furnished a good clue, being as follows:

"Presented to Lieut. P. F. Hodge by the members of Co. A, 55th Pa. Vols., July 15, 1863."

He wrote at once to Adjutant Gene-

ral Stewart at Harrisburg, who is also at this time the national commander of the Grand Army of the Republic. He also sent an inquiry to the National Tribune, the soldiers' paper published in Washington. From both sources he heard that an old soldier named Patrick F. Hodge was living at Swissvale, Alleghany county, Pa.

An interesting correspondence followed, pursuant to which Lieut. Harrison dined with Lieut. Round on Thursday, and the sword which by the stern fortunes of war fell from the grasp of Lieut. Hodge, as a minie ball struck him in the face, May 16, 1864, was returned to him by Adams Express.

It seems that when Mr. Hodge was promoted from first sergeant to lieutenant the members of his company presented him an elegant sword. He had possession of it ten months and one day, when the two armies got badly mixed up in the "fog fight" along the Petersburg and Richmond R. R. In the mixup the Confederates came out ahead and Hodge and some of his men were taken in and rushed back to the rear. Mr. Round, by another coincidence, was nearby at the time, a corporal in the Connecticut Battery, but owing to the dense fog the artillery could render no assistance, though they could tell from the increasing roar of the battle that their friends were being forced backward. Later in the day his battery put in a few shots to warn the visitors to attempt no further conquests.

It is interesting to note that when Harrison returned home in spring, 1865 it was his own mother who suggested the idea that he hunt up Lieut. Hodge and return the sword. His duties on the farm, however, were pressing, and after a time he left the homestead and the sword was missing when it again came into his mind. He supposed some relic hunter had confiscated it, when recently it was found with a pile of rubbish in the attic of the Harrison homestead near Haymarket. The sword was shown to Governor Montague and other distinguished guests at the horse show, to whom as well as our citizens, it was an object of special interest. Lieutenant Hodge expresses great gratification at his singular good fortune and Lieutenant Harrison sends his best wishes for health and happiness, along with the sword to his former foeman. The three lieutenants are planning a reunion at Manassas some time in 1904.

REGIMENTAL REUNION.

[Daily Record, Oct. 10, 1003.]

The thirty-seventh reunion of the 143d Regt. of Pennsylvania Volunteers, one of the fighting regiments of the Civil War, occurred at Carbondale yesterday. Although the weather was far from inviting a large proportion of the surviving members of this historic regiment was present. The feature of the occasion was the presence of General J. L. Chamberlin of Maine, who led the brigade of which the 143d was a part in the hopeless and almost annihilating charge at Petersburg.

General Chamberlin, some seventy-five years of age, a continual sufferer from wounds received in the charge mentioned, is one of the grand old men who yet remain to inspire all who meet them with true patriotism and lofty purpose. His address was one from comrade to comrade, full of humor at times, at times thrilling and pathetic. He told those present why they were the men chosen to strike the first blow at Petersburg, which charge he declared was not excelled in bravery by the charge of the Light Brigade at Balaklava.

Arthur L. Collins of Scranton was the orator of the day, and he reviewed in a masterly way the history of the regiment and the lessons of their achievements. The poet of the occasion was Theron G. Osborne, principal of schools of Luzerne Borough, and he recited the following poem:

THE GLORY OF PENNSYLVANIA.

The glory of Pennsylvania is not in her
    clanging mills,
The wealth of her treasured carbon or
    the iron veins of her hills;
Not in her scenic beauty or bounty of
    vale and plain,
Not in her cities teeming with millions
    athirst for gain;
Tho' the smoke and flame of her forges
    be industry's flag unfurled.
Tho' energy leap from her bosom to move
    the wheels of the world.
Tho' her mountains blue be beauty's own
    and from her slopes, sun-kissed,
Her lakelets gleam like maiden's eyes
    thro' lashes of woods and mist,
And streams wind seaward, silver threads
    bedecking her mantle green.—
'Tis not in these, tho' we prize them well,
    her greatness is truly seen:
The glory of Pennsylvania is the record
    her sons have made
In halls of state and toils of war.—Liberty's high crusade.

The arch that our father's builded in that
    old heroic day
Grows on my sight, out-peering, in col-
    umns of gold and gray.
Block by block those columns, slowly,
    sublimely rise
Till they tower six for freedom and six
    for compromise.
Bowed each to each they tower; a span
    and the arch is done:
Shall it win a King's approval, or a
    world's applause be won?
How now, Oh. Pennsylvania, what shall
    the verdict be?—
Speak thro' the lips of Morton, shall the
    West be bond or free?
Lo! on the waiting vision, over a mist of
    doubt,
A glow like a hint of morning, a light-
    gleam leaping out,
And now a flood of glory as within the
    waiting space
Gemmed like the brand Excalibur, the
    Keystone falls in place.

Gates have been made for heroes in the
    walls of Greece and Rome,
Gates of triumphal entry when their sons
    came marching home
From fields of glory and conflict; but this
    arch of the old Thirteen
By the deeds of our fathers builded is the
    grandest ever was seen.
Not here. not there is it stationed, but up
    from the heart of each State
It grows when the people conjure to wel-
    come their heroes late.
To-day it is called into being here in this
    beauteous dale,
Splendor not of the sun or moon, but
    brightness that makes pale
All orbs celestial; turn your gaze, ye sol-
    diers of the past,
Gaze on that arch of beauty and glory
    and import vast,
Flashing with pearl and diamond, ruby
    and amethyst.
And all rare jewels that should shine on
    Liberty's fair breast.

And see! there cometh Franklin, that
    glorious portal thro',
Foster child of our soil, wise, unselfish.
    true,
Bearer of parchment and pen, voice that
    spake from our strand
To the peoples beyond the ocean and
    taught them to understand.
And who are those that follows? Sages
    and statesmen gray.
Traitors and rebels to kings, but patriots
    in the fray.
All as fearless as one the tyrant to scorn
    and defy,
Eager for Freedom to live. ready for
    Freedom to die.

Veterans, tattered and worn in swift re-
    view now come,
Flint-locks clasped in rigid hands, voice-
    less fife and drum,
Faded banners, eloquent of those whose
    lips are dumb.
Strong defenders of eighteen-twelve,
    heroes of forty-eight,
Warriors stanch of Indian wars, grim
    arbiters of fate,
Follow in proud possession those first, the
    immortal ones,
Virtue and valor of noble sires revealed
    again in the sons.
Steel of the front of battle, oppression to
    overthrow,
Strength to maintain the vantage, steel,
    'gainst the lurking foe,
Heart of the nation keep them! When
    shall their stories fade,
Written in letters of gold, or dust of the
    wilderness ambuscade.
When shall a band as worthy approach
    where their glories be?
Why trembles the vibrant ether to a glow
    of expectancy?
Why kindles the dear old archway with a
    sweeter, diviner light?
Why thrill your warming bosoms—what
    vision is this on your sight?
A stream of flashing bayonets above a
    line of blue—
Behold the men of the Civil War, a part
    of which were you.
O veterans, wherefore speak of fame on
    history's pages bright?
Is not that your glorious ensign of many
    a stubborn fight?
To tread the way "their feet have worn,"
    the brave, the true, the great,
Who fought to found the nation you have
    helped perpetuate,
Is honor enough to repay the years, the
    the tears, the lives you gave,
And prove that the path of glory leads
    to something more than the grave.

Let fall the curtain; a transient view has
    passed before your eyes
Of that which points where the glory of
    Pennsylvania lies,
And to you who have right to question
    what posterity will do,
With the heritage bequeathed to it by you
    and such as you,
I say: Whatever plant upsprings from
    loam, or clay or clod,
Shall put forth chivalry's blossom, 'neath
    the smile of the past and God,
And I pledge you that Pennsylvania, the
    Keystone ever shall be
In the arch that our fathers builded of
    Union and Liberty.

THE REGIMENT.

The 143d Pennsylvania Volunteers was

recruited for the most part in old Luzerne
County. Its colonel was Hon. E. L. Dana,
a veteran of the Mexican War and afterwards president judge of Luzerne County.
Its total enrollment during the war was
1,492 men. Out of this number 757 were
either killed in battle or died of disease.
It is one of the 300 regiments known as
the "fighting regiments" of the war.

REMARKABLE WILL.

[Daily Record, Oct. 10, 1903.]

What is probably the shortest will on
record (five words outside of the signa-
tures) is recorded in the court house in
this city. But what is probably the long-
est will that was ever seen in Wilkes-
Barre was one shown at the meeting
of the Historical Society last night.
The will is that of Redmond Conyngham, grandfather of the late Judge
John N. Conyngham of the Luzerne
County bar. The will was made in Ireland and was probated in 1784. It is
engrossed on seven sheets of parchment (or "animal skins," as the ac-
knowledgment shows), each thirty
inches square. In connection with the
curious old document Rev. Horace Edwin Hayden read some entertaining
Revolutionary reminiscences of David
Hayfield Conyngham (son of the above
Redmond), who lived from 1750 to 1832.
He was a member of the firm of Conyngham & Nesbitt, a business house in
Philadelphia which rendered distinguished financial assistance to the
struggling colonies during the Revolutionary War. In 1780, when Washington's army at Valley Forge was in
great need of food, and in danger of
being disbanded, the crisis was averted
by the generous patriotism of the Conyngham & Nesbitt firm. In the dire
distress of the time Washington wrote
to Richard Peters, Esq., telling him of
the condition of affairs. Mr. Peters
called on Conyngham & Nesbitt and
laid the statement of Gen. Washington
before them. Mr. Nesbitt replied that
Mr. Howe of Trenton had offered to
put up pork for them if paid for in
hard money. He accordingly contracted with Howe to buy all the pork and
beef he could get, to be paid for in
gold. Howe executed the contract and
was paid in gold. Mr. Nesbitt told
Judge Peters that Washington could
have all this meat, and also the cargo
of a valuable prize vessel which had
arrived, laden with provisions captured
from the British on the high seas. This
timely assistance of the firm saved
Washington's army. In addition to this

assistance the firm subscribed £5,000 for the public use. The firm owned numerous vessels and sent out privateers. Among these were the Surprise and Revenge. commanded by Capt. Gustavus Conyngham, who created great devastation in British commerce. Capt. Conyngham was captured by the British, but was afterward released on threats of the American government to make reprisals. Capt. Conyngham unfurled the first American flag in the British Channel on the Surprise. This flag was subsequently presented to the State of Pennsylvania and hung over the chair of the speaker of the House of Representatives. but it has since been lost. Mr. Hayden's sketch of the Conyngham family will appear in the next volume of transactions.

A. F. Berlin of Allentown was to have been present to read a paper on "Smoking Pipes of Indians" and show several specimens, but owing to the serious illness of his wife he could not attend. Secretary Hayden received a letter to that effect, which stated that Mr. Berlin hoped to be able to deliver his address at the spring meeting.

The following persons were elected resident members: Mrs. Eckley B. Coxe. Drifton; Miss Myra Poland. Mrs. Henry H. Derr. Miss Emily Jenkins. Wyoming; Charles F. Hill. Hazleton; E. L. Bullock, Audenried; Hon. G. H. Troutman. Dr. W. G. Weaver. As corresponding member, T. L. Montgomery, State librarian.

Announcement was made of death during the year of the following members: Hon. Charles A. Miner, Dr. Nathaniel G. Parke. Miss Martha Bennet. Mrs. Priscilla Lee Bennett.

Rev. Dr. Henry L. Jones presented the following resolution on the death of the late Hon. Charles A. Miner, a former president and trustee of the society:

"Resolved. That in the decease of the late Hon. Charles A. Miner, a member of this society from its formation, at one time its president, and for many years one of the trustees, we have lost a valued friend whose deep interest in all the affairs of the society was always manifest, and whose counsel and support were ever freely given. Our heartfelt sympathy is extended to those most sorely bereaved."

The resolution was unanimously adopted.

H. H. Ashley was elected a trustee in place of the late Charles A. Miner.

INDIAN RELICS.

Christopher Wren of Plymouth made a formal presentation to the society of his valuable collection of over 5,000 Indian relics. Mr. Wren states that with few exceptions the collection is made up of implements made and used by the local Indian tribes who lived along the Susquehanna River, and special care has been taken to separate such specimens from those in the collection that came from other States.

The trustees of the society have passed a resolution thanking Mr. Wren and accepting with great pleasure his valuable gift. The collection of Indian relics in the society rooms is now, with the recent Wren collection, one of the finest in the State. The collection is handsomely arranged and contains many fine specimens. The collection now numbers 15,000 and the society is to be congratulated upon having such a complete and invaluable assortment.

Mr. Wren stipulated that if ever the Historical Society should cease to exist his collection should pass entire to the University of Pennsylvania.

PRESENTATIONS.

A fine portrait of H. Baker Hillman, by Walter Carpenter, has been presented to the society by the Hillman family. The society has also procured a fac simile of the Declaration of Independence, and another fine crayon picture of the old tall gate at the end of the Easton turnpike above Georgetown. The picture is by G. W. Leach and is a fine copy of a small photograph.

William Puckey has presented the society with a large collection of tin. iron and copper specimens taken from mines in Wales.

MRS. KUNKLE DEAD.

[Daily Record, Oct. 16, 1903.]

Mrs. Mariette Goss Kunkle died on Wednesday morning at the country home of her daughter on the North Mountain, near Central, in Columbia County. She was ill for nearly five years of valvular disease of the heart and death relieves her of great suffering.

She was the widow of Maj. Wesley Kunkle, at one time a prominent manufacturer and politician of Luzerne County. Soon after her marriage to Maj. Kunkle she and her husband went to live at what is now known as the village of Kunkle. the town having grown up around industries which Maj. Kunkle, and later his brother, Conrad Kunkle, established there. All of her

eight children, excepting the youngest, were born there, and she, the late Mrs. Reed of Philadelphia, was born on the old Kunkle homestead at Dallas, at present Col. Dorrance's famous Meadow Brook Farm.

Mrs. Kunkle's ancestors since before the War of the Revolution were of the New England element which came into Wyoming Valley before that period. Previous to the massacre of Wyoming her grandfather, together with many other of the families of early settlers, moved down into Huntington Valley. He settled at Huntington Mills, where he erected the flour and woolen mills which gave the place its name and which are still in operation. Mrs. Kunkle was born at that place on June 29, 1820.

Through her grandmother, Thankful Hale, she was descended from the Connecticut family of that name, forever made famous in American history by the noble young patriot, Nathan Hale. She is survived by five children, Adelaide, wife of Rev. E. C. Hoag of New York; Arthur P., the well known insurance agent of Wilkes-Barre; Dr. F. P. of Culiacan, Mexico; William W. of Phoenix, Arizona, and Anna of Wilkes-Barre; and by ten grandchildren and two great-grandchildren and a daughter-in-law; and also by two sisters, Mrs. Almina Tubbs of Jeanesville and Mrs. Rhoda Drumheller of Wilkes-Barre.

In her youth Mrs. Kunkle united with the Baptist Church, which relation she maintained until her death. For many years, however, she was an attendant of the Presbyterian Church of Kingston, and funeral services will be conducted by Rev. Mr. von Krug, pastor of that church, in the M. E. Church at Dallas on Friday morning at 11 o'clock. Interment, which will be private, will take place in Wardan Cemetery at Dallas.

LUTSEY REUNION.

On Labor Day the descendants of John Lutsey held their first reunion in Slocum, the original homestead of the family. A pleasant time was spent in talking over old times and in tracing the genealogy of the family. There are now over 500 descendants in Luzerne, Lackawanna and Columbia counties. An elaborate dinner was served. After the spread it was decided to form a permanent organization. Samuel Houck of Berwick was elected temporary chairman. Replying in a brief historical sketch of the family he told of the hardships endured in subduing the

wilderness. The reminiscence was so touching at different points that tears were seen on some of the faces of the older persons present.

John Lutsey of Scranton, who bears the name of his grandfather, was elected president; W. L. Houck of Berwick, secretary. An executive committee, consisting of S. Myers, A. Moore, J. Lutsey, N. Stair and S. M. Engle, was appointed.

This committee appointed Labor Day next year and the old homestead as the time and place for the next reunion.

John Lutsey, the founder of the family, came to this country in 1777, being 17 years old. He married Elizabeth Gilbert. They had five children, from whom are descended many of the prominent families of this region, and a considerable branch in Wisconsin. He settled in that part of the country on a section of land secured by patent from the Commonwealth of Pennsylvania in 1789. The postoffice now called Slocum was originally called Lutsey, and many of the old landmarks of that region are monuments of the Lutsey family.

At the next reunion a complete list of the descendants will be read, when an endeavor will be made to have as many present as possible.

Those present were:

Mr. and Mrs. Samuel Stair, Mr. and Mrs. W. S. Myers and daughters Ethel and Marjorie and sons Clyde and Bruce, Mrs. Rachel Lutsey, Mrs. Adaline George, Mr. and Mrs. Frederick Seigle, Mr. and Mrs. Oscar Stair, Clive Stair, Mrs. Ellen Lutsey, Mr. and Mrs. M. S. Engler and children, Miss C. Lutsey, Mr. and Mrs. J. E. Lutsey, Miss Nellie Lutsey, Mr. and Mrs. Arthur Moore, Mr. and Mrs. Abraham Engler, Mr. and Mrs. Ed Whitebread, Helen Whitebread, Mr. and Mrs. Norman Stair, Mamie Stair, Mr. and Mrs. W. A. Fairchilds, Mrs. Cora Grant, Myrtle Fairchilds, Mr. and Mrs. Eldridge Engler, Lyman, Edward and Harry Deets, Andrew Payne, Wapwallopen; Mr. and Mrs. Ed Lutsey and daughter Nellie, Clark's Green; Mr. and Mrs. F. F. Sprague and son Edward, Mrs. Henry Greenwalt, Mr. and Mrs. J. L. Lutsey and son Frank of Scranton; Mr. and Mrs. Samuel Houck, Dr. Harry Houck, William Houck, Dr. John Houck, Mr. and Mrs. Edgar Lutsey, Mr. and Mrs. E. L. Lutsey, Mrs. William Stout of Berwick; Mr. and Mrs. S. E. Stair, Eva M. Stair, Elsie Stair, Mr. and Mrs. Burton Stair, Mr. and Mrs. Jacob Kleinsmith and sons Edward, Arthur and Ralph, Mr. and Mrs. Norman Buckwalter and sons Eugene and Rowland, Francis Reynolds, Mr. and Mrs. Harry Zeiser and daughters Margaret

and Myra and son Bruce, Mr. and Mrs. John Myers, Mr. William Lueder, Miss Anna Lutsey, Mr. and Mrs. A. C. Lueder, Esther and Carl Lueder, Mr. C. W. Lueder of Wilkes-Barre, Mr. and Mrs. V. B. Zeiser, Miss Mame Zeiser of Nescopeck; Mrs. Harry Gibler, Mrs. Rosa Ruth of Wanamie, Mrs. S. L. Lueder of Nanticoke; Mr. and Mrs. Fred Reese and daughters Ruth and Hazel of Alden; Miss Clauda Clark and Mrs. Sue Clark of Towanda; Mary Whitebread, Ward Whitebread, Mr. and Mrs. Deets, Gussie Jones, Charles Jones, Harry Jones and Mattie Jones, all of Wapwallopen.

CHARLES BOWMAN WHITE DEAD.

[Daily Record, Oct. 23, 1903.]

Charles Bowman White. one of the best known newspaper men of this city, died at his residence, 296 South River street, at 11:40 a. m., Oct. 22, of liver trouble and dropsy, after an illness of several weeks. The deceased was born in Ashley on Oct. 21, 1859, and was 44 years old, in the prime of life and in the midst of a promising newspaper career when cut down by the grim reaper.

Deceased was a son of Rev. John White and Melinda Collins Blackman White, descendants of old Revolutionary families and pioneers of the Wyoming Valley, both of whom preceded him in death, his mother, to whom he was greatly attached, dying in December last. He is survived by his wife, Elizabeth A., (nee Forsman) to whom he was married in June, 1889. He is also survived by one brother, W. D. White, the well known druggist, and a sister, Mrs. Mame A. Williams of Ashley.

Charles White was active, rugged looking and energetic during his long newspaper career until March, 1902, when he met with an accident during the flood, which was a shock to his constitution, and he had not been well since. His residence on Carey avenue was flooded at the time, and going to the cellar steps to examine the height of the water, he slipped on the slimy ooze left by the flood and fell into the cellar, sustaining injuries from which he never fully recovered. Since that time his health has been failing and for the past three months he was scarcely able to attend to his duties. He worked bravely, made little complaint and was at his desk in the Leader office for the last time a week ago yesterday. Since that time he failed rapidly, complications set in

and despite every care and attention he sank into unconsciousness on Wednesday, in which state he lingered until death relieved him.

Charles B. White was one of the most popular newspaper men in Wyoming Valley and was well known in this section of the State. He was a practical printer and rose from the "case," developing into a pleasing and entertaining writer. For eleven years he was city editor of the Wilkes-Barre Times, being at the helm of the news department of that paper almost since it was established. About five months ago he took a position on the editorial staff of the Wilkes-Barre Leader and was with that paper at the time of his death.

He learned his trade as a printer with the late H. B. Beardsley on the old Luzerne Union nearly thirty years ago. Later he worked as a printer on the Pittston Comet, the Luzerne Union, and for the late J. C. Coon at Pittston, and in this city on the Plain-Dealer, now the News.

Some twenty odd years ago he became connected with the Wilkes-Barre Leader as printer and Ashley correspondent, in time becoming foreman of the composing room of that paper, a position he held for several years. He also held a reportorial position with the Ashley Observer about that time and was a correspondent for other newspapers. He left the newspaper business for a few years and worked as a painter in the Ashley shops of the C. R. R. of N. J. He returned to the Leader, where he worked as printer and foreman until 1893, when he became city editor of the Wilkes-Barre Times, a position he held for nearly eleven years.

LETTER FROM COLUMBUS BALD-WIN.

Norwalk, O., Oct. 28, 1903.

Friend L.: Great events have marked the passing years since we were boys together; and in common with the general experience of others, our fondest hopes have not always been realized, neither has life's pathway always been strewn with flowers, as we have from time to time been called upon to bid adieu to loved ones who have preceded us in the crossing of the dark river.

Credit me with the inclosed $2, which will complete my fiftieth year's subscription to the Record. My subscription to the paper dates back to 1854,

then published by my esteemed friend, the late William P. Miner. My first communication to the Record of the Times was published about that time, and my scrap book will give proof of the fact that I have written many scores of articles for that paper. The place of my nativity; the scenes of my childhood days; where I spent the years of my earlier manhood and where repose the bones of my ancestors—of thee I can truty exclaim (barring Quayism) "My dear old Pennsylvania, I love thee still!"

I notice that you have commenced the construction of a new court house to be more in keeping with the wealth and population of your flourishing county. I take exceptions to the location, which is too secluded. A structure of such magnitude and grandeur should be located where it would prove an ornament to the city and a credit to the county. The writer was the first occupant of the present court house, having moved from the old stone "fire proof" building located on the Square, into the then new court house on Jan. 1, 1859.

Back in those days Luzerne was generally Democratic by about fifteen hundred majority. In the fall of '58 the Democrats were considerably dissatisfied with their ticket, resulting in the election of several Republicans. as follows, to wit: W. W. Ketcham and Ario Pardee, to the State legislature; T. M. Harding, prosecuting attorney; John Blanchard Ross, commissioner, and the writer, clerk of the courts. George W. Scranton was elected to Congress by a majority of 4,000. The district then consisted of Luzerne, Wyoming, Columbia and Montour counties.

The court house officials in 1860 were: J. N. Conyngham, president judge; Barnum and Bristol, associates; J. B. Stark, sheriff; D. L. Patrick, prothonotary; G. M. Harding, prosecuting attorney; Thomas Atherton, register of wills; Edmund Taylor, treasurer; Wesley Kunkle, recorder; John Blanchard, Stephen Davenport and Benjamin Pfouts, commissioners; Sidney Eicke, court crier; Charles Behler, janitor, and the writer, clerk of the courts. All having been summoned to appear before that higher court, from whose decision there is no appeal, excepting Judge Harding and myself.

Yours truly,

C. J. Baldwin.

MRS. WM. KIRBY DEAD.

[Daily Record, Nov. 2, 1903.]

Unconsciously and without pain Mrs. William Kirby passed yesterday into the great beyond at the residence of her son on River street. Mrs. Kirby had not been well for a year or two and her demise is attributed to an enfeebled condition of heart and kidneys. She had been a resident of Wilkes-Barre since 1885, at which time she came here with her husband, William Kirby, and her only son, F. M. Kirby. Her husband died in February, 1895. Mrs. Kirby's maiden name was Angeline Elizabeth Slater, and she was a daughter of Joseph Slater of Hounsfield, Jefferson County, N. Y. She was born there Dec. 10, 1832, and spent her life in that neighborhood until coming to Wilkes-Barre nineteen years ago. Her father was from Vermont and was one of the pioneers of the northern tier of New York counties. Mrs. Kirby is the last of a family of three brothers and sisters. A niece to whom she was much attached, Mrs. Knight of Black River, Col., arrived a few hours too late to see her aunt alive.

Mrs. Kirby was one of those quiet, domestic mothers such as we all love. She was a devoted wife and mother and much given to good works. She had a remarkable memory and was always bright and cheerful, even in her sickness. She possessed a beautiful disposition and to know her was not only to enjoy her company and admire her many excellencies of character, but to love her. She was a woman of deep religious conviction and was a communicant of St. Stephen's Episcopal Church.

LUZERNE CO. NEWSPAPERS.

[Daily Record, Nov. 2, 1903.]

Speaking of the Record's thirtieth anniversary as a daily, Mr. C. F. Lathrop of Carbondale, who nearly sixty years ago published the Wilkes-Barre Advocate, out of which the Record grew, says in his Carbondale Leader:

The writer (Mr. Lathrop) well remembers the difficulties and discouragements which attended the daily issue at its commencement and for several years after, during which the most strenuous efforts were necessary to keep it in motion.

Up to that time the newspapers in this region of country were of a decidedly primitive character. What enterprise there was connected with the

business was confined to the large
cities, and the country press was appreciated by few persons outside of the
politicians and others who had axes to
grind. One will have to go but a few
years back to see in the papers piteous
appeals to delinquent subscribers, and
even offers to take wood, vegetables and
other commodities on subscription account. Business men were slow to ad-
vertise and what little patronage they
bestowed in that way must be taken
out in trade. This enabled publishers
to eke out a bare existence, but cash
was necessary to buy paper and ink and
to replenish worn out materials.

In these circumstances it may well be
believed that printing a country newspaper in early times involved a lot of
hardship, not to say humiliation, for its
proprietor.

The enterprising young men who have
built up the Record to its present proud
and influential position, we are pleased
to say, have not had to pass through
the dark days we have described, but
have reaped a generous reward from an
appreciative public who no longer de-
spise the printer, nor look upon him as
an object of charity.

In this connection it may be said that
the old-time newspaper editor was not
a whit behind those of the present day
in brainy qualities. We recall some of
the men who were prominent in Pennsylvania journalism fifty years ago, and
even longer, who were the peers of the
brightest and most profound writers of
more recent times. The change in
newspaper conditions is more in the
business line, corresponding with the
hustling enterprise which characterizes
the age in which we are now living. In
no department in the business world
has there been greater advancement
than in that of newspaper making; and
the Wilkes-Barre Record is a fair sam-
ple of progress in that line.

HISTORIC DOCUMENTS.

[Daily Record, Nov. 11, 1903.]

Harrisburg, Nov. 10 —Two papers,
connected with the early history of the
Commonwealth of Pennsylvania and
now of great historic interest, were recently discovered among the records of
the Department of Internal Affairs by
Theodore B. Klein, secretary of the department. The first paper is dated July
3, 1792, and contains articles of agreement between Governor Thomas Mifflin
and the contractors for clearing the
Susquehanna River, and making it

navigable from Wright's Ferry to Swatara Creek. The second paper is the report of the inspectors upon the completion of the work, and is dated Dec. 5, 1797.

The making of this contract was one of the first important acts of Governor Mifflin, who has the honor of being the first governor of Pennsylvania elected under the Constitution of the State. He became chief executive in 1790. In it Messrs. Robert Morris, William Smith, Walter Stewart, Samuel Meredith, John Steinmertz, Lench Francis, John Nicholson, John Donaldson, Samuel Miles, Timothy Matlack, David Rittenhouse, Alexander James Dallas, William Bingham, Henry Miller, Abraham Whitmer and Robert Harris each bound themselves to make a clear water way from Wright's Ferry to Swatara Creek, for the sum of £5,250.

The contract comprised the building of a canal at Conewago Falls, at a width of forty feet, and a depth of not less than four feet, with safe and navigable locks. The contractors were also to remove the obstructions at Chickie's Falls and Haldeman's Ripples. All the work was to be completed by Jan. 1, 1796. In connection with the building of the canal the men were to keep it in constant repair. On the first of January the canal was to be opened as a public highway for boats, rafts and vessels of transportation of every description. They were to have free and safe passage through the locks and the use of the entire water way without the payment of tolls.

The inspectors' report is signed by John Hall, "agent of information on the completion of the Conewago Canal." As the report is dated Dec. 5, 1797, it is evident that the canal was not completed at the time specified. Mr. Hall, in this report, gave an exhaustive account of the inspection of the canal, which was found to be built according to plans and specifications. According to the report the trip of inspection was a thrilling one. It was made in the month of December and the boats in which the inspectors rode were obliged to break through a thin layer of ice, which had formed on the canal. Shortly after the party had started a snow storm was encountered and the remainder of the trip was made with great difficulty.

Governor Mifflin, with a number of other State officials, accompanied the inspectors in a separate boat, and scrutinized closely the work on the canal and the working of the locks.

The discovery of these relics of the early history of the Commonwealth of Pennsylvania has. afforded Mr. Klein much pleasure, and he is preparing a paper on them which he will read before the Dauphin County Historical Society.

PIONEER BAPTISTS.

[Daily Record, Nov. 12, 1903.]

At the recently held eighteenth anniversary of the Immanuel Baptist Church of Edwardsville, the pastor, Rev. John T. Griffith, D. D., made an admirable historical address, tracing the Baptist movement in Wyoming Valley from its inception in 1762, down to the present. The portion of the address dealing with the early history is appended:

The first person who preached to the white people of the Wyoming Valley was Elder William Marsh. It is true that missionaries were sent before Elder Marsh for the purpose of converting the Indians. A man named Rev. John Sargeant, from the Massachusetts Indian School, came in 1741 to the Wyoming Valley with a few Christians from the Mohegan tribe, but failed in his attempt. In the next year, 1742, Count Zinzendorf, that noble Moravian missionary, visited this valley to labor among the Indians, but he remained only a few weeks, and was evidently not encouraged to return by the reception that was given to him. It was with a company of Connecticut colonists that William Marsh came in 1762. He was their preacher and teacher. They located at Mill Creek. In the fall they returned East to spend the winter, but the next spring they came back 150 strong. Then they opened settlements at Wilkes-Barre, Kingston, Pittston and Hanover. On October 15, 1763, the hostile Delawares moved against the white settlers, killing thirty of them at Mill Creek. Among those who were killed was the Rev. Wm. Marsh. His name appears in the minutes of the old Philadelphia Baptist Association for 1761-'62-'63 and then disappears.

In 1769, and later with the return of the whites who had fled from the valley after the Mill Creek massacre and the killing of Marsh, other ministers of different denominations visited the valley, and among them was a man named John Stafford, a Baptist licentiate from Dutchess county, New York. He came here in the year 1773, and preached in the township of Kingston. In the same

year, according to "Pearce's Annals,"
a Baptist minister named Gray
preached in Kingston Township and
subsequently in the vicinity of Pittston. In 1776 Elkanah Holmes of Kings-
wood, New Jersey, also came to the
Wyoming Valley as a missionary. He
came from the Philadelphia Conference
and preached in the valley for a season. The records of the Baptist
Church of Goshen, now Warwick,
Orange county, New York, show that
brethren at Westmoreland, a territory
including all northeastern Pennsylvania embraced in the counties of
Luzerne, Lackawanna, Wyoming, Susquehanna and Bradford, with a population at that time of 2,000, desired
help. It was then voted to send Elder
James Benedict and two other brethren
to answer this request. The records of
the same church further show that in
December of the same year, 1776, Elder
Benedict did as directed; and finding
twelve of their own members, with
fourteen others in good standing, he
baptized six others, and then constitu-
ted the Pittston Baptist Church, with a
membership of thirty-two persons. Soon
after the organization of the Pittston
Church Elder Benedict returned to
Warwick, but subsequently came back
to Pittston and built a cabin near the
stone quarry at the foot of Parsonage
street. He remained until after the
massacre of July 3, 1778, and then returned to Warwick, and resumed his
former pastorate there. The new
church was nearly broken up by the
Indian troubles. Doubtless many members were killed and others were scattered, but upon the return of the settlers into the valley the meetings of
the church were resumed.

Among those who early came from
Warwick soon after the massacre were
David Mitchell. He had served through
the Revolutionary War, and in 1785 set
his face westward to find a home in a
newer section of the country. His
wife's maiden name was Sarah Patterson. She was born in Litchfield, Conn.,
in 1759. They settled on the flats below the present site of Coxton upon
land belonging to John Phillips, one of
the most active of the early members
of the Pittston Church. Mrs. Mitchell
sent for Elder James Benedict and he
baptized her in the Susquehanna. The
names of the six constituent members
of the Pittston Church who had been
baptized by the Rev. James Benedict
before this time are not known, so Mrs.
Mitchell's baptism is the first authen-
ticated baptism in this section. Mr.

Mitchell died soon after settling here, and Mrs. Mitchell became the wife of Abram Frear and the grandmother of the late Dr. George Frear, of Wilkes-Barre.

In 1792 a man named Thomas Smiley, who had been a Revolutionary soldier, was baptized at Plymouth by the pastor of the Pittston Church. He became a very useful Baptist minister and was the pioneer of the Baptists in the White Deer Creek Valley and the Northumberland Association, Pa. In 1842 a regular Baptist church was organized at Wilkes-Barre. It was known by the name of the Wilkes-Barre and Kingston Church.

[See an article entitled "The fathers of the Wyoming Association," written by the late Hon. Theodore Hart of Pittston.]

Thus we see that Baptist preaching dates far back in this section and that a great deal of early pioneer work was done here by our Baptist fathers, yet we have no account of any special Baptist organization on the west side of the river from Wilkes-Barre prior to 1868, when the Welsh Baptists organized at Plymouth, and 1873, when the Welsh Baptists organized at Edwardsdale.

The address has been printed in neat pamphlet form and will be sold for the benefit of Immanuel Church.

DEATH OF A CENTENNARIAN.

[Daily Record, Nov. 19, 1903.]

In the person of Patrick Corrigan, who died at his home, 48 Jones street, on Monday, probably the oldest man in Luzerne County passed away, he having reached the remarkable age of 102 years. That he possessed a wonderful constitution goes without saying. He was born in Westport, County of Mayo, Ireland, on the 19th day of March, 1801, and had he lived until March, 1904, he would have been 103 years old.

Mr. Corrigan's parents died when he was in his teens. He was the eldest of a family of four sons and one daughter and he kept the family together by hard work until his brothers and sister were grown up. He secured employment in a stone quarry and learned the masonry trade. At the age of 40 he was married and five years later came to the shores of America with his wife. He settled in Philadelphia and was employed at the navy yard, building docks and doing other masonry work. He worked there during the administra-

tion of Buchanan and was well acquainted with the President.

· His brothers and sisters are all now dead. One brother and the sister came to America and settled at what is now Penn Haven Junction. The former died when he was 40 years of age, while the sister reached the three score and ten mark.

Mr. Corrigan lived for fifteen years with his wife and family in Philadelphia and then came to Wilkes-Barre. This was in the year 1868. The war was then over. Had he not been beyond the age limit he would have taken part in the struggle. He was acquainted with President Lincoln and told interesting stories about him.

When he came to Wilkes-Barre the town was a hamlet and the old canal was then in full operation. Mining for coal was in its infancy and he was employed in building many of the foundations for coal breakers. He was employed by the Jersey Central Railroad and the Lehigh Valley Railroad for many years, doing masonry work along the road, building abutments for bridges along the roads from Mauch Chunk to Falling Springs. He continued at his trade until about twenty years ago, when he gave up active work. He located with his family on Jones street, where the family has since resided. Rolling Mill Hill at that time was wooded and there was · an abundance of game.

Being five feet six inches tall, he had the strength of a giant and prided himself on this fact. He greatly amused his hearers with tales of his native land, of how he worked in the stone quarries and bested all the men employed, by being able to carry a heavier burden of stones on a barrow than any of the rest of them. He also related many anecdotes of early days in Philadelphia, portraying the life of the Quakers, who were then the principal residents.

His good wife, who is now 93 years of age, is still quite hearty. She was the mother of twelve children, of whom four sons and two daughters survive.

Although Mr. Corrigan spent the greater portion of the last years of his life at his home and seldom went anywhere, he was always active. He would carry railroad ties and timbers from the mines and railroad near his home, on his back up the hill, and would then split the wood with an ax and always had a huge pile of fire wood in the yard and in the cellar.

He enjoyed being in the open air and
had no fear of the rain. His familiar
figure on a rainy day could be seen
on the sidewalk in front of his home,
cleaning out the gutter so that the
water would have a free course.

He was always in good health and
never knew what sickness was. Up to
six months ago his sight was exceedingly good. He never wore glasses and
was able to thread a needle as well as
a youngster. He also had full possession of his other faculties and enjoyed life up to the last. He took particular enjoyment in smoking his pipe,
and his prolonged years are due to a
great extent to the fact that he did
not over indulge in anything, led a regular life and had no bad habits.

He was able to be up and around
until only seven weeks ago, and it was
only two weeks before his death that
he became bedfast. He suffered but
little and was conscious up to within
an hour of his death. The doctors
stated that his death was not due to
any particular cause, but came from
general debility, brought on by his advanced years.

Of the children surviving the oldest
is Mrs. Joseph Brown of Philadelphia,
who is 59 years of age; Patrick, the oldest son, never married. He lives at
home and is an engineer on the Lehigh
Valley R. R. He is 53 years of age.
John, the next oldest, who is 51, is now
in Alaska prospecting. The youngest
son, Austin, who also resides at home,
is 49, while the youngest in the family
is Mrs. Jacob Staitz, aged 40, who resides with her family at 60 Jones street.

COMPANY B'S ANNIVERSARY.
[Daily Record, Dec. 1, 1903.]

The twenty-fifth anniversary of the
organization of Co. B, 9th Regt., which
was known at the time of organization as the Wilkes-Barre Fencibles,
was celebrated at Redington's hotel
last evening with a pleasant reunion
and banquet. There was a large number of members, ex-members and
friends of the company present, nearly one hundred, and several toasts were
responded to in addresses filled with
patriotic sentiment and with reminiscences of twenty-five years ago, when
the organization was founded in the
spirit of patriotic and military ardor.
Co. B has become one of the foundation stones of the present superb 9th
Regt. Its record is an honorable one
and the observance of its anniversary

was a fitting recognition of its worth
and of the men who have kept its
escutcheon bright and its glory un-
dimmed.

The members of the present company,
officers of the regiment, original members of the company and guests were
seated at two long tables in the main
dining room, and at the conclusion of
the feasting, at 10 o'clock, the after
dinner festivities began and continued
until after midnight, when they ended
with the singing of "Auld Lang Syne."

THE FIRST CAPTAIN.

Oscar J. Harvey, the first captain of
the company, presided as toastmaster,
and his introductions were witty and
were filled with many reminiscences of
an historical nature.

COLONEL RIPPLE SPEAKS.

Colonel Ripple of Scranton, adjutant
general on the staff of Governor Pen-
nypacker, was pleasantly introduced as
the first speaker, his toast being "Our
neighbors, the 13th.," and he responded
in a graceful manner. He began by
paying a compliment to Co. B as part
of the 9th Regt., and then gave a rather
thrilling narrative of the riots and
scenes of disorder which resulted in the
formation of the 13th and 9th Regts.
He told of the railroad riots and other
troubles that seemed to rise like a
wave of anarchy and threatened the
welfare of the nation. He told how
this disorder was suppressed in Scranton by the vigorous stand of the then
mayor, McCune, who with his little
posse of town guards checked the progress of the mob and maintained law
and order until the arrival of troops.
He said the 9th and 13th Regts. were
necessary to each other as comrades in
arms and he hoped both would keep
memories of a glorious past.

THE OLD ARTILLERISTS.

Toastmaster Harvey next introduced
Capt. T. C. Parker of this city, who as
captain of the old Wyoming Artillerists
mustered Co. B into the State service.

Capt. Parker proved an interesting
as well as humorous speaker and related many historical facts in connection with the early formation of the
National Guard. He told of the horrors
of war, that there never was a good
war and there never was a bad peace,
and that notwithstanding the progress
of civilization war is just as possible
to-day as it was twenty centuries ago.
He told of the hard work of officers and
men in the Guard and the slim recom-
pense which their service brings.

THE NINTH'S COLONEL.

Col. C. B. Dougherty was introduced as the next speaker, his toast being "The Ninth Regiment,' and in his introduction the toastmaster read from a New York paper, praising the rapid mobilization of the regiment at the time of the Lattimer trouble in 1898, and also a portion of an address of Gen. Gobin to the regiment when it was leaving Hazleton, in which he said that never before had soldiers made such a quick response to duty.

Col. Dougherty made an able response. He told how he enlisted as a private in Co. B when barely 21 years old, and remained continuously in the service until to-day, at 43. If you put two and two together, said the colonel, you can realize that the greater portion of my life has been devoted to the building up of the regiment. Nothing is so dear to me, except my little family, as the 9th Regt.

The colonel referred to the dark days of trouble in 1877, when the militia turned out to suppress the riots, and that Gen. Hartranft, who came on from the West to take charge of affairs, said the National Guard of Pennsylvania was the best citizen soldiery in the country. To that general, said the speaker, is due the splendid standing of the Pennsylvania militia to-day, because he started it right. The colonel told of the progress of the 9th Regt. from a position at the foot of the ladder to a place at the head. He paid a tribute to Col. Ripple as one of the best types of American citizenship, and to Col. G. M. Reynolds, the first colonel of the local regiment. He told how the 9th always did its duty and related instances of its remarkable mobilization and prompt response when called to duty. And then when the call came to fight for the country in the war with Spain nearly 87 per cent. of the regiment volunteered. The boys were sent to Chickamauga and held as a reserve, but some of them did not come back, and the graves they fill are as honored graves as any of those who fell for the flag. He said it was an honor to be a member of the regiment and it is going to be a greater honor still under the new National Guard law, which makes the militia a second defense of the nation.

UNABLE TO BE PRESENT.

The toastmaster read letters from the following named (unable to be present), containing pleasant reminiscences and expressing interest in the welfare of Co. B, and hopes for a successful and honorable future:

Col. G. Murray Reynolds, the first colonel of the 9th Regt.

Col. E. A. Hancock of Philadelphia, quartermaster general N. G. P., 1879-83, an honorary member of the civic organization and second vice president of the same.

Gen. Paul A. Oliver, first vice president of the civic organization of the Fencibles and the giver of several prizes to be competed for by members of the company.

Col. R. B. Ricketts, an original honorary member of the Fencibles.

Dr. Harry Hakes, an original honorary member of the Fencibles, who in 1874 presented the company with a handsome flag.

Judge Stanley Woodward, an original honorary member of the Fencibles.

A. D. Moore, original second lieutenant of the Fencibles and the first adjutant of the 9th Regt.

MEMBER OF FENCIBLES.

A. R. Brundage was introduced as an honorary member of the old Fencibles company, and responded to the toast "The Fencibles' Honorary Members." He said that few realize the close connection between the military and the judiciary, the the military is a reserve to the civil authorities for the upholding and enforcing of the law, and is the bulwark of our liberties. He closed by saying that he hoped and believed that the time is not far distant when the necessities for military organizations will have passed away, and that when the twentieth century has passed the difficulties of nations will be subject to the law of love and arbitration. In the meantime we are right in keeping an organization that can and will take care of us and keep us from falling back into lawless disorder.

THE PRESS GANG.

The toastmaster next introduced Dr. F. C. Johnson of the Record to respond to the toast "The Press Gang," and he explained the press gangs of old that

COL. C. BOW DOUGHERTY.

pressed citizens into the army and navy, but which were succeeded by a press gang of a different kind.

Dr. Johnson replied briefly, related some interesting reminiscences of the early military days as he remembered them as a boy and closed by saying that Co. B dated originally back to 1878, but that it had its inspiration fully seventeen years earlier. When the Civil War had burst upon the country

the small boys of Union street had become imbued with the military spirit and they not only watched the organization of local companies and followed their departure to the stations, but they organized a juvenile company, with Oscar J. Harvey as captain. They had their camps and their drills and imagined themselves a part of the great military force of the country. One of their diversions was to march to Reichard's brewery, draw up in line and give three cheers for Capt. John Reichard, who never failed to return the compliment by treating the boys to sarsaparilla. It was in this boy company that Oscar Harvey got his first military conception and out of it grew the Fencibles and the 9th Regt. Dr. Johnson closed by quoting the following from Charles Miner, the historian of Wyoming:

"In my opinion America owes her independence to the militia system which existed in the colonies. Pennsylvania cannot too sedulously encourage and preserve that right arm of her power, the militia of this great Commonwealth."

ONE OF THE SERGEANTS.

Capt. Harvey read a humorous account of a battalion drill of the military companies existing here in 1845, some of which in the absence of guns carried corn stalks, and then introduced attorney W. L. Raeder as a sergeant of the old Wilkes-Barre Fencibles. Mr. Raeder's subject was "The Fencibles and the females," and he made a brief but pleasing response, wit and sentiment mingling. He closed by reciting a German dialect poem on "Barbara Frietchie."

MAJOR STEARNS.

Maj. Irving A. Stearns, a former private in Co. B., also spoke briefly, told of several interesting experiences he had with the company on its first encampment and his pride in being a member of the company, but there was pathos in his voice as he referred indirectly to the death of his son, who died from typhoid fever contracted at Chickamauga while captain of the same Co. B.

OTHER SPEAKERS.

Capt. Polen, Capt. Marshall and Quartermaster Sauermilch of the old Fencibles made brief responses and told of interesting experiences while members.

THE PRESENT CAPTAIN.

The last speaker on the toast list was Capt. James C. Kenny, the present commanding officer of the company. His toast was "Co. B, now and later," and he gave praise to the members of his command for their soldierly qualities and spoke of the praise bestowed on them by Gen. Miles during the big parade in New York and the praise of their commanding general for their appearance at the last State encampment. He gave some figures as to the number of men who enlisted in the past twenty-five years and the work of the officers in training the new men. He closed by thanking all for their attendance and hoped the spirit of good fellowship would grow.

The anniversary closed by the singing of "Auld Lang Syne."

HISTORY OF FENCIBLES.

The Wilkes-Barre Fencibles were organized in September and October, 1878. Nov. 15, 1878, orders were issued by the adjutant general for the election of officers and the mustering in of the company. Capt. T. C. Parker, commanding the Wyoming Artillerists of Wilkes-Barre, was designated to hold the election and muster in the company. This was done in due form in the armory of the Artillerists in Music Hall block on Thanksgiving night (Nov. 28), 1878. Fifty men were mustered in at that time. The following officers were elected at that time: Captain, Oscar J. Harvey; first lieutenant, Henry Crandall; second lieutenant, Arthur D. Moore. The following served as captains, in order of succession, since that time: Henry Crandall, Stephen J. Polen, oJhn C. Horton, deceased; Walter S. Marshall, Stewart L. Barnes and L. Denison Stearns, deceased.

The following are the present commissioned officers of Co. B: Captain, James C. Kenny; first lieutenant, John A. Kenny; second lieutenant, Bruce B. Dimmick.

When organized the company was not assigned to any regiment and in special orders from 3d Brigade headquarters it was directed that it be "designated by name instead of by regiment and letter." The name "Wilkes-Barre Fencibles" was adopted a few days later.

The company first appeared in public (although not yet uniformed) Dec. 6, 1878, under orders to proceed to Scranton for inspection. Its first ap-

pearance in uniform was on Jan. 11, 1879, in a street parade. In the evening of that day, at Music Hall, the famous Mendelssohn Quintet Club of Boston gave a concert under the auspices of the Fencibles. Gen. W. H. McCartney, in behalf of Dr. H. Baker, presented the Fencibles with a handsome flag.

Jan. 21, 1879, the Fencibles attended at Harrisburg the inauguration of Governor Hoyt and took part in the parade.

June 29, 1879, orders were issued for the formation of a new regiment, to be known as the 9th, the Fencibles to be Co. B, and July 26, 1879, G. Murray Reynolds was elected colonel of the new regiment.

Co. B furnished to the 9th Regt. the following officers: Its first adjutant, A. D. Moore; its first quartermaster, I. A. Stearns; its first commissary, Oscar J. Harvey, and its present colonel, C. B. Dougherty; also Charles L. Peck, who was lieutenant and then captain of Co. A of the 9th, and later lieutenant colonel of the 7th provisional regiment, was a member of Co. B.

DEATH OF ANDREW J. BALDWIN.

[Daily Record, Dec. 5, 1903.]

Andrew Jackson Baldwin, one of Wilkes-Barre's most prominent residents, a man who built thousands of miles of telegraph lines in the United States and the first cable line in this country, died shortly before midnight last night at the home of his daughter, Mrs. Charles A. Jackson, 30 West Ross street.

Mr. Baldwin about ten years ago suffered a stroke of paralysis and since that time had been in poor health. A few days ago he took a turn for the worse and failed rapidly until his death.

Mr. Baldwin traced his descent from a long line of English forefathers, his earliest American ancestry dating less than two decades after the first arrival of the Mayflower. His great-grandfather, Elijah Baldwin, was born in 1717 in Newark, N. J., where the family resided during the greater part of the eighteenth century.

A. J. Baldwin, the second son of Jared R. Baldwin, was born on the Baldwin farm at Trucksville, Pa., in 1824. After his early farm life, interspersed with country schooling, he at the age of thirteen began the work of mail carrying between Wilkes-Barre

and White Haven. This work he continued for three years. He then entered Cisty's printing office in Wilkes-Barre, where after he had mastered the printer's trade he became a partner in the concern, which then went under the name of Cisty & Baldwin. Later the large cities drew him, and we find the young man in Philadelphia as telegraph operator and in New York in a position on the Journal of Commerce.

While working in the former position an interest in electrical matters seized him, which lasted throughout his life.

He was at one time superintendent of a telegraph line, of which the well known Col. Speed was president. It was about the year 1853 that he began the practical work of building telegraph lines, and he has himself calculated this work as covering nearly nine thousand miles in various parts of the country east of the Mississippi, including two lines between New York City and New Orleans.

Mr. Baldwin deserves the distinction of having laid the first cable in the United States, a short line of six miles between Wood's Hole and Vineyard Haven, Martha's Vineyard. A second cable was laid by him between Monomoy and Grand Point, Nantucket, a distance of twenty-five miles. This line was swept away, but not before it had transmitted its first message, he news of the bombardment of Sevastopol, in 1855.

During the past ten years Mr. Baldwin has resided in Wilkes-Barre, where his failing health has made active life impossible.

Mr. Baldwin was married to Mary Hyde Collings, daughter of Daniel Collings, and sister of Samuel P. Collings. His wife and the following children survive him: Mrs. Charles A. Jackson, Wilkes-Barre; Mrs. Andrew G. Raub, Luzerne Borough; George P. Baldwin, Brooklyn, N. Y.; Harry H. Baldwin, Lehman, and Alexander G. of Luzerne Borough.

OF REVOLUTIONARY STOCK.

[Daily Record, Dec. 7, 1903.]

In the death of Mrs. Elizabeth Carpenter of West Pittston about midnight on Friday, from an attack of heart disease and general debility, Wyoming Valley loses one of its oldest residents.

The deceased was a native of this valley, being born in Exeter Borough Sept. 3, 1818, her ancestry being of Revolutionary stock. She was the fifth of a family of nine children and was the last of her

family. She resided in the upper section of Wyoming Valley all her life.

Mrs. Carpenter was a descendant of the old Schooley family. She was born in a house in the Sturmerville section of Exeter Borough, which was erected over one hundred years ago and is still standing. In 1849 she was married to John Sharps Carpenter, also of Revolutionary descent, who died five years ago, and for a time they lived in Kingston, later removing to the upper part of the valley, where they kept what was known as the Head-of-the-Valley Hotel, a famous hostelry in the days of the stage coach between Wilkes-Barre and Tunkhannock, and where the relays of horses were changed.

In 1866 the family removed to West Pittston, and she had since resided there. Early in life Mrs. Carpenter became a member of the Presbyterian Church and remained steadfast in that faith.

Those surviving the deceased are a son, Jesse B. Carpenter, three grandchildren, Jesse B. Jr., and Elizabeth and Joseph B. Welch.

NOW HAS A MONUMENT.

[Daily Record, Dec. 7, 1903.]

Gen. Samuel Meredith's remains and those of his wife now repose beneath the granite blocks of the foundation of the monument being reared to his memory by the State in Triangle Park, Pleasant Mount, Wayne County. The monument is to cost $3,000, and will be dedicated on May 30, 1904, when Governor Pennypacker has promised to attend.

Gen Meredith was the first treasurer of the United States, having been appointed by President Washington in 1798. In 1789 he gave $25,000 to the fund for the support of Washington's army and himself participated in several battles of the Revolution.

At the outbreak of the Revolution he organized the Silk Stocking company of Philadelphia, and was made major of his regiment. He took part in the battles of Trenton and Princeton. In 1777 he was made a brigadier general by Washington and as such was in the battles of Germantown and Brandywine, near his old home in Philadelphia.

After the war Gen. Meredith made his home on what is known as Belmont Terrace, near Pleasant Mount, and there Gen. Washington, while President, was wont to come. The closest friendship existed between Washington and Gen. Meredith and in 1798, after

the adoption of the Constitution, President Washington tendered Gen. Meredith the portfolio of treasurer, which he accepted.

After Washington's term Gen. Meredith retired to private life, and died in the early part of the nineteenth century. He, with his wife, was buried near the homestead, on what is known as Belmont Manor.

As the years went by the grave of the patriot was forgotten. It was moss grown and overrun with wood-vines until the little marble slab was barely discernible. Some few years ago a movement was started to build a monument to fittingly mark Gen. Meredith's grave and the measure was put through the legislature and an appropriation of $3.000 made.

The bodies of the almost forgotten patriot and his wife were removed to their new resting place recently. The removal was made under the direction of Mrs. Sarah Maria Graham of Tunkhannock, a granddaughter of the Merediths.—Towanda Review.

NEW ENGLAND SOCIETY BANQUET.

[Daily Record, Dec. 23, 1903.]

The landing the Pilgrims on Plymouth Rock in 1620 was celebrated last evening by the New England Society of Northeastern Pennsylvania for the seventeenth time. The society meets once a year and the occasion is devoted to a dinner, in which such New England accessories as cider and pumpkin pie are not omitted from the bill of fare. The dinner was given in Scranton at the Hotel Jermyn and the banqueting room was hung with flags and bunting and further made beautiful with plants and flowers. Prior to the dinner the members of the society and their invited guests gathered for an informal reception. The dinner began at 7 and the menu was one that would have made the starving Pilgrim Fathers drop over in a faint to see its gastronomic elaboration. After it had been duly stowed away under the waistbands of the modern pilgrims, coffee and cigars introduced the speechmaking.

The presiding officer for the current year was Dr. F. C. Johnson of Wilkes-Barre and he was seconded by Thomas H. Atherton, Esq., Wilkes-Barre, who admirably and entertainingly discharged the duties of toastmaster. The toasts were as follows:

"Pilgrims and Pure Food, by Dr. Har-

vey A. Wiley of Washington, chief of
the bureau of chemistry, U. S. Department
of Agriculture.

"The Relations of Pennsylvania and
New England," by Hon. Hampton L.
Carson of Philadelphia, attorney general
of Pennsylvania.

"A Puritan Potpourri," by Col. Edwin
B. Hay of Washington.

"The Puritans and Education" was to
have been responded to by Dr. S. J.
McPherson of Lawrenceville, N. J., but
he was compelled to cancel his acceptance.

"The Puritan of To-day," Rev. E. J.
Morris, pastor of the Puritan Congregational
Church, Wilkes-Barre.

Throughout the evening there was
vocal and instrumental music, the latter
by Bauer's orchestra, the former
made up of college songs.

PRESIDENT'S ADDRESS.

The presiding officer after a few
words of introduction mentioned that
up to a fortnight ago the ranks of the
society had been unbroken by death
since the last meeting, but on Dec. 12
Col. Henry M. Boies was suddenly
and fatally stricken at Wilkes-Barre
while returning from Washington,
whither he had gone for a conference
with the President of the United States.
Col. Boies was 66 years of age, was a
soldier in the Civil War and as a resident
of Scranton he was prominently
identified with its social, commercial,
literary, military and religious life. The
assemblage at this point rose and drank
a silent toast to the memory of Col.
Boies.

Some letters of regret were presented,
one being from John Weaver, mayor of
Philadelphia.

As two of the officers have just withdrawn
from active duty after serving
a dozen years, A. C. Fuller as treasurer
and J. H. Fisher as secretary, each was
made the recipient of a loving cup.

Dr. Johnson then proceeded with a
consideration of the New England town
of Westmoreland, attached nominally to
Connecticut but located on Pennsylvania
soil and wiped off the map when
Pennsylvania conciliated the Connecticut
claimants after a thirty years' war.
An effort was made to show that Westmoreland
not only contributed liberally
of patriot troops but she played some
part in shortening that great struggle.
The speaker related a dramatic incident
in the life of his great-grandfather,
Rev. Jacob Johnson, first settled
pastor in the Westmoreland region. An
explanation was given why the British

destroyed Wyoming and mention was
made of Ethan Allen's project to erect
a new State out of Westmoreland as
compelling Pennsylvania to finally
make suitable concessions to the
Yankees and thus end the Pennamite
war.

Following are extracts:

During the Revolution the spot in
Pennsylvania which we occupy to-night
was in the New England town of Westmoreland. It occupied soil that was
claimed by two States. It was part of
Pennsylvania's unbroken territory and
it was separated from Connecticut by
only the projecting lower portion of
New York State. Seventy miles square,
bounded on the north by the New York
line and on the east by the Delaware
River, Westmoreland County (for the
town subsequently became a county),
had a population of about 2,000 souls.
The same territory now has a population 350 times as great, or close to three-
quarters of a million. It was a part of
the nearest Connecticut county, and its
members of the legislature had to go on
horseback nearly 200 miles, much of
the distance through a wilderness. It
was for this fair region that Pennamites
and Yankees struggled in civil war for
a generation. The governor of Connecticut issued a proclamation forbidding all settlements in Westmoreland
except under the authority of Connecticut, while the governor of Pennsylvania
warned all intending settlers that the
claims of Connecticut were only pre-
tensions and that no other authority
than that of the Penns must be recognized. The Indians had always been
opposed to the settlement of this region
by the whites and made dire threats
that were executed many times by
bands of prowling savages. The inter-
necine struggle between Connecticut
and Pennsylvania was waged for a
third of a century and was never interrupted except during the Rovlution-
ary War, when by common consent
both parties suspended their local strife
and joined in a common defense against
the growing oppressions of Great
Britain. When the war clouds of the
Revolution were gathering, but had not
yet burst, a Connecticut man who was
afterwards to play a part in the Westmoreland settlement, was a missionary
among the Six Nations. A treaty was
in progress—one of great national importance, as one of its purposes was to
fix a permanent boundary between the
Indians and the whites. The council
was held in the colony of New York and
was attended by the governors of the

interested colonies and by some 3,000 Indians. It was dominated by the Penns, John Penn, a son of William Penn, being present. He wanted the lands in northeastern Pennsylvania which were claimed by Connecticut and which had been bought by Connecticut from the Indians some years previous. The commissioners had boatloads of gold and guns and gewgaws, and besides these an abundance of that argument so potent with the Indians then and ever since—rum. It is needless to say the Penn interests prevailed. As Connecticut was not invited to the council which was to wrest from her a part of her ex-territorial possession, the Wyoming region, this Connecticut missionary undertook—entirely without authority, however,—to defend the Connecticut interest by dissuading the Indians from selling to the Penns the land which Connecticut claimed.

While the treaty was in progress the king's agent, Sir William Johnson, gave a banquet and the missionary, by reason of his sacred office, rather than by reason of his being a New England man, was among the invited guests. The feast was made the occasion of bursts of eloquence as to the greatness of England and toasts were drunk to the health of King George III. Amid the noisy merrymaking of the convivial company the Connecticut missionary could hear the muttering of the gathering storm, he could already feel with Patrick Henry that the next breeze from the north was to bring to their ears the clash of resounding arms. So when the adulations of the king were all over and the preacher from Connecticut was called upon, the scene was not unlike that on the night when in the revel at Babylon there appeared, written across the wall in letters of fire, those words which foretold the doom of Belshazzar. These are the missionary's thrilling sentences: I drink to the health of King George III of Great Britain, comprehending New England and all the British colonies in North America, and I mean to drink such a health so long as his royal majesty shall govern the British and American subjects according to the great charter of English liberty, and so long as he hears the prayers of his American subjects. But in case his British majesty (which God in great mercy prevent) should proceed contrary to charter rights and privileges, and govern us with a rod of iron, and the mouth of cannons and utterly refuse to consider our humble prayers, then I should consider it my indispensable

duty to join my countrymen in forming a new empire in America."

It does not surprise us to learn that in after years when the missionary was pastor at Westmoreland he denounced the Pennamite outrages with such vehemence that he was dragged before the court and compelled to give bonds for his peaceable behavior.

Two resolutions of the Westmoreland people in town meeting assembled soon after the shock of Lexington and Bunker Hill deserve to be remembered —one "to make any accommodation with the Pennsylvania party that shall conduce to the best good of the whole, and come in common defense of liberty in America," and the other was "to act in conjunction with our neighboring towns within this and the other colonies in opposing the measures to enslave the colonies, and that we will unanimously join our brethren in America in the common cause of defending our liberty." This resolve was more than lived up to, for Westmoreland not only raised her quota of troops for the Continental Army, but she sent more and she kept on sending until she was left defenseless herself, except for a home guard, made up of such of her remnant of men and boys as were either too young or too old for service in the army. More than this, she out of her scanty resources armed and equipped such companies as she sent to the front.

Throughout the war the New Englanders in Pennsylvania were greatly irritated by certain of their neighbors who were not in sympathy with the revolt against the mother country. It must be admitted that the Yankees of Westmoreland were pretty severe on these Tories, for the latter were repeatedly expelled as spies and in some instances their properties were confiscated. Driven from their farms by the Yankees, these Loyalists had no other recourse than to seek shelter at the nearest British stronghold, which was Fort Niagara. Their tales of the pernicious activity of the Westmoreland "rebels" in raising troops and in persecuting the Loyalists inspired the expedition which destroyed Wyoming in 1778 —an expedition made up of a motley force of British soldiers, painted Indians and smarting Tories.

When news came from Niagara of the threatened invasion by the British, the Westmoreland officers and men in Washington's army pleaded to be allowed leave of absence that they might hasten to the defense of their families,

On the ground that the public safety required their presence at the front the permission was not granted. As Miner says: "History affords no parallel of the pernicious detention of men under such circumstances. Wives wrote to their hsubands, begging them to come home, and many responded to the piteous call. Who can blame them for placing the pleadings of wives and children above the cruel order of their superiors to remain at the front?" The fears of invasion were only too well founded. Butler and his combined force came down the valley of the Susquehanna and destroyed the settlement. Some of the patriots who had hastened to defend their families fell in the memorable battle. Out of the 400 Connecticut men in the fight only 100 came out alive, and John Butler stated in his official report that his Indians had taken 227 scalps. The destruction of Wyoming by uncontrollable savages, led by a British officer, sent a thrill of horror through the civilized world and a protest went up against such barbarous methods, methods entirely foreign to what we call modern and enlightened warfare. The people of England instantly joined in denunciation of the turning loose of savages upon defenseless frontiers and the tomahawking and scalping of fellow Anglo-Saxons. That the commander of the British invading force should in cold blood report that his Indians had taken hundreds of scalps—scalps for which the king was offering pay—caused the people of the mother country to cry out in shame against such inhuman warfare between civilized belligerents—belligerents, too, of the same blood. The sentiment in England in favor of the American colonies was strengthened, not only among the people, but on the floor of Parliament, three of whose statesmen, Pitt and Wilkes and Barre, have been honored by having their names incorporated in two of our Westmoreland cities—Wilkes-Barre and Pittston. It is not going too far when we assert that this revulsion in England against the employment of savages by British officers had an influence in bringing the Revolution to a close.

Not only was the Revolution shortened by the reaction of the people of England from the destruction of Wyoming by savages, but it was perhaps shortened still further by the campaign the next year, when in order to make such horrors as that at Wyoming impossible of repetition, Washington sent Gen. Sullivan with an expedition which

ravaged the country of the Six Nations
so completely that the great Indian
Confederacy never engaged in another
battle. Had it not thus been crushed
the Indian allies of the British might
have harassed the frontiers indefinitely
and thus prolonged the revolution.

While we are considering how the
comparatively insignificant frontier post
of Westmoreland was a factor in the
Revolutionary War we may perhaps
consider that the occupancy of the
Wyoming region by the Moravian missionaries for the two decades prior to
the Revolution had an influence in
shortening the struggle by holding some
of the Indians friendly to the colonies,
or at least bringing about their neutrality.

Throughout the entire Revolutionary
War the Indians devastated the region
with fire and hatchet, but the close of
that great struggle witnessed no cessa-
tion of suffering for the Connecticut
settlers. The Pennsylvania government, which no longer had to fight a
foreign enemy, now turned again with
ferocity upon the Connecticut settlers,
who were already impoverished by war.
The climax of the Pennamite cruelty
was reached when the soldiers obliter-
ated the Connecticut boundaries and at
the point of the bayonet dispossessed
all the Connecticut claimants, and
drove men, women and children across
the wilderness to Connecticut on foot.

How did the civil strife end? It ter-
minated as strife usually ends, by compromise. After a thirty years' war,
with loss of life on both sides, the con-
testants came to an agreement. The
legislature of Pennsylvania a little
prior to 1800 enacted several laws calculated to settle all differences fairly
and justly. All Connecticut claimants
who were actual settlers were given
title from Pennsylvania on the payment
of small sums. It took many years for
Pennsylvania to recognize the rights of
the Connecticut people and to make
such concessions as would pacify them.
The Connecticut people, roused to des-
peration, had undertaken to form a
new State out of northeastern Pennsylvania. The movement was so far-
reaching as to be aided by such prominent men as Oliver Walcott, Joel Bar-
low and Ethan Allen of Ticonderoga
fame. Pennsylvania became alarmed
at a movement which threatened to dis-
member the State for a constitution
had been drawn and officers decided
upon by the revolutionists. Under this
pressure Pennsylvania made concessions that were satisfactory to the

Yankees. With the erection of the new Pennsylvania county of Luzerne the New England town of Westmoreland disappeared from the map and remained only as a memory.

It would be interesting to trace the results that might have followed the formation of a New England State on soil claimed by Pennsylvania. Ethan Allen boasted that he had made one new State and that with 100 Green Mountain boys and 200 riflemen he could repeat Vermont in spite of Pennsylvania. Had not Pennsylvania nipped the project in the bud by conciliating the Yankees, a civil war, more far-reaching in its consequences than the Pennamite war, would have resulted. Turbulent Yankees from all over New England would have rallied around Ethan Allen and a struggle would have ensued which might have involved the Union in its disastrous consequences.

It is interesting to know that of the Penn claim to Westmoreland there is a portion of the Sunbury Manor along Harvey's Creek in Luzerne County still in the possession of the Penn heirs in line of succession under William Penn.

THE PURITAN OF TO-DAY.

Following is a brief synopsis of the excellent response by Rev. E. J. Morris, pastor of the Puritan Congregational Church:

In all essentials of character the Puritan of to-day is just such a man as the Puritan of the seventeenth century, and his mission in the world is to carry on and perfect the work of his illustrious predecessors. The victories of Cromwell and the experiments of the Commonwealth in Great Britain and of the early settlements of New England were turning points in the great world battle for freedom, not the crowning victory. The crowning victory is yet to come even in our own beloved country. The Puritans gave our country a good start not only in free government but also in the conduct of life and in the improvement of society. In these matters also the Puritan of to-day is well fitted to continue their work.

Considering everything, perhaps we have no great reason to complain or to fear about anything in the present state of the country. But it is well to be on our guard and to give heed to the warnings of the wise. The distinguished philosopher who passed away a few days ago, Mr. Herbert Spencer, spoke words of very sharp warning to us and to our kinsmen beyond the sea almost with his last breath. His last book,

"Facts and Comments," published last year, is a startling arraignment of things we are apt to be proud of—"Rebarbarization" is the heading of one of his chapters, and by that strong word he characterizes some leading tendencies of our civilization. Mr. Spencer prescribed no specific remedies for the evils he saw in our life, public and private. From his point of view it would have been extremely difficult to do so. But there is very little risk in saying that a new infusion of clear Puritanism would prove an admirable tonic just now for our country and for every Christian country in the world.

The old historical Puritanism was a combination of intense religious enthusiasm with the instinct of self government and personal freedom. But the religious enthusiasm was the dominant and effective element. The instinct for self government had existed in the English people from the first, even before they arrived in Britain. In every age of England's history it had asserted itself and struggled with every new despotism. But victory crowned its efforts only when, by the placing of the English bible in the hands of the people, the whole nation learned to claim its freedom not merely as a natural right but as a divine trust and the necessary condition of realizing its true life.

The Puritan of to-day is a true Puritan just so far as he also has learned that his whole life, public and private, is sacred; that the aim of his politics should be to make God's will prevail on earth; and that, in the smallest things as in the greatest, he should live, like the great poet of Puritanism, John Milton, "as ever in the Great Taskmaster's eye." A general revival of this strict Puritanism would seem to many narrow and severe, as did the movement which succeeded the "spacious times of great Elizabeth." But those old Puritans achieved their results through their so-called narrowness, that is to say, through their earnestness and moral concentration. Self denial at the behest of faith can bring no real loss—must bring great gain. But is real faith in a living and righteous God, not only reigning in heaven but also ruling on earth, possible to-day? That is the most pressing question of the hour for the individual and for the nation, as we are told in an impressive sentence in Morley's Life of Gladstone, where the old statesman says that "the great battle of mankind is being fought now not in politics but in the world of thought."

MR. WILEY'S ADDRESS.

Dr. Harvey A. Wiley of Washington, D. C., made a capital address, a few extracts following:

How the Pilgrim Fathers preserved their food history does not state, for borax, salicylic acid and formaldehyde were unknown. Game and corn were not abundant, and so their first care must have been devoted to the soil. The struggle for food is the first fight that man must make, and it is one which is never ended and is not a curse. More than half of all the effort exerted by man is for food. Other things can come later, but food we must have first and ever after. While the struggle for food is an important factor in the evolution of man, the character of the food has an important effect. The plain, unadulterated food of the Pilgrims must have been an element of importance in their character. Their meat was cured by salt and smoke, and not by borax and acid.

Thus with wholesome food and labor in the open air they found health and strength.

As to the intolerance of the Pilgrims, the speaker said intolerance was better than license. They were fond of hard cider containing 7 per cent. alcohol, yet they would look upon the drinking of a mug of beer containing 3 per cent. as a crime.

The acts of the adulterator are coming into vogue. Instead of hard cider we have apple juice kept sweet with salicylic acid. Maple syrup has been displaced by glucose. Pumpkin pie is made with mashed turnips. No longer is there a minister at the head of Harvard. The farms of New England have poured out their population to other States.

Dr. Wiley's address was full of humorous allusions to the Pilgrims and was received with evident favor.

OFFICERS, COMMITTEES.

Following are the officers and committees:

Officers—President, Dr. F. C. Johnson; vice president, Mr. A. D. Blackinton; secretary, Mr. J. H. Fisher; treasurer, Mr. W. J. Torrey; historian, Mr. H. F. Paine; chaplain, Rev. George E. Guild, D. D.

Committee of arrangements—William A. Wilcox, Esq., Capt. Dolph B. Atherton, Mr. Arthur L. Collins, Mr. George B. Dimmick, Russell Dimmick, Esq.

Committee on speakers—Mr. Alvah De O. Blackinton, Rev. George E. Guild, D. D., Hon. Alfred Hand, Mr. Charles D. Sanderson, William A. Wilcox, Esq.